P9-CLR-539

WRITING SKILLS
Problem Solver

Carol H. Behrman

**THE CENTER FOR APPLIED
RESEARCH IN EDUCATION**
West Nyack, New York 10994

Property of Oxford
MCAS Summer Camp
Middle/Secondary

Library of Congress Cataloging-in-Publication Data

Behrman, Carol H.
   Writing skills problem solver: 101 ready-to-use writing process
activities for correcting the most common errors / by Carol H.
Behrman.
      p. cm.
   ISBN 0-13-021716-6 (spiral wire)   ISBN 0-13-060039-3 (paper)
   1. English language--Composition and exercises--Study and teaching
(Elementary) Problems, exercises, etc.   I. Title.
   LB1576.B427 1999   99-33440
   372.62'3--dc21   CIP

Acquisitions Editor: *Connie Kallback*
Production Editor: *Mariann Hutlak*
Interior Design/Formatter: *Dee Coroneos*

© 2000 *by* The Center for Applied Research in Education, West Nyack, New York

All rights reserved.

Permission is given for individual classroom teachers to reproduce these activities and projects for classroom use. Reproduction of these materials for an entire school system is strictly forbidden.

Every effort has been made to ensure that no copyrighted material has been used without permission. The author regrets any oversights that may have occurred and would be happy to rectify them in future printings of the book.

Printed in the United States of America

10 9 8 7 6 5 4 3 2 1   10 9 8 7 6 5 4 3 2 1

ISBN 0-13-021716-6 (spiral wire)   ISBN 0-13-060039-3 (paper)

ATTENTION: CORPORATIONS AND SCHOOLS

The Center for Applied Research in Education books are available at quantity discounts with bulk purchase for educational, business, or sales promotional use. For information, please write to: Prentice Hall Special Sales, 240 Frisch Court, Paramus, NJ 07652. Please supply: title of book, ISBN number, quantity, how the book will be used, date needed.

**THE CENTER FOR APPLIED RESEARCH
IN EDUCATION**
West Nyack, NY 10994

http://www.phdirect.com

DEDICATION

To a new generation of excellent writers:

Patrick and Luke Beezer
Matthew and Jonathan Behrman
Rose Maisner

A SPECIAL THANKS TO:

my terrific editor, Connie Kallback
my husband, Edward, best critic, proofreader, and inspiration

ABOUT THE AUTHOR

Carol H. Behrman was born in Brooklyn, New York, graduated from City College of New York, and attended Columbia University's Teachers' College, where she majored in education. She married Edward Behrman, an accountant, and moved to Fair Lawn, New Jersey, where they raised three children. They currently reside in Sarasota, Florida. For many years, Behrman taught grades five through eight at the Glen Ridge Middle School in New Jersey, where she created a program utilizing a writing process that combined language arts with word-processing instruction. She has written nineteen books, fiction and nonfiction, for children and young adults, and has conducted numerous workshops on the writing process for students, teachers, and aspiring writers. She has served as writer-in-residence at Chautauqua Institution and has been an adjunct lecturer at Seton Hall and New York University's Writing Center.

Mrs. Behrman is also the author of *Writing Activities for Every Month of the School Year* (1997), *Write! Write! Write!* (1995), and *Hooked on Writing!* (1990), all sponsored by The Center for Applied Research in Education.

PREFACE

This writing resource is designed to help teachers and students deal with writing problems—on an individual basis or as an entire class.

Students in the same class or grade vary greatly in their writing ability. It is difficult for the teacher to address writing problems adequately that are specific to one or two students. Chris's writing may contain sentence fragments. Kim's subjects and predicates don't always agree. Carlos can't seem to construct a simple essay. The list goes on and on. These difficulties, and others, occur regularly, even though the material may have been adequately covered in classroom lessons and assignments.

No matter how excellent their writing teacher, inevitably there will be students who continue to struggle with inadequate and incorrect writing techniques. If a significant percentage of the class demonstrates a particular problem, most teachers will review and reteach these lessons. Usually, however, it is impossible to devote extra class time to the writing needs of individual students. Even if every student in a class demonstrates faulty writing, each one's errors may occur in completely different areas of writing expertise. Ideally, every student should master a specific writing technique before going on to the next. In practice, however, this is seldom, if ever, possible in a classroom situation.

This resource is an answer to this dilemma. It is intended to help the teacher address individual writing problems without encroaching upon precious class time. When a student displays a weakness in writing techniques, that student can be given a series of individualized exercises and activities that promote improvement in that particular area.

It is the author's belief, however, that exercises alone do not always change incorrect writing habits. The new knowledge needs to be incorporated into expanded writing projects in order to become ingrained into a student's natural writing technique. Therefore, wherever possible, the activities in this resource utilize a writing process that has been shown to be the most effective way of acquiring competence in writing. Many activities follow at least some of the steps of the writing process (organizing ideas, writing a first draft, revising, and writing a final copy).

As in the author's previous writing resources *(Hooked on Writing, Write! Write! Write!,* and *Writing Activities for Every Month of the School Year)* the activities have been structured and designed to spark student interest and to make the writing process exciting. As with any remedial resource, of course, it is not always possible to avoid a certain amount of ordinary drill, but an attempt has been made in all cases to take the young person's point of view into consideration and to elicit enthusiasm.

All of the activities in this resource are not only individualized for specific writing problems, but are also designed to be used with little or no teacher involvement. The instructions are clear and simple. The activities are structured to allow students to work on their own. This makes them ideal for home instruction, as well as for use in the classroom. Additionally, these activities can be used by the teacher in conjunction with the general writing curriculum.

Please note that this is not a complete grammar textbook. It does not lay out all, or even most, of the rules for writing English correctly. Its goals are to identify the most common writing errors among students and to provide a varied assortment of easy-to-follow material that the teacher can use to correct individual writing problems.

HOW TO USE
THIS RESOURCE

There could be no easier, more effective way of addressing individual writing problems than by using this resource, nor one that takes less preparation time on the part of the teacher. Just follow these easy steps:

1. Identify one or more specific writing problems in a student's work.

2. In the table of contents, locate the section (or sections) appropriate to that problem. Each section covers specific areas of writing and grammar, such as Word Usage Help, Punctuation Help, Sentence Writing Help, Spelling Help, and so on.

3. Under the listing for that section, locate the description and number of the activity (or activities) that specifically address the problem. For example, if a student uses *accept* for *except*, or *passed* for *past*, look under Word Usage Help. There you will find several activities for Words Often Confused.

Some problems may be covered in more than one section. For example, while the correct use of punctuation is addressed in Punctuation Help, there are also activities involving punctuation in the unit on Grammar. The same is true of Sentence Help. The column labeled *Type of Error* in the table of contents will help locate the appropriate activities required.

> **NOTE:** In addition to the table of contents, each section is preceded by a listing of the specific problems covered in that section and the appropriate activities. These Section Guides provide more details than the general table of contents and can be of assistance when seeking a specific activity.
>
> **EXAMPLE:** Section One (Word Usage Help) contains ten activities for "Words Often Confused." The Section Guide offers a list of the actual words covered in each activity.

4. Copy the easy-to-reproduce activities and distribute for individual student use. Most activities contain solution keys to the exercises for the student to use in self-correction and self-evaluation.

5. In many cases, more than one activity is available for a specific error. The more practice a student receives in areas of writing that require remediation, the more likely it is that the correct method will be retained.

6. In cases where an activity can be useful in correcting problems on a class basis, follow the steps just outlined and distribute worksheets to all the students.

CONTENTS

Section One
WORD USAGE HELP

Section Two
PUNCTUATION HELP

ACTIVITY TITLE	TYPE OF ERROR	ACTIVITY NUMBER
Punctuation Expert *Review*	Punctuation Review	**25B**
Find the Lost Punctuation *Review*	Punctuation Review	**26A**
The Punctuation Expert *Review*	Punctuation Review	**26B**

Section Three
SPELLING HELP

TEACHER'S GUIDE—ALPHABETICAL LISTING OF SPELLING
PROBLEMS AND THEIR ACTIVITY NUMBERS . . . . p. 69

ACTIVITY TITLE	TYPE OF ERROR	ACTIVITY NUMBER
I Hear with My Ear *Explanation and Exercises*	Homonyms	**27A**
I Hear with My Ear *More Homonyms*	Homonyms	**27B**
I Hear with My Ear *Using Homonyms in a Paragraph*	Homonyms	**27C**
A Pair of Pears *Explanation and Exercises*	More Homonyms	**28A**
A Pair of Pears *Explanation and Exercises*	More Homonyms	**28B**
They Sound the Same *Simple Common Homonyms*	Simple Homonyms	**29A**
They Sound the Same *Simple Common Homonyms*	Simple Homonyms	**29B**
Same Sound, Different Meaning *Paragraph—First Draft*	Homonym Review	**30A**
Same Sound, Different Meaning *Paragraph—Revising and Writing a Final Copy*	Homonym Review	**30B**
IE or EI? *Explanation and Exercises*	Words with ie or ei	**31A**

ACTIVITY TITLE	TYPE OF ERROR	ACTIVITY NUMBER
IE or EI? *Explanation and Exercises*	Words with ie or ei	**31B**
IE or EI? *Review Exercises*	Words with ie or ei	**31C**
From One to Many *Explanation and Exercises*	Plurals	**32A**
From One to Many *Additional Exercises*	Plurals	**32B**
Plurals with Y *Explanation and Exercises*	More Plurals	**33A**
Plurals with Y *Additional Exercises*	More Plurals	**33B**
Chiefs and Thieves *Explanation and Exercises*	Plurals: Final F	**34A**
Chiefs and Thieves *Additional Exercises*	Plurals: Final F	**34B**
Always Begin Big! *Rules and Exercises*	Capitalization	**35A**
Always Begin Big! *Additional Rules and Exercises*	Capitalization	**35B**
Always Begin Big! *Review and Exercises*	Capitalization	**35C**
The Word Garden—1	Words Commonly Misspelled	**36A**
The Word Garden—2	Words Commonly Misspelled	**36B**
Spelling Demons—1 *List and Exercises*	Words Commonly Misspelled	**37A**
Spelling Demons—2 *List and Exercises*	Words Commonly Misspelled	**37B**
Spelling Demons—3 *A Search for Misspelled Words*	Words Commonly Misspelled	**37C**
Don't Put Us Together!	Writing Two Words as One	**38**
Happy Endings *Rules and Exercises*	Adding Suffixes	**39A**
Happy Endings *Rules and Exercises*	Adding Suffixes	**39B**

Section Four

GRAMMAR HELP

Section Five
SENTENCE WRITING HELP

ACTIVITY TITLE	TYPE OF ERROR	ACTIVITY NUMBER
Putting It Together *Explanation and Exercises*	Recognizing a Complete Sentence	**59A**
Putting It Together *Explanation and Exercises*	Recognizing a Complete Sentence	**59B**
Putting It Together *Exercises*	Recognizing a Complete Sentence	**59C**
Broken Apart *Explanation and Exercises*	Sentence Fragments	**60A**
Broken Apart *Exercises*	Sentence Fragments	**60B**
Broken Apart *Paragraph—First Draft*	Sentence Fragments	**60C**
Broken Apart *Paragraph—Revising and Writing a Final Copy*	Sentence Fragments	**60D**
Putting It Together *Simple Exercises*	Sentence Fragments: Simple Exercises	**61**
Running Past the Base *Explanation and Exercises*	Run-on Sentences	**62A**
Running Past the Base *Paragraph—First Draft*	Run-on Sentences	**62B**
Running Past the Base *Paragraph—Revising and Writing a Final Copy*	Run-on Sentences	**62C**
Running Past the Base *Additional Explanation and Exercises*	Run-on Sentences	**62D**
We Must Agree! *Explanation and Exercises*	Agreement of Subject and Verb	**63A**
We Must Agree! *Editing a Paragraph*	Agreement of Subject and Verb	**63B**
We Must Agree! *Explanation and Exercises*	Agreement of Subject and Verb: Collective Nouns	**63C**

Section Six
PARAGRAPH HELP

TEACHER'S GUIDE—ALPHABETICAL LIST OF PARAGRAPH
PROBLEMS AND RELEVANT EXERCISES . . . . p. 183

ACTIVITY TITLE	TYPE OF ERROR	ACTIVITY NUMBER
Mix And Match *Explanation and Exercises*	Sentence Order	**72A**
Scrambled Paragraphs *Additional Exercises*	Sentence Order	**72B**
Scrambled Paragraphs *Another Exercise*	Sentence Order	**72C**
What's It All About? *Explanation and Exercises*	Topic Sentence	**73A**
What's It All About? *Additional Exercises and Paragraph Draft*	Topic Sentence	**73B**
What's It All About? *Writing a Paragraph—Final Copy*	Topic Sentence	**73C**
Sum It Up! *Explanation and Exercises*	Concluding Sentence	**74A**
Sum It Up! *Additional Exercises*	Concluding Sentence	**74B**
The Paragraph Story *Prewriting*	Organizing a Paragraph	**75A**
The Paragraph Story *Writing a First Draft*	Organizing a Paragraph	**75B**
The Paragraph Story *Revising and Writing a Final Copy*	Organizing a Paragraph	**75C**
No Switching Allowed *Explanation and Exercises*	Consistency of Tense	**76A**
No Switching Allowed *Explanation and Exercises*	Consistency of Tense	**76B**
Either You or I *Explanation and Exercises*	Consistency of Pronoun	**77A**
Either You or I *Paragraph—First Draft*	Consistency of Pronoun	**77B**

Section Seven

ESSAY WRITING HELP

Section Eight
LETTER WRITING HELP

WORD USAGE HELP

TEACHER'S GUIDE—
ALPHABETICAL LISTING OF WORD USAGE PROBLEMS
AND WORDS OFTEN CONFUSED
AND THEIR ACTIVITY NUMBERS

Section One covers problems with word usage, such as:

Words Often Confused	Activities 1–11 *(see below)*
Idiomatic Expressions	Activity 12
Colloquialisms	Activity 13
Illiteracies	Activity 13
Slang	Activity 13
Triteness	Activity 14
Double Negatives	Activity 15

To simplify access to a specific problem, here is an alphabetical listing of words often confused, together with the activity numbers where they can be found.

WORDS OFTEN CONFUSED	ACTIVITY NUMBER
accept or except	1A, B, C
advice or advise	4A, B
affect or effect	1A, B, C
agree to or agree with	11A, B
all ready or already	1A, B, C
altogether or all together	4A, B
among or between	1A, B, C
as or like	11A, B
beside or besides	4A, B
breath or breathe	7A, B, C
bring or take	6A, B
capital or capitol	5A, B, C
clothes or cloths	9A, B

WORDS OFTEN CONFUSED	ACTIVITY NUMBER
conscience or conscious	7A, B, C
convince or persuade	9A, B
desert or dessert	2A, B
fewer or less	11A, B
in or into	6A, B
its or it's	8A, B
learn or teach	2A, B
lend or loan	9A, B
maybe or may be	2A, B
passed or past	3A, B, C
persecute or prosecute	11A, B
principal or principle	5A, B, C
proceed or precede	5A, B, C
quite or quiet	6A, B
raise or rise	6A, B
stationery or stationary	3A, B, C
than or then	3A, B, C
there or their or they're	10A, B
through or thorough	10A, B
whose or who's	8B
your or you're	8A, B

Name _____ Date _____

ARE YOU ALL READY ALREADY?
Explanation and Exercises

Are you sometimes confused about whether to use:

accept	or	*except*
affect	or	*effect*
all ready	or	*already*
among	or	*between*

Lots of people get these words mixed up, but they are easy to remember. You just need to know what each one means.

Accept means "to take," as I *accept* your gift.
Except means "other than," as Everyone went home *except* me.

Affect (a verb) means "to influence," as Absences *may affect* my marks.
Effect (a noun) means "result," as Studying had a good *effect* on my marks.

All ready means "all are ready," as The girls are *all ready* to leave.
Already means "earlier or before," as They had *already* left.

Among is used with *more than two things,* as in We were not *among the crowd.*
Between is used with *two things,* as in The race was *between* Jim and Joe.

TRY IT OUT: Fill in the blank spaces below.

1. The senator walked _____ the people in the crowd. (among or between)

2. The movie star will happily _____ the award. (accept or except)

3. Does the weather ever ____ your mood? (effect or affect)

4. What _____ does ice have on the ski slope? (effect or affect)

5. Matthew was _____ a rock and a hard place. (among or between)

6. Is the family _____ to leave for our trip? (all ready or already)

7. At 8:30 I was _____ late for school. (all ready or already)

8. Everyone _____ Bill was at the party. (accept or except)

9. Your attitude will _____ your success. (effect or affect)

10. Jeff's name appeared _____ the ten finalists. (between or among)

*Check Your Answers on Activity 1B.

© 2000 by The Center for Applied Research in Education

Name _____ Date _____

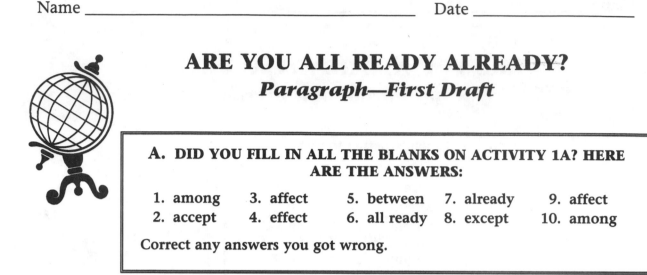

ARE YOU ALL READY ALREADY?
Paragraph—First Draft

**A. DID YOU FILL IN ALL THE BLANKS ON ACTIVITY 1A? HERE
ARE THE ANSWERS:**

1. among	3. affect	5. between	7. already	9. affect
2. accept	4. effect	6. all ready	8. except	10. among

Correct any answers you got wrong.

B. In this activity, you are going to write a paragraph, using at least three of the words listed in Activity 1A. In your paragraph, describe three or more things (or people) that you see
in your classroom, as in this example:

> There are some unusual things in this classroom. Did
> you ever notice the waste basket that stands <u>between</u>
> the teacher's desk and the chalkboard? It is shaped like
> a dolphin. Speaking of boards, every chalkboard is green
> <u>except</u> the one in the back. That one is black. Also, there
> is a lot of dust on the big white clock. I wonder if that
> has any <u>effect</u> on its accuracy. I hope the strange
> objects in this room don't <u>affect</u> my concentration.

C. Write your paragraph below. This is just a first draft, so don't worry about perfect spelling
or grammar. Just concentrate on getting your thoughts down on paper. *Be sure to use at least
three of the words on your list.* (Indent at the beginning of the paragraph.)

_____

_____

_____

_____

_____

_____

_____

_____

_____

© 2000 by The Center for Applied Research in Education

Name _____ Date _____

ARE YOU ALL READY ALREADY?
Paragraph—Revising and Writing a Final Copy

> **WORDS OFTEN CONFUSED**
>
> | | |
> |---|---|
> | accept, | except |
> | affect, | effect |
> | all ready, | already |
> | among, | between |

© 2000 by The Center for Applied Research in Education

A. Revise and edit the paragraph you wrote for Activity 1B, using the following questions as guidelines:

1. Does your beginning (topic) sentence tell what the paragraph is about? If not, change it.

2. Do you describe *at least three* objects or people in the room? Is there another interesting one you could add?

3. Do you use at least three of the words on the list above? Can you find a place in the paragraph to use another of these words?

4. Can you add any descriptive words that would make the object or person more real to a reader?

5. Are your sentences complete? Do the subjects and verbs agree?

6. Are there any words you are not sure how to spell? Consult a dictionary.

B. When your paragraph is as good as you can make it, write your final copy below. (Indent at the beginning of the paragraph.)

Name _____ Date _____

DESSERT IN THE DESERT
Explanation and Exercises

Here are more words that are sometimes confused:

| *maybe* or *may be* | *learn* or *teach* | *desert* or *dessert* |

You won't be confused once you know the correct meaning of each word.

> *May be* are two separate words used to show possibility or chance, as
> Bobby *may be* the next person to travel to the moon.

> *Maybe* is one word that means "perhaps", as
> *Maybe* you'll be the one to travel to the moon.

On the line below, write a sentence with the word *maybe*, meaning "perhaps":

_____

Write a sentence below using *may be,* showing possibility or chance:

_____

> *Learn* means "to receive information or knowledge," as
> Matthew will *learn* how to speak French next year.

> *Teach* means "to give out information or knowledge," as
> The professor will *teach* a course in history.

Write a sentence below with the word *learn,* meaning to receive knowledge:

_____

On the next line, write a sentence using *teach,* to give information:

_____

> *Dessert* is the sweet, yummy course at the end of a meal, as
> Rocky Road ice cream is my favorite *dessert*.

> A *desert* is a dry, sandy place, as
> I'd like to ride a camel across the *desert*.

> Desert also means to "abandon" as
> The soldier will never *desert* his buddies.

Write a sentence below that contains the word *dessert* (food):

_____

On the next line, write a sentence with *desert* (dry, sandy place):

_____

Below, write a sentence containing *desert,* meaning to abandon:

_____

© 2000 by The Center for Applied Research in Education

Name _____ Date _____

DESSERT IN THE DESERT
Additional Exercises

maybe	or	*may be*
teach	or	*learn*
dessert	or	*desert*

A. Fill in the correct word from the list above.

1. The Dodgers _____ pennant winners next year.   (may be or maybe)

2. Mr. Smith _____ our homeroom teacher next year.   (may be or maybe)

3. _____ I'll go to the game with you.   (may be or maybe)

4. You can't _____ an old dog new tricks.   (teach or learn)

5. I'm going to _____ to do a new card trick.   (teach or learn)

6. I'll _____ you a lesson you'll remember.   (teach or learn)

7. Would you _____ me when I need you?   (desert or dessert)

8. _____ is the best part of the meal.   (desert or dessert)

9. The Sahara _____ is in Africa.   (desert or dessert)

10. It's hard to grow food in the _____.   (desert or dessert)

B. In the paragraph below, fill in the blank spaces with words from the list at the top of the page.

I like to _____ new things, but I don't like it when my older brother tries to _____ me. _____ he's always right, but I don't care. It _____ that I'll never catch up to him. He even finishes dinner before me. He is already eating _____ while I'm still on the main course. I love my brother, and I'd never _____ him if he needed me, but it's no fun being the youngest.

Answers: *Sentences*—1. may be,   2. may be,   3. maybe,   4. teach,   5. learn, 6. teach,   7. desert,   8. dessert,   9. desert,   10. desert. *Paragraph*—learn, teach, Maybe, may be, dessert, desert

© 2000 by The Center for Applied Research in Education

Name _____ Date _____

YOU PASSED THE TEST!
Explanation and Exercises

What words are most commonly confused with each other? Here are some contenders for top honors:

then	or	*than*
passed	or	*past*
stationery	or	*stationary*

Even good writers sometimes confuse these, but once you know the precise meaning of these words, you'll never mix them up again.

Then is an indication of time. It is an adverb (a word that modifies a verb), as
We had lunch at McDonald's and *then* went to the movies.
Than is always used for comparison, as
Mike is taller *than* Bobby.

Passed is the past tense of the verb "to pass", as in
Last semester, I *passed* all my courses. OR
We *passed* Billy's house on the way home.
Past is a verb participle; it is used with a helping verb, as
We went *past* Billy's house.
Past can also be used as a noun, as in
We should be able to learn from the *past*.

Stationery always refers to writing paper, as in
Maggie took out her new box of *stationery* to write a letter.
Stationary always means "not moving," as in
The bleacher seats are nailed to the ground and *stationary*.

Check the meanings above, and fill in the blank spaces in these sentences.

1. My dad has a _____ bike in his exercise room.
   (stationery or stationary)
2. In the _____ I always got good grades in science.
   (past or passed)
3. Don't try to move that rock because it is _____.
   (stationery or stationary)
4. History teaches us what happened in the_____.
   (past or passed)
5. This basketball hoop is higher _____ the one in the schoolyard.
   (then or than)
6. Promise you'll never tell and _____ I'll tell you the secret.
   (then or than)
7. I _____ Ellen's house on my way to the mall.
   (past or passed)

*SEE ACTIVITY 3B FOR ANSWERS.

© 2000 by The Center for Applied Research in Education

Name _____ Date _____

YOU PASSED THE TEST!
Paragraph—First Draft

> ### A. DID YOU FILL IN ALL THE BLANKS ON ACTIVITY 3A?
> ### HERE ARE THE ANSWERS:
>
> | | |
> |---|---|
> | 1. stationary | 5. than |
> | 2. past | 6. then |
> | 3. stationary | 7. passed |
> | 4. past | |
>
> **If you got them all correct, then you have passed the test in good word usage.**

B. Look at the paragraph that is begun below. The first sentence states the topic *(a ride in the car).*

Complete the paragraph in your own words. Tell what happens in the car and describe what you see along the way. Add at least four more sentences.

Include at least *three* of the following words in your paragraph:

> passed, past, then, than, stationery, stationary

This is a *first draft,* so concentrate on getting your thoughts down on paper. Don't be concerned about spelling or punctuation, except for the words on the list above.

I went for a ride in the car with my Mom. On the way, _____

_____

_____

_____

_____

_____

_____

_____

_____

_____

_____

© 2000 by The Center for Applied Research in Education

Name _____ Date _____

YOU PASSED THE TEST!
Revising and Writing a Final Copy

A. Revise and edit the paragraph you wrote for Activity 3B, using the following questions as guidelines:

1. Does the rest of the paragraph discuss the subject that is stated in the first sentence? Take out anything that is not appropriate to that subject.

2. Have you added *at least four* more sentences? Can you think of any more than would make this paragraph more interesting?

3. Do you use *at least three* of the words on the list? Are they used correctly? If you are not sure, check the word meanings in Activity 3A.

4. Can you find a place to add one more word from the list?

5. Can you add any striking or colorful words that will make your description more interesting and vivid?

6. Are your sentences complete? Do subjects and verbs agree?

7. Are there any words you are not sure how to spell? Consult a dictionary.

B. When the paragraph is as good as you can make it, write your final copy below. (Be sure to indent at the beginning of the paragraph.)

© 2000 by The Center for Applied Research in Education

Name _____ Date _____

TAKE OUR ADVICE!
Explanation and Exercises

Many people are sometimes confused about whether to use

advice	or	*advise*
altogether	or	*all together*
beside	or	*besides*

You will always use the right word if you know its meaning.

Advice is a noun. It means "something given," as Always take good *advice*.
Advise is a verb meaning "to give advice to," as The teacher *advised* him.

Altogether means "completely," as Are you *altogether* satisfied with that purchase?
All together means "everybody in one place" as, The family was *all together*.

Beside means "by the side of," as The dog sat *beside* the fire.
Besides means "also," as I don't like to go there, and *besides* I feel sick.

TRY IT OUT: Fill in the blank spaces below.

1. My family will be _____ at Thanksgiving. (altogether or all together)

2. I like to sit _____ my cousin, Matt. (beside or besides)

3. The food is always good, but I'm not _____ happy about going. (altogether or all together)

4. My Uncle Harry always like to give me _____ . (advice or advise)

5. I wish he wouldn't _____ me all the time. (advice or advise)

6. _____, I don't think Uncle Harry is as smart as my Dad. (Beside or Besides)

7. My Dad usually gives me good _____. (advice or advise)

8. Why do grown ups always feel they have to _____ kids? (advice or advise)

9. Thanksgiving would be _____ better without Uncle Harry. (altogether or all together)

Answers: 1. all together; 2. beside; 3. altogether; 4. advice, 5. advise; 6. Besides; 7. advice; 8. advise 9. altogether

© 2000 by The Center for Applied Research in Education

Name _____ Date _____

TAKE OUR ADVICE
Additional Exercises

altogether	all together
beside	besides
advise	advice

A. Fill in the correct word from the list above.

1. I'm going to _____ my father to stop smoking.

2. It's bad for his health, and _____ it smells horrible.

3. The chorus teacher said, "Now, let's sing _____.

4. A family picture stands_____ the clock on the shelf.

5. I am_____ too sleepy to finish my homework.

6. Dr. Smith gives _____ about health on the radio.

7. I'm going to sit _____ my friend at the movie theater.

8. There were _____ too many people at the party.

9. Would you _____ me to wear a warm coat today?

In the paragraph below, fill in the blank spaces with words from the list at the top of the page.

Here is some good _____. Join the chorus at our school. The teacher,

Mr. Crow, gives everyone a good grade. _____, it is fun to sing in a group.

Mr. Crow lets everyone choose places, so you could stand _____ me.

When the chorus sings _____, it really sounds cool. Being in chorus is

_____ great! So do as I _____, and join up soon.

© 2000 by The Center for Applied Research in Education

Answers: *Sentences*—1. advise; 2. besides; 3. all together; 4. beside
5. altogether; 6. advice; 7. beside; 8. altogether; 9. advise
Paragraph—advice, Besides, beside, all together, altogether, advise

Name _____ Date _____

DON'T LOSE IT!
Explanation and Exercises

Do you ever confuse the words *lose* and *loose? Lose* is a verb (action word) that means "to no longer have something," as Don't *lose* your money. *Loose* means "not fastened tightly," as This belt is too *loose* on me.

Other words often confused are

Capitol is a building, such as the *Capitol* in Washington, D.C., where Congress meets.
Capital means "a city," such as Albany, the *capital* of New York State.
Capital can also mean "money," as You need *capital* to start a business.

Principal can be an adjective, meaning "chief or main," as His *principal* reason for
   working is to earn money.
Principal also means "someone in charge," such as the *principal* of a school.
Principle means an "idea or ideal," such as moral *principles*.

Proceed means "to move along," as Please *proceed* to finish the test.
Precede means "to come before," as A short lecture will *precede* the film.

TRY IT OUT: Fill in the blank spaces below.

1. She likes to wear _____-fitting clothes. (loose or lose)

2. A marching band _____ the float in the parade. (proceeded or preceded)

3. Do you believe honesty is a good _____? (principal or principle)

4. Washington, D.C. is the _____ city of the United States. (capitol or capital)

5. When I was there, I visited the _____ building. (capitol or capital)

6. Mrs. Bick is the _____ of our school. (principal or principle)

7. Jay sat down and _____ to eat his whole meal. (proceeded or preceded)

8. Hold on to your wallet or you will _____ your money. (lose or loose)

9. My Dad needs more _____ to go into business. (capitol or capital)

10. Do you have any _____ change in your pocket? (lose or loose)

11. My _____ reason for working is to earn money. (principal or principle)

© 2000 by The Center for Applied Research in Education

Answers: 1. loose; 2. preceded; 3. principle; 4. capital; 5. Capitol; 6. principal; 7. proceeded; 8. lose; 9. capital; 10. loose; 11. principal

Name _____ Date _____

DON'T LOSE IT!
Paragraph—First Draft

Look at the paragraph that is begun below. The first sentence states the topic, which is *A walk down the street.*

Complete the paragraph in your own words, following these directions:

1. Add *at least four* more sentences: The final sentence should sum up the topic, as *"A walk down the street can be exciting if you really observe what is happening."*

2. Include at least *three* of the following words in your paragraph:

> ****capital, principal, principle, loose, lose, proceed, precede****

3. This is a *first draft,* so concentrate on getting your thoughts down on paper. Don't be concerned about spelling or punctuation, except for the words on the list.

<u>It's amazing how many interesting sights you can see while walking down the street.</u>

© 2000 by The Center for Applied Research in Education

Name _____ Date _____

DON'T LOSE IT!
Paragraph—Revising and Writing a Final Copy

A. Revise and edit the paragraph you wrote for Activity 5B, using the following questions as guidelines:

1. Does the rest of the paragraph discuss the subject that is stated in the first sentence? Take out anything that is not appropriate to that subject.

2. Have you added *at least four* more sentences? Can you think of any additional sentences that would make this paragraph more interesting?

3. Does your last sentence refer back to the topic?

4. Do you use *at least three* of the words on the list. Are they used correctly? If you are not sure, check the word meanings in Activity 5A.

5. Can you find a place to add one more word from the list?

6. Are your sentences complete? Do subjects and verbs agree?

7. Are there any words you are not sure how to spell? Consult a dictionary.

B. When the paragraph is as perfect as you can make it, write your final copy below. (Be sure to indent at the beginning of the paragraph.)

© 2000 by The Center for Applied Research in Education

Name _____ Date _____

ARE YOU QUITE QUIET?
Explanation and Exercises

quite,	quiet
raise,	rise
bring,	take
in,	into

The pairs of words above can sometimes be tricky. Do you always use them correctly? You will, if you know the exact meaning of each.

Quite means "very," as in Jenna is *quite* happy with her gift.
Quiet means "silent," as in It was *quiet* during the movie.

Here is a sentence that uses both of these words: It was *quite quiet* during the movie—meaning that it was very silent.

Raise means "to lift up or make higher," as in Let's *raise* the roof.
Rise means "to go up," as in Steam will *rise* from the boiling pot.

Bring means "to come here with something," as *Bring* me the tools.
Take means "to go there with something," as in *Take the plates away.*

In shows where something is, as *Maria is in the house.*
Into shows movement from one place to another, as *Go into the house.*

TRY IT OUT: Fill in the blank spaces below.

1. The boss will _____ Matt's salary.   (raise or rise)

2. Julia will _____ to become president of the company.   (raise or rise)

3. How many eggs are _____ that cake?   (in or into)

4. I am going to put four eggs _____ the cake.   (in or into)

5. I am waiting for you to _____ the groceries to me.   (bring or take)

6. _____ the soda to Mrs. Adams in the next apartment.   (bring or take)

7. It is _____ warm in this room.   (quiet or quite)

8. It is peaceful and _____ in this room.   (quiet or quite)

9. The boys are _____ Jon's room.   (in or into)

10. Don't let the dog go _____ that room.   (in or into)

11. Don't forget to _____ out the garbage.   (bring or take)

12. _____ your hand if you know the answer.   (raise or rise)

*ANSWERS ON ACTIVITY SHEET 6B.

© 2000 by The Center for Applied Research in Education

Name _____ Date _____

ARE YOU QUITE QUIET?
Additional Exercises

quiet, quite	raise, rise	bring, take	in, into

© 2000 by The Center for Applied Research in Education

A. Answers to *Try It Out* on activity 6A:

1. raise	2. rise	3. in	4. into	5. bring	6. Take
7. quite	8. quiet	9. in	10. into	11. take	12. Raise

B. FIND THE ERROR! The following paragraph uses six words from the list at the top of the page incorrectly. Can you find and circle these mistakes?

Yesterday, I came home from school and went in my house. It was awfully quite. I called, "Mom!" There was no answer. I rised my voice and called again, but again there was silence. It was clear that there was no one else into the house. Then I remembered. Mom had gone to bring a cake to the sick lady down the block. I knew she'd be back quiet soon.

(Did you circle all six mistakes? Here are the correct words: into, quiet, raised, in, take, quite)

C. FOR THE EXPERTS. Now that you are expert in using these words, write your own sentence on the line following each word. (Don't forget to begin each sentence with a capital letter and end with a period or question mark.)

1. quite _____

2. quiet _____

3. in _____

4. into _____

5. rise _____

6. raise _____

7. bring _____

8. take _____

Name _____ Date _____

THE BREATH OF LIFE
Explanation and Exercises

| breath, breathe | conscience, conscious | lay, lie | sit, set |

A. Do you know the difference between *breath* and *breathe*?

Breath (rhymes with *death*) means "the air you draw into and out of your lungs," as in
His *breath* smells like pizza.
Breathe (with a long *e* like *feet*) means "the act of drawing air into your lungs," as in
You must *breathe* to live.

The other words listed above can also sometimes be confusing, but not if you know the correct meanings.

Conscience is that inner voice that tells you right from wrong, as in
My *conscience* won't let me tell a lie.

Conscious means being awake or aware of your surroundings, as in
The victim was still *conscious* after the accident.

Lay means "to put down somewhere," as in *Lay* your book on the table.
Lie means "to rest or put yourself in a prone position," as in
You should *lie* down and go to sleep.

Sit means to take a seat, as in *Sit* down on the chair.
Set means to put something down, as in *Set* the forks on the table.

B. TRY IT OUT: Fill in the blank spaces below.

1. Criminals don't seem to have a _____. (conscience or conscious)

2. Are you _____ of the people around you? (conscience or conscious)

3. The movers should _____ the piano in that corner. (sit or set)

4. If you are tired, you can _____ on that bench. (sit or set)

5. After the two-mile run, I was out of _____. (breath or breathe)

6. The patient was able to _____ with a respirator. (breath or breathe).

7. Don't _____ down on top of the new bedspread. (lay or lie)

8. I shall _____ the new bedspread upon the bed. (lay or lie)

9. I need a _____ of fresh air. (breath or breathe)

10. If you hurt her, it will be on your _____. (conscience or conscious)

11. Are you _____ of the harm you have done? (conscience or conscious)

Answers: 1. conscience, **2.** conscious, **3.** set, **4.** sit, **5.** breath, **6.** breathe, **7.** lie, **8.** lay, **9.** breath, **10.** conscience, **11.** conscious

© 2000 by The Center for Applied Research in Education

Name _____ Date _____

THE BREATH OF LIFE
More Explanations and Exercises

Even when you understand the difference between *lay* and *lie*, it is possible to get mixed up when using other forms of these verbs.

The past tense of *lay* (meaning "put") is *laid*, as in I *laid* the book on the table an hour ago.
The past tense of *lie* (meaning "to rest") is *lay*, as in
  Last night I *lay* down and went right to sleep.

What is this? Is the past tense of the verb *lie* the same as the present tense of the verb *lay*? That's right! Here are some more examples:

Tonight I am going to *lie* down on my shiny new sheets. (present tense)
Last night, I *lay* down on my shiny new sheets. (past tense)

I am going to *lay* the plate on the table. (present tense)
Yesterday, I *laid* the plate on the table. (past tense)

TRY IT OUT: Fill in the blank spaces in the sentences below with *lay, laid,* or *lie*.

1. Can you _____ that package down without making any noise?

2. Anita wants to _____ down on her sister's bed because it's so soft.

3. Yesterday, the twins _____ down in the same bed to take a nap.

4. Last Christmas, Santa _____ the gifts under the tree.

5. In the summertime, I like to _____ under a tree and read.

6. The paper boy _____ the newspaper on the front step.

Answers: 1. lay, 2. lie, 3. lay, 4. laid, 5. lie, 6. laid

Now that you are an expert with the present and past tenses of *lay* and *lie*, you are ready to learn the participle forms of these words.

The participle form of *lay* (meaning to put) is *laying*, as
  Are you laying the forks on the table correctly?
The participle form of *lie* (meaning to rest) is *lying*, as
  Mom is lying down now because she is tired.

TRY IT OUT: Fill in the blanks in the following sentences with *lying* or *laying*.

1. The children are _____ in the grass and telling stories.

2. Dad is _____ down bricks for our new patio.

3. The princess was _____ in her beautiful four-poster bed.

4. The injured quarterback was _____ on the football field.

Answers: 1. lying, 2. laying, 3. lying, 4. lying

© 2000 by The Center for Applied Research in Education

Name _____ Date _____

THE BREATH OF LIFE
Exercises for Experts

breath, breathe   lay, lie   sit, set   conscience, conscious
(also: laying, lying, and laid)

Now that you are an expert in using these words, you should be able to ace the following exercise.

Fill in the blank spaces in the sentences below.

1. Are you _____ of the meaning of your actions?   (conscience, conscious)

2. Can you _____ down your glass without spilling the water?   (lie, lay)

3. It is hard to _____ naturally when one is nervous.   (breath, breathe)

4. Ask your guest to _____ on the most comfortable chair.   (sit, set)

5. Have you done anything that troubles your _____ ?   (conscience, conscious)

6. _____ the new TV on the stand that came with it.   (sit, set)

7. I slid into home base and could hardly catch my _____ .   (breathe or breath)

8. After lunch, I _____ down for a nap.   (lie, lay, laid)

9. The accident victim was _____ on the ground near the car.   (laying or lying)

10. Do you _____ through your nose or your mouth?   (breathe or breath)

11. The salesperson _____ the necklace on the counter.   (lay or laid)

12. The ushers _____ the chairs in rows.   (sit, set)

13. He was _____ the bowl on the table when it slipped from his fingers.
(laying, lying)

14. Pete _____ the fork on the napkin when he was setting the table.   (lay, laid)

15. You can _____ a sigh of relief because this is the last sentence.
(breath or breathe)

Answers: 1. conscious,   2. lay,   3. breathe,   4. sit,   5. conscience,   6. set.
7. breath,   8. lay,   9. lying,   10. breathe,   11. laid,   12. set,
13. laying,   14. laid,   15. breathe

© 2000 by The Center for Applied Research in Education

Name _____ Date _____

IT'S A SNAP!
Explanation and Exercises

A. Do you sometimes have trouble knowing whether to use *it's* or *its?* Join the club! These are two of the most frequently misused words in the language. The strange thing is that knowing which to use is really a snap. You just need to know the simple rules.

> *Its* always shows possession, as in The dog wagged *its* tail.
> *It's* stands for *it is* or *it has,* as *It's* a lovely day. *(It is)* or *It's* been a great party. *(It has)*

Isn't that easy? You should have no trouble with the exercise below. Just remember that you should always be able to substitute *it is* or *it has* for *it's.* Otherwise, use *its.*

B. Use the correct form of *its* or *it's* in the spaces below:

1. The weather forecast said that _____ going to rain.

2. _____ been a very hot summer.

3. The Raggedy Ann doll lost one of _____ arms.

4. _____ the sixth inning and our team is ahead.

5. The elephant lifted _____ trunk.

6. Dad thinks _____ too late for me to go out.

C. Do you always know when to use *your* or *you're?* The rule is similar to the one above.

> *Your* shows possession, as Is that *your* hat?
> *You're* always means *you are,* as *You're* late to school.

D. Fill in the blank spaces below with *your* or *you're.* Remember that *you're* always stands for *you are.*

1. Do you give _____ word that _____ telling the truth?

2. What is _____ name?

3. Did you know that _____ sitting in the wrong seat?

4. The teacher said that _____ his best student.

5. What was _____ grade in English last year?

6. On _____ mark! Get ready! Go!

ANSWERS TO EXERCISES B AND D ON ACTIVITY SHEET 8B.

© 2000 by The Center for Applied Research in Education

Name _____ Date _____

IT'S A SNAP!
Explanation and Exercises

A. ANSWERS TO EXERCISES ON ACTIVITY SHEET 8A:

Exercise B: 1. it's, 2. it's, 3. its, 4. It's,
5. its, 6. it's

Exercise D: 1. your; you're, 2. your, 3. you're,
4. you're, 5. your, 6. your

B. WHO'S? WHOSE? The rules for using *who's* or *whose* are similar to those for *it, it's* and *your, you're*.

Whose shows possession, as *Whose* book is this?

Who's means *who is,* as *Who's* coming with me? or *who has,* as
Who's left the dirty dishes in the sink?

C. TRY IT OUT: Fill in the blank spaces below. Remember, *who's* always stands for *who is* or *who has*.

1. _____ going to answer the question?

2. _____ taken the car?

3. _____ answers are always correct?

4. Papa Bear asked, " _____ been sitting in my chair?"

5. _____ chair is next to mine?

D. EXERCISES FOR EXPERTS: Fill in the blank spaces with the correct word.

1. _____ that knocking at my door?   (who's or whose)

2. Give me _____ hand.   (your or you're)

3. Give the mail to _____ mother.   (your or you're)

4. _____ fun to go to the movies.   (its or it's)

5. Tell Marty that _____ going to his party.   (your or you're)

6. The cat went straight to _____ food dish.   (its or it's)

7. _____ sweaters are in the washing machine?   (whose or who's)

8. _____ often rained on my birthday.   (its or it's)

Answers to Exercise C: 1. Who's, 2. Who's, 3. Whose, 4. Who's, 5. Whose
Answers to Exercise D: 1. Who's, 2. your, 3. your, 4. It's, 5. you're, 6. its,
7. Whose, 8. It's

© 2000 by The Center for Applied Research in Education

Name _____ Date _____

LEND OR LOAN?
Explanation and Exercises

A. Do you ever have trouble knowing when to use

clothes	or	*cloths?*
lend	or	*loan?*
convince	or	*persuade?*

Here is what you need to know to use these words correctly.

Clothes are things one wears, as She wears expensive *clothes*.
Cloths refers to materials, as Her dresses are made from fine *cloths*.

Lend is a verb meaning "to borrow," as *Lend* me some money.
Loan is a noun; it is something one gets, as Give me a small *loan*.

One is *convinced* to see things a certain way, as Ethan *convinced* his sister that ice cream is the best dessert.
One is *persuaded* to *do* something, as Ethan *persuaded* his sister to eat chocolate ice cream.

B. TRY IT OUT: Fill in the blank spaces below.

1. I am _____ that honesty is the best policy.   (convinced, persuaded)

2. Can you _____ the cat to come inside?   (convince, persuade)

3. The class _____ the teacher to give less homework.   (convinced, persuaded)

4. Don't wear torn _____ to school.   (clothes or cloths)

5. You could never _____ me to cheat on a test.   (convince or persuade)

6. The painters use drop _____ to protect the rug.   (clothes or cloths)

7. Did you ever _____ money to a friend?   (lend or loan)

8. They _____ books at the library.   (lend or loan)

9. I got a _____ of $100 from the bank.   (lend or loan)

10. Can you _____ the bank to give me a _____?   (convince or persuade);
    (lend or loan)

Answers: 1. convinced,   2. persuade,   3. persuaded,   4. clothes,   5. persuade,   6. cloths,   7. lend,   8. lend,   9. loan,   10. persuade; loan

© 2000 by The Center for Applied Research in Education

Name _____ Date _____

LEND OR LOAN?
Paragraph—First Draft

A. Fill in each of the blank spaces in the paragraph below with one of the words from the following list (or the appropriate form of that word, such as convinces, loaned, etc.):

cloths	convince	lend
clothes	persuade	loan

   Every morning, I wake up and try to _____ myself that it is a school holiday. Then my Mom comes in and _____ me to get dressed, so I put on my _____. I feel better after breakfast, especially if I can _____ Mom to cook pancakes. Then, after I get my brother to _____ me his new baseball cap, I'm ready to go.

*ANSWERS AT THE BOTTOM OF THE PAGE.

B. Now you are going to write your own paragraph, describing some part of your day. It can be morning at home, like the one above, or your trip to school or a school day or an afternoon with your friends or any other part of your day you choose. Begin the paragraph with a topic sentence, which tells what the paragraph is about. Add at least three more sentences. Include at least three of the words from the list at the top of the page.

   Write your paragraph here. (This is a first draft, so concentrate on getting your thoughts down on paper. Don't be too concerned about grammar or spelling, except for the words on the list.)

_____

_____

_____

_____

_____

_____

_____

_____

Answers to Exercise A: convince, persuades, clothes, persuade, lend

© 2000 by The Center for Applied Research in Education

Name _____ Date _____

LEND OR LOAN?
Paragraph—Revising and Writing a Final Copy

WORDS OFTEN CONFUSED		
cloths	convince	lend
clothes	persuade	loan

A. Revise and edit the paragraph you wrote for Activity 9B, using the following questions as guidelines:

1. Does your beginning (topic) sentence tell what the paragraph is about? If not, change it.

2. Do you use at least three of the words on the list above? Can you find a place in the paragraph to use another of these words?

3. Does your final sentence sum up the topic?

4. Are your sentences complete? Do the subjects and verbs agree?

5. Are there any words you are not sure how to spell? Consult a dictionary.

B. When your paragraph is as good as you can make it, write your final copy below. (Indent at the beginning of the paragraph.)

© 2000 by The Center for Applied Research in Education

Name _____ Date _____

THERE YOU ARE!
Explanations and Exercises

A. *They're* wearing *their* best clothes *there* at the party.

They're, their, and *there,* are sometimes confused, but the sentence above clearly shows how each should be used.

They're means "they are" (The apostrophe shows the missing letter *a*), as in *They're* all coming to my party.

Their shows possession and is followed by a noun or noun phrase, as in The team won *their* final game.

There shows direction and means "in or at that place," as in *There* is my house.

B. TRY IT OUT: Fill in the blank spaces below with *there, their,* or *they're.*

1. _____ will be a party at Anita's house tomorrow.

2. All her friends will be _____.

3. _____ going to bring presents for Anita.

4. _____ expecting good food to eat.

5. They hope that Anita will like _____ presents.

6. Anita's brother, Ricardo, will be _____, too.

7. _____ going to play games at the party.

8. After the party, _____ parents will pick them up.

9. Anita and Ricardo will have to clean up _____ house.

*ANSWERS ON ACTIVITY SHEET 10B.

C. Two other words that are sometimes confused are *thorough* and *through.*

Thorough means "complete or all that is needed," as in They did a *thorough* cleaning of the house.

Through means "by way of or from one end to the other" as in They went *through* the house with a vacuum cleaner. *Through* can also mean *finished.*

D. TRY IT OUT: Fill in the blanks with *through* or *thorough.*

1. We drove _____ the whole town in one hour.

2. The police made a _____ search of the crime scene.

3. They searched _____ the whole area before they were _____.

4. Did you make a _____ study of the assigned chapters?

*ANSWERS ON ACTIVITY SHEET 10B.

© 2000 by The Center for Applied Research in Education

Name _____ Date _____

THERE YOU ARE!
Additional Exercises

A. ANSWERS TO EXERCISES ON ACTIVITY SHEET 10A:

Exercise B. 1. There,   2. there,   3. They're,
4. They're, 5. their,   6. there,
7. They're, 8. their,   9. their

Exercise D. 1. through,   2. thorough,
3. through, through,
4. thorough

B. Fill in the blanks in the paragraph below using words from the following list:

there	they're	through
their		thorough (or thoroughly)

The Smiths want _____ house to be _____ clean for their big New

Year's party. _____ hiring a cleaning service to do the job. _____

expecting a hundred people and hope _____ will be enough room for all.

Everyone they know will be _____, including _____ whole family.

When the cleaners are _____, they hope that _____ house will be

sparkling. If the cleaners do not do a _____ job, they will not be hired again.

*ANSWERS AT THE BOTTOM OF THE PAGE.

C. Use the same list of words to fill in the blanks in these sentences.

1. My friends are happy because _____ going to New York.

2. They have wanted to go _____ for a long time.

3. Now, _____ dream is coming true.

4. _____ parents are planning lots of sightseeing for them.

5. _____ are many interesting sights in New York.

6. _____ hoping to do a _____ visit and see everything.

7. The hope to go _____ all the museums.

*ANSWERS AT THE BOTTOM OF THE PAGE.

© 2000 by The Center for Applied Research in Education

Answers to Sentences: 1. they're,   2. there,   3. their,   4. Their,   5. There,
6. They're, thorough,   7. through

Answers to Paragraph: their, thoroughly, They're, there, there, their, through,
their, thorough

Name _____ Date _____

AS YOU LIKE IT!
Explanation and Exercises

A. "As You Like It" is a play by William Shakespeare. It is a wonderful name for a play, but do you know the correct use of the words *as* and *like?*

> *as* is used when comparing phrases, as in
> Maria has just as much trouble with homework *as* I do.
> That boy is *as* noisy *as* a herd of elephants.

> *like* is used when comparing nouns and pronouns, as in
> Joe is just *like* his father.
> The ballerina is *like* a graceful bird.

B. Here are some more words and phrases that are often confused.

> *fewer* is used with things that can be counted, as in
> Mr. Pace's class has *fewer* tests than ours.
> That store employs *fewer* than fifteen workers.

> *less* is used with a general quantity, as in:
> The Oteros have *less* money to live on than the Browns.
> My mom wants me to spend *less* time playing basketball.

> *agree to* is used with an action, as in
> The referee *agreed to* change the rules.
> I won't *agree to* do anything stupid.

> *agree with* is used with someone, as in
> Sam always *agrees with* his best friend.
> Marta *agreed with* Sarah.

> *persecute* means to treat someone badly or unfairly, as in
> The Nazis *persecuted* the Jews during World War II.
> Joe thought he was being *persecuted* by the bullies in his class.

> *prosecute* means to be charged in a court of law, as in
> The district attorney *prosecutes* criminals.
> If you break the law, you will be *prosecuted.*

C. Fill in the blank spaces below with the correct word.

1. Jack is tall _____ his father.   (*as* or *like*)

2. Carla _____ help Helen with her homework.   (*agreed with* or *agreed to*)

3. People usually eat _____ fat on a diet.   (*fewer* or *less*)

4. Criminals will be _____ if they steal.   (*prosecuted* or *persecuted*)

*ANSWERS ON ACTIVITY 11B.

© 2000 by The Center for Applied Research in Education

Name _____ Date _____

AS YOU LIKE IT!
Additional Exercises

A. ANSWERS TO EXERCISE C ON ACTIVITY 11A:
1. like   3. less
2. agreed to   4. prosecuted

as or *like*	*less* or *fewer*
agree with or *agree to*	*persecute* or *prosecute*

B. Write a sentence using each of the words or phrases in the above list.

1. (as)   _____

2. (like)   _____

3. (agree with)   _____

4. (agree to)   _____

5. (less)   _____

6. (fewer)   _____

7. (persecute)   _____

8. (prosecute)   _____

C. Check the correct sentence in each of the following groups:

1. a. There were less people in the audience on Sunday.
   b. There were fewer people in the audience on Sunday.

2. a. That witness will be prosecuted because he lied.
   b. That witness will be persecuted because he lied.

3. a. I agreed with my friend, Jimmy.
   b. I agreed to my friend, Jimmy.

4. a. Sometimes my brother is as a two-year-old.
   b. Sometimes my brother is like a two-year-old.

5. a. There are fewer calories in low-fat food.
   b. There are less calories in low-fat food.

*SEE ANSWERS BELOW.

Answers to Exercise C: 1. b   2. a   3. a   4. b   5. a

© 2000 by The Center for Applied Research in Education

Name _____ Date _____

AGREE TO WHAT?
Explanation and Exercises

Do you know what an idiom is? That's *idiom*, not idiot! Of course, you don't have to be an idiot not to know the meaning of an idiom.

An *idiom* is a group of words used in a special way in a particular language. Through usage and tradition, these phrases have come to have certain meanings. Spanish idioms are different from English idioms. People learning English often have difficulty using idiomatic expressions. Here are some idioms commonly used in English: *birds of a feather, dark horse, horse of a different color, all thumbs, get one's back up.*

Sometimes, people are confused about the correct use of idiomatic expressions, as in these examples

Agree *to,* as in agree *to* a proposal
Agree *on,* as in agree *on* a method
Agree *with,* as in agree *with* a friend

Differ *with,* as in differ *with* a person
Differ *from,* as in differ *from* something else (comparison)
Differ *about,* as in differ *about* a question

TRY IT OUT: Fill in the blank spaces below.

1. I agree _____ my father's opinions on most things.

2. Dad and I differ _____ how much allowance I should get.

3. We finally agreed _____ ten dollars a week.

4. I would not agree _____ settle for less.

5. My family differs _____ yours in many ways.

6. I often differ _____ my father about things like allowances.

*CHECK YOUR ANSWERS ON ACTIVITY 12B.

Here are more idiomatic expressions that are sometimes troublesome.

acquainted *with* (not *to*)
graduated *from* (not *graduated*)
according *to* (not according *with*)
desirous *of* (not desirous *to*)

TRY IT OUT AGAIN: Fill in the blank spaces below.

1. Are you acquainted _____ my cousin, Carlos?

2. He graduated _____ high school in June.

3. According _____ Carlos, it's easy to get into college.

4. Carlos is desirous _____ becoming a computer engineer.

*CHECK YOUR ANSWERS ON ACTIVITY 12B.

© 2000 by The Center for Applied Research in Education

Name _____ Date _____

AGREE TO WHAT?
More Idioms

> **A. ANSWERS TO EXERCISES IN ACTIVITY 12A:**
> *Try It Out:* 1. with, 2. about, 3. on, 4. to,
>   5. from, 6. with
> *Try It Out Again:* 1. with, 2. from, 3. to, 4. of

B. MORE IDIOMATIC EXPRESSIONS

> impatient *for* something that one wants to get or happen
> impatient *with* somebody else
> impatient *at* someone's behavior
>
> rewarded *for* something one has done
> rewarded *with* a gift or a medal
> rewarded *by* someone else

TRY IT OUT: Fill in the blank spaces in the sentences below.

1. The audience was impatient _____ the movie to begin.
2. The substitute teacher was impatient _____ the unruly class.
3. Olympic athletes are rewarded _____ medals.
4. Jack was rewarded _____ finding and returning Mrs. Jones' purse.
5. The sitter was impatient _____ the naughty behavior of the kids.
6. Jack was rewarded _____ Mrs. Jones for returning her purse.

*CHECK YOUR ANSWERS ON ACTIVITY SHEET 12C.

ADDITIONAL IDIOMS: Here are other idiomatic expressions that are sometimes a problem.

> among *themselves* (not among one another)
> in search *of* (not in search for)
> cannot help *talking* (not cannot help but talk)
> prefer something *to* something else (not prefer it over something else)
> authority *on* (not authority about)

TRY IT OUT AGAIN: Fill in the blank spaces in the sentences below.

1. People cannot help _____ about unusual events.
2. My social studies teacher is an authority _____ the Civil War.
3. I prefer swimming in a pool _____ swimming in the ocean.
4. The people in the audience were talking among _____.
5. I was looking through the closet in search _____ my hat.

*CHECK YOUR ANSWERS ON ACTIVITY SHEET 12C.

© 2000 by The Center for Applied Research in Education

Name _____ Date _____

AGREE TO WHAT?
Using Idioms in a Paragraph

> **A. ANSWERS TO EXERCISES IN EXERCISE 12B:**
>
> *Try It Out:* 1. for,   2. with,   3. with,   4. for,   5. with,   6. by
>
> *Try It Out Again:* 1. talking,   2. on,   3. to,   4. themselves,   5. of

B. USING IDIOMS CORRECTLY IN A PARAGRAPH: The paragraph that follows contains five idiomatic expressions that are not correct. Can you find all five of them? First, circle the words that are wrong. Then, write the complete paragraph correctly on the lines below.

> Yesterday, I got into trouble. It all started when I got impatient at my little brother, Andy, for pestering me. I was in my closet in search for a book I needed. Andy burst into my room. He wanted me to agree to him that our sister, Amy, is a pest. Andy said, "Just because she graduated high school doesn't mean she knows everything!" I was so annoyed at the interruption that I couldn't help but talk in a loud voice. In fact, I yelled. Mom heard me and that's how I got into trouble.

Did you find all *five* incorrect idioms? If you are not sure, you can check the key at the bottom of this page. Then, copy the complete paragraph correctly on the lines below. (Don't forget to indent at the beginning of the paragraph)

_____

_____

_____

_____

_____

_____

_____

(Did you correct all the errors in the paragraph? Here they are:

impatient at should be impatient with; in search for should be in search of; agree to him should be agree with him; graduated high school should be graduated from high school; couldn't help but talk should be couldn't help talking.)

© 2000 by The Center for Applied Research in Education

Name _____ Date _____

NOWHERE! NOHOW!
Illiteracies: Explanation and Exercises

The language you may hear out on the street is not always acceptable for written English. There are some kinds of word usage you want to avoid. *Illiteracies* are words and phrases that are incorrect in both spoken *and* written English. Here are some common illiteracies. These are not real words and should *never* be used!

---

ain't should be isn't, aren't, or am not, as in *he isn't, I am not, they aren't*

anywheres should be anywhere, as in I'm not going *anywhere.*

nowheres should be nowhere, as in I am going *nowhere.*

nohow could be at all, as in I can't do that work *at all.*

brung should be brought, as in I *brought* in the mail.

drownded should be drowned, as in She *drowned* in the ocean.

this here should be this, as in *This* is my brother.

couldn't of should be couldn't have, as in I *couldn't have* done it without help.

I been should be I have been, as in *I have been* hungry all day.

B. FIX IT! Each of the following sentences contains one illiteracy. Circle the word or phrase that is wrong. Then, write the complete sentences correctly on the lines below.

1. Did you hear about the man who drownded in the lake yesterday?

_____

2. Jerry ain't going to make the team this year.

_____

3. Robin brung the books back to the library on time.

_____

4. You couldn't of seen me because I wasn't there.

_____

5. I been in the park all morning.

_____

6. Julio couldn't find his sneakers anywheres.

_____

© 2000 by The Center for Applied Research in Education

Answers: 1. *drownded* should be *drowned,* **2.** *ain't* should be *isn't,* **3.** *brung* should be *brought,* **4.** *couldn't of* should be *couldn't have,* **5.** *been* should be *have been,* **6.** *anywheres* should be *anywhere*

Name _____ Date _____

NOWHERE! NOHOW!
Illiteracies: Explanation and Exercises

A. Here are some more words and phrases you may hear on the street, but which are NOT correct English.

1. *Goes* means that someone or something is moving. It should NEVER be used to show speech. The correct word to use is *says*.

    WRONG: Magda *goes,* "I can't come to your house today."
→ **RIGHT:**   Magda *says,* "I can't come to your house today."

2. There is no such word as *snuck*. The past tense of sneak is *sneaked*.

    WRONG: Matthew *snuck* into his room.
→ **RIGHT:**   Matthew *sneaked* into his room.

3. Never say *alls I know* when you mean *all I know*.

    WRONG: *Alls I know* is that I can't find my book.
→ **RIGHT:**   *All I know* is that I can't find my book.

4. Never say *in regards to*. The correct phrase is *in regard to* or *regarding*.

    WRONG: I'll speak to the teacher *in regards to* my homework.
→ **RIGHT:**   I'll speak to the teacher *in regard to* my homework.
→ **RIGHT:**   I'll speak to the teacher *regarding* my homework.

B. Rewrite each sentence correctly on the line below.

1. My mom always goes, "Tell the truth."

_____

2. Alls I know is that I'm not the one who did that.

_____

3. Do you have any information in regards to our new neighbors?

_____

4. Last night, I snuck into the kitchen for a late-night snack.

_____

© 2000 by The Center for Applied Research in Education

Name _____ Date _____

NOWHERE! NOHOW!
Colloquialisms and Slang: Explanation and Exercises

A. *Colloquialisms* are words or phrases that are acceptable for use in conversation, but should usually be avoided in written work unless they are used for some specific purpose, such as humor or dialogue. Some common colloquialisms are

> *show up* should be come or attend, as in He *came* late to class.

> *take a try at* should be try, as in I will *try* cooking dinner tomorrow.

> *alongside of* should be alongside, as in He pulled up *alongside* the bus.

> *flabbergast* should be surprise or amaze, as in
> Sally was *surprised* when she got an A in English.

B. SLANG: Everyone uses some slang in conversations, but slang is not suitable for written English for several reasons. First, slang is always changing. A word or phrase that is popular today may not be recognized by anyone in a couple of years. Slang meanings can vary from group to group or place to place, so a slang word you use in California may not be understood by someone in New York. Also, slang can be an excuse for not using the best word or phrase. It is not always wrong to use slang, but most of the time a better way can be found. Here are some common slang expressions that should usually be avoided in written work.

> psych out, corny, egghead, scram, mod, lousy, swell, jerk, goof off, blow one's top, rip off, cool it.

C. FIX IT: Circle any colloquialisms or slang in the following paragraph. Then, copy the paragraph on the lines below, using better English.

> My Uncle Ethan is a swell guy. He offered to drive me to school. We were almost there when a car pulled up alongside of us on the road. The lousy jerk inside tried to psych us out by screaming out the window. Uncle Ethan blew his top and yelled back. I told him to cool it, and the other car scrammed.

_____

_____

_____

_____

(Did you circle and change the following colloquialisms and slang? swell, alongside of, lousy, jerk, psych us out, blew his top, cool it, scrammed)

© 2000 by The Center for Applied Research in Education

Name _____ Date _____

GOOD AS GOLD
Explanation and Exercises

A *trite* word or phrase is one that has become worn out with use. Sometimes these words or phrases are called *cliches*. Here are some phrases that have been used so much they have become TRITE.

> green as grass, good as gold, brave as a lion, cold as ice, bigger and better things, beat around the bush, butterflies in my stomach, honest to goodness, last but not least, live it up, necessary evil, nip in the bud, raining cats and dogs, sad to relate, the time of my life, worse for wear, through thick and thin, in this day and age, goes without saying, fond memories

FIX IT!: Each of the following exercise contains a trite phrase. Rewrite the sentence on the line below using a better phrase.

1. My aunt's new baby is as good as gold.

   _____

2. I had butterflies in my stomach before I had to go on stage.

   _____

3. I forgot my gloves, and my fingers were as cold as ice.

   _____

4. My old typewriter is none the worse for wear.

   _____

5. Homework is a necessary evil.

   _____

6. I looked out the window and saw it was raining cats and dogs.

   _____

7. Joanna had the time of her life at the party.

   _____

8. I will remain your friend through thick and thin.

   _____

9. This is an honest to goodness genuine diamond.

   _____

© 2000 by The Center for Applied Research in Education

Name _____ Date _____

WHEN *NO* MEANS *YES*
Explanation and Exercise

© 2000 by The Center for Applied Research in Education

A. DOUBLE NEGATIVE: Did you ever hear anyone state, "I don't want no broccoli"? That person is saying the opposite of what he means. When he says he doesn't want *no* broccoli, that means he wants *some* broccoli. What he should say is, "I don't want *any* broccoli" or "I don't want broccoli."

This is called a *double negative*. If you don't want to say the opposite of what you intend, you must never use double negatives.

Here are some more examples of double negatives, and the correct version for each.

Marlon did not see nobody in the room.	(WRONG!)
Marlon did not see anybody in the room.	(CORRECT) ←
Don't give me none of that nonsense.	(WRONG!)
Don't give me any of that nonsense.	(CORRECT) ←
Jack did not want nothing to do with Jill.	(WRONG!)
Jack did not want anything to do with Jill.	(CORRECT) ←
A criminal should not get no respect.	(WRONG!)
A criminal should not get any respect. (or)	(CORRECT) ←
A criminal should not get respect.	(CORRECT) ←
Carrie will not do none of her homework.	(WRONG!)
Carrie will not do any of her homework.	(CORRECT) ←

B. Each of the following sentences contains a double negative. Rewrite each sentence correctly on the line below.

1. Jesse would not answer none of the teacher's questions.

   _____

2. Matt did not fail no tests in English this year.

   _____

3. I don't have to do no homework tonight.

   _____

4. I have not had no luck today.

   _____

5. Alice won't do nothing to help her mother.

   _____

Answers: 1. Jesse would not answer any of the teacher's questions. **2.** Matt did not fail any tests in English this year. **3.** I don't have to do any homework tonight. **4.** I have not had any luck today. **5.** Alice won't do anything to help her mother.

PUNCTUATION HELP

TEACHER'S GUIDE—
ALPHABETICAL LISTING OF PUNCTUATION PROBLEMS
AND THEIR ACTIVITY NUMBERS

Here is a list of the punctuation problems addressed in this section, and the relevant exercises.

PUNCTUATION	ACTIVITY NUMBER
Apostrophe	18A, B, C, D
Colon	19
Comma	16A, B, C, D, E, F
Dash	17
Ellipsis	23A, B
Exclamation Point	24A, B, C
Hyphen	21
Parentheses	23A, B
Period	24A, B, C
Question Mark	24A, B, C
Quotation Mark	22A, B, C, D
Semicolon	20A, B
Slash	23A, B
Punctuation Review	25A, B
Punctuation Review	26A, B

Name _____ Date _____

LISTS AND SEPARATORS
Explanation and Exercises

Do you ever throw commas into a sentence any old way because you think they are needed but are not sure where they belong? Putting a comma in the wrong place can make a sentence as confusing as using no commas at all. In this activity you will learn some rules to simplify the use of commas.

> **IN GENERAL, A COMMA IS USED TO SEPARATE WORDS OR PHRASES TO MAKE THEIR MEANING MORE CLEAR.**

➤ **RULE 1**   A comma is used to separate words in a series or list.

Examples: Mary, Jenna, and Kristen are all coming to my party.
His hobbies are sports, reading, and stamp collecting.

➤ **RULE 2**   Do not use a comma before the first word in a list or after the last word in a list.

Wrong: I had, juice, eggs, and milk, for breakfast.

Right: I had juice, eggs, and milk for breakfast.

Here are some exercises for you to do for *Rules 1 and 2.* In the following sentences, put commas where they are needed.

1. Bobby's favorite periods in school are English Gym and Lunch.

2. Chris has lived in New York California and Florida.

3. Apples oranges and pears are fruits that are good to eat.

4. His shirt had blue white and black stripes.

*ANSWERS ON ACTIVITY SHEET 16B.

➤ **RULE 3**   Commas are used to separate phrases in a series.

Examples: I have two books, three pens, and one notebook.
He is either in his house, at the playground, or at school.

In the following sentences, insert commas where necessary to separate phrases in a list.

1. There are three oak trees two rose bushes and one vegetable garden in the backyard.

2. This afternoon, I shall watch TV eat dinner and do my homework.

3. Jack plans to visit his aunt go to the shore and read three books during the summer.

4. I am going to take a shower get dressed and eat breakfast.

*ANSWERS ON ACTIVITY SHEET 16B.

© 2000 by The Center for Applied Research in Edueation

Name _____ Date _____

LISTS AND SEPARATORS
Additional Rules and Exercises

ANSWERS TO EXERCISES ON ACTIVITY SHEET 16A:

RULES 1 and 2:

1. Bobby's favorite periods in school are English, Gym, and Lunch.
2. Chris has lived in New York, California, and Florida.
3. Apples, oranges, and pears are fruits that are good to eat.
4. His shirt had blue, white, and black stripes.

RULE 3:

1. There are three oak trees, two rose bushes, and one vegetable garden in the backyard.
2. This afternoon, I shall watch TV, eat dinner, and do my homework.
3. Jack plans to visit his aunt, go to the shore, and read three books during the summer.
4. I am going to take a shower, get dressed, and eat breakfast.

→ **RULE 4**   Use commas to enclose a word or phrase that follows a noun (or pronoun) to identify or describe it. This is called a word (or phrase) in apposition.

Examples: We visited Aunt Anne, my mother's sister, yesterday.
Mr. Wiley, my math teacher, is very strict.

(Notice that if you leave out the *words in apposition* the sentence would still be complete and make sense.)

In the following sentences, insert commas to set off the word (or phrase) in apposition:

1. Albany the capital of New York is a large city.
2. Andy my best friend lives on the next block.
3. I went to visit Mrs. Adams our neighbor in the hospital.
4. The last book I read *Tom Sawyer* was humorous.
5. George Washington the first president of the United States was a great man.

*ANSWERS ON ACTIVITY SHEET 16C.

→ **RULE 5**   Use a comma before (or after) a quotation, as in dialogue.

Examples: Jeff said, "I'll race you to the corner."
"Okay," I replied.

IN THE FOLLOWING DIALOGUE, INSERT COMMAS WHERE REQUIRED:

Linda opened the door and said "Come on in."

I walked into the living room. "Let's do our homework" I suggested.

"Okay" Linda replied. "What should we do first" she asked.

"I'd like to work on math first" I told her.

ANSWERS ON ACTIVITY SHEET 16C.

© 2000 by The Center for Applied Research in Education

Name _____   Date _____

LISTS AND SEPARATORS
Additional Rules and Exercises

A. ANSWERS TO EXERCISES ON ACTIVITY SHEET 16B

RULE 4   1. Albany, the capital of New York, is a large city.
2. Andy, my best friend, lives on the next block.
3. I went to visit Mrs. Adams, our neighbor, in the hospital.
4. The last book I read, *Tom Sawyer,* was humorous.
5. George Washington, the first president of the U.S., was a great man.

RULE 5   Linda opened the door and said, "Come on in."
I walked into the living room. "Let's do our homework," I suggested.
"Okay," Linda replied. "What should we do first," she asked.
"I'd like to work on math first," I told her.

→ **RULE 6**   Use a comma after an introductory word or a phrase at the beginning of a sentence to separate it from the main part of the sentence.

Examples: When I saw my school photo, I laughed out loud.
If you see Erin, tell her I'll be home late today.
After you get there, wait for me.
Usually, I get home at three o'clock.

B. Insert commas in the following sentences to separate the introductory clause from the rest of the sentence.

1. When you finish your homework go to sleep.
2. After I get home I'll call Kevin.
3. Before you leave put on your coat.
4. If I get there first I'll wait for you.
5. As soon as I get home I'll call you.
6. However I may get home earlier.

*ANSWERS ON THE BOTTOM OF THIS PAGE.

Answers to Exercises for Rule 6:

1. When you finish your homework, go to sleep.
2. After I get home, I'll call Kevin.
3. Before you leave, put on your coat.
4. If I get there first, I'll wait for you.
5. As soon as I get home, I'll call you.
6. However, I may get home earlier.

© 2000 by The Center for Applied Research in Education

Name _____ Date _____

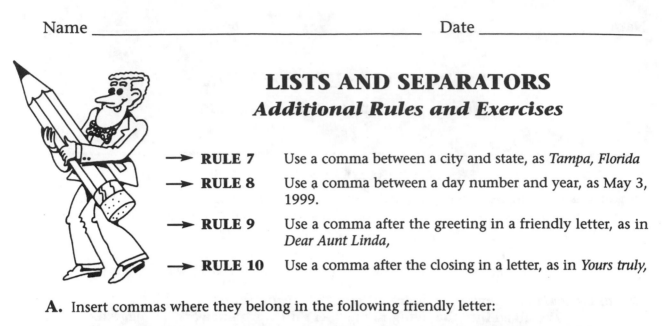

LISTS AND SEPARATORS
Additional Rules and Exercises

→ **RULE 7** Use a comma between a city and state, as *Tampa, Florida*

→ **RULE 8** Use a comma between a day number and year, as May 3, 1999.

→ **RULE 9** Use a comma after the greeting in a friendly letter, as in *Dear Aunt Linda,*

→ **RULE 10** Use a comma after the closing in a letter, as in *Yours truly,*

A. Insert commas where they belong in the following friendly letter:

> 25 Maple Street
> Oakville NY 10950
> December 1 2000
>
> Dear Kevin
>
> I hope you are happy in your new house. What is it like to live in Philadelphia Pennsylvania? In school all the kids miss you. Do you remember the tall blonde kid Pat Sawyer? Yesterday he asked where you were. When you come back for the holidays don't forget to call me.
>
> Your friend
> Andy

CHECK YOUR PUNCTUATION WITH THE ANSWER AT THE BOTTOM OF THIS PAGE.

B. Insert commas where they belong in the following sentences:

1. Did you ever visit Disney World in Orlando Florida?
2. When I was a little kid we lived in Denver Colorado.
3. We moved here on April 5 1998.
4. My sister was born on February 17 1995.

Answers:

In the letter: Commas should appear in the following places: Oakville, NY   December 1, 2000
Dear Kevin,   Philadelphia, Pennsylvania
In school,   tall, blonde kid, Pat Sawyer   Yesterday,   Your friend,   holidays,

In the sentences: Commas should be used after these words:
1. Orlando,   2. Kid, Denver,   3. April 5,   4. February 17,

© 2000 by The Center for Applied Research in Education

Name _____ Date _____

LISTS AND SEPARATORS
Additional Rules and Exercises

➤ **RULE 11**   Use a comma between two adjectives modifying the same noun, as *I came to a strange, far-off city.*

Note: Use the comma only if you are able to use the word *and* in its place (a strange *and* far-off city). If you could not use "and" between the adjectives, do not use a comma, as *He wore a dark blue jacket.* (No comma—you could *not* say dark *and* blue.)

➤ **RULE 12**   Use a comma after introductory words in a sentence, as in *Oh, there you are!*

A. Insert commas where they belong in the following sentences:

1. Really I cannot understand a word you say.

2. Here give this to your brother.

3. That tree has ripe delicious fruit.

4. She wore a light blue dress.

5. He is a tall handsome man.

6. Lara why are you late?

7. It was a wonderful interesting trip.

8. No I can't go to the party tomorrow.

9. Look at the starry moonlit sky!

10. Last night I saw a scary exciting movie.

11. Rex come here right now!

© 2000 by The Center for Applied Research in Education

Answers: Commas should be inserted after the following words:

1. Really,   2. Here,   3. ripe,   4. no comma   5. tall,   6. Lara,   7. wonderful,   8. No,   9. starry,   10. scary,   11. Rex,

Name _____ Date _____

LISTS AND SEPARATORS
Review

This activity contains exercises to help you review what you have learned about using commas.

A. Complete these sentences by putting in commas where needed.

1. When I get home I'm going to walk the dog finish my homework and eat dinner.

2. By the middle of the next century we'll all be traveling in space.

3. My favorite computer game "Battling the Bad Guy" is on sale today.

4. Looking at his mom's face Gary knew he was in trouble.

5. My friend Tom Hansen is moving away.

*ANSWERS AT BOTTOM OF THIS PAGE.

B. Insert commas wherever they are needed in the following paragraph:

> Yesterday I noticed my friend Ellen in the library. She was sitting at a table with two books three magazines and two pens. "Hi" I said. When she saw me she smiled. "Hello" she replied. I asked her if she was working on a report for Mr. Simons our social studies teacher. Nodding her head she remarked that parts one two and three of the report were the hardest. "Once I get that part done I'll be home free" she said.

© 2000 by The Center for Applied Research in Education

Answers:

A. 1. When I get home, I'm going to walk the dog, finish my homework, and eat dinner.
2. By the middle of the next century, we'll all be traveling in space.
3. My favorite computer game, "Battling the Bad Guy," is on sale today.
4. Looking at his mom's face, Gary knew he was in trouble.
5. My friend, Tom Hansen, is moving away.

B. Yesterday, I noticed my friend, Ellen, in the library. She was sitting at a table with two books, three magazines, and two pens. "Hi," I said. When she saw me, she smiled. "Hello," she replied. I asked her if she was working on a report for Mr. Simons, our social studies teacher. Nodding her head, she remarked that parts one, two, and three of the report were the hardest. "Once I get that part done, I'll be home free," she said.

Name _____ Date _____

SET IT OFF
Explanation and Exercises

A. *Dashes* set off ideas that are separate from the main sentence. They are similar to commas but interrupt the sentence more forcefully and emphasize the additional thought, as

1. Aunt Emma—a wild and funny lady—is my mother's younger sister.

2. The New York Giants—Alan's favorite team—is winning again.

3. June Masterson—a really annoying person—sits behind me in class.

Dashes can also be used to introduce a word—or group of words—you want to emphasize, as

1. Dennis needs one thing to make his life complete—a new bike.

2. Mom asked if I had everything I needed for the trip—my sleeping bag, a change of clothing, and my camera.

3. The person I least wanted to see showed up for the party—Lucy Grant.

B. Rewrite these sentences on the line below, inserting dashes where needed.

1. Ellen knows how to cook three things spaghetti, scrambled eggs, and hamburgers.

_____

2. Mr. Jacobs my favorite teacher in the world was absent today.

_____

3. Sweet-smelling flowers roses and gardenias grew in the garden.

_____

4. Are you sure you have the right address 23 Cranshaw Road?

_____

5. One emotion stands out above all the rest love.

_____

© 2000 by The Center for Applied Research in Education

Answers to Exercise B:

1. Ellen knows how to cook three things—spaghetti, scrambled eggs, and hamburgers.
2. Mr. Jacobs—my favorite teacher in the world—was absent today.
3. Sweet-smelling flowers—roses and gardenias—grew in the garden.
4. Are you sure you have the right address—23 Cranshaw Road?
5. One emotion stands out above all the rest—love.

Name _____ Date _____

WHOSE IS IT?
Explanation and Exercises

The *apostrophe* has two meanings. It either shows possession or means that a letter has been left out.

A. POSSESSION: The apostrophe shows ownership by someone or something, as

> *Jake's* dog is tearing up our yard. (The dog belongs to Jake.)
> The *children's* clothing department is busy. (The clothing belongs to the children.)

Put the apostrophe *after* the *s* in plural words, as

> The *ladies'* room is down the hall. (Room belongs to ladies.)
> The *students'* tests are on the *teacher's* desk. (Tests belong to the students—plural.
>   Desk belongs to the teacher—singular.)

Do not use an apostrophe with personal possessive pronouns—*my, mine, your, yours, his, her, hers, its, our, ours, your, yours, their, theirs*—since these already show possession without the apostrophe, as

> Janie left *her* book on the table.
> The book is *hers*.
> The dog obeys *its* owner.

B. Complete the following sentences by inserting the correct word:

1. The _____ crown is on her head.   (The crown belongs to the Queen.)

2. The _____ medal was pinned to his coat.   (The medal belongs to the hero.)

3. You will recognize the bakery by _____ heavenly aroma.   (*its* or *it's*)

4. The _____ howling was frightening.   (The howling belongs to the wolves.)

5. Is this lunchbox _____?   (The lunchbox belongs to you.)

6. The _____ bouquet is beautiful.   (The bouquet belongs to the bride.)

7. The _____ stalls have been cleaned.   (The stalls belong to the horses.)

8. This pen is _____.   (The pen belongs to me.)

9. _____ team is the best in Little League.   (The team belongs to Patrick.)

10. My _____ store is on this block.   (The store belongs to the parents.)

*See Activity 18B for Answers.

© 2000 by The Center for Applied Research in Education

Name _____ Date _____

WHAT'S LEFT OUT?
Explanation and Exercises

> **A. ANSWERS TO ACTIVITY 18A:**
> 1. Queen's, 2. hero's, 3. its, 4. wolves', 5. yours, 6. bride's,
> 7. horses', 8. mine, 9. Patrick's, 10. parents'

B. The apostrophe is used to show that something (a letter) has been left out, as

It's going to be the most important game of the year.
(*It's* stands for *it is*. The apostrophe takes the place of the *i* in *is*.)

I *don't* want to miss that game.
(*Don't* means *do not*. The *o* in *not* is left out. The apostrophe takes its place.)

He's going to have a great birthday party.
(*He's* means *he is*. The apostrophe takes the place of the *i* in *is*.)

Words that use the apostrophe to show omitted letters are called *contractions*. Some additional contractions are: wasn't (was not), isn't (is not), can't (cannot), doesn't (does not), didn't (did not), she's (she is), aren't (are not), and I'm (I am).

C. Complete the following sentences by filling in the correct contraction:

1. _____ wearing my most comfortable shoes on the hike.

2. Look at Meg! _____ running down the street.

3. The game is long. _____ going into extra innings.

4. Ethan _____ want to go on the trip.

5. Sally _____ go to school because she's sick.

*ANSWERS AT BOTTOM OF THIS PAGE.

> **D.** Two of the most commonly misused words are *it's* and *its*. Here is a good way to remember how to use these words correctly. *It's* always stands for *it is*. If *it is* makes sense in the sentence, write *it's*. If *it is* does not fit in, write *its*.

E. Complete these sentences with either *its* or *it's*.

1. _____ time to leave for school.

2. _____ clear that he doesn't know the answer.

3. The dog is wagging _____ tail.

4. The wagon lost _____ front wheel.

> **Answers to E:** 1. It's,   2. It's,   3. its,   4. its
>
> **Answers to C:** 1. I'm,   2. She's,   3. It's,   4. doesn't   5. can't

© 2000 by The Center for Applied Research in Education

Name _____ Date _____

TO APOSTROPHE OR NOT TO APOSTROPHE!
Additional Exercises

A. The following paragraph contains fourteen errors using apostrophes. Sometimes a necessary apostrophe has been omitted. Sometimes an apostrophe appears where it doesn't belong.

Circle all the apostrophe errors. Then, rewrite the paragraph correctly on the lines below.

> Im sorry to tell you that you're familys dog is causing a problem in the neighborhood. Its going into the neighbors yard's and making messes. Also, it's loud barking is a real nuisance. We know that the dogs name is Barney. Its not really Barneys fault. Its your family's responsibility to control your pets behavior. The problem is your's, and all you're neighbors hope you will take care of it.

B. Did you find all fourteen apostrophe errors? (If you missed any, check the answers at the bottom of this page. Then, copy the complete paragraph correctly on the lines below.)

_____

_____

_____

_____

_____

_____

_____

_____

_____

Answers: Line 1: I'm, your, family's Line 2: It's, neighbor's Line 3: yards, its Line 4: dog's, Line 5: It's Barney's, It's Line 6: pet's, yours Line 7: your

© 2000 by The Center for Applied Research in Education

Name _____ Date _____

TO APOSTROPHE OR NOT TO APOSTROPHE!
Additional Exercises

A. Check the correct sentence in each group below:

1. ☐ a.   Megans dog is wagging it's tail.
   ☐ b.   Megan's dog is wagging it's tail.
   ☐ c.   Megan's dog is wagging its tail.

2. ☐ a.   Eds brother is the teams star player.
   ☐ b.   Ed's brother is the team's star player.
   ☐ c.   Ed's brother is the teams star player.

3. ☐ a.   Your dog's food is in it's dish.
   ☐ b.   Your dog's food is in its dish.
   ☐ c.   Your dogs food is in it's dish.

4. ☐ a.   It's clear that Mike's story is best.
   ☐ b.   Its clear that Mike's story is best.
   ☐ c.   It's clear that Mikes story is best.

5. ☐ a.   Mikes team has already won two pennant's.
   ☐ b.   Mike's team has already won two pennants.
   ☐ c.   Mike's team has already won two pennant's.

6. ☐ a.   I dont think this is Jennifer's book.
   ☐ b.   I don't think this is Jennifers book.
   ☐ c.   I don't think this is Jennifer's book.

7. ☐ a.   Sarahs brother said that she's sick today.
   ☐ b.   Sarah's brother said that shes sick today.
   ☐ c.   Sarah's brother said that she's sick today.

8. ☐ a.   I don't always agree with my parent's rules.
   ☐ b.   I dont always agree with my parents' rules.
   ☐ c.   I don't always agree with my parents' rules.
   ☐ d.   I don't always agree with my parents rules.

© 2000 by The Center for Applied Research in Education

Answers: 1. c   4. a
2. b   3. b
5. b   6. c
   7. c
   8. c

Name _____ Date _____

COMING ATTRACTIONS
Explanation and Exercises

A *colon* (:) is used to prepare the reader for something that follows. Think of a colon as a ramp inviting you to continue onto the road.

A. A colon introduces a word or phrase that explains or illustrates the preceding statement, as *Joe has a problem: to remain at the party or leave.* Note: The statement before the colon should be able to stand by itself (*Joe has a problem*).

B. A colon may introduce a list, as *Here is what you will need for school: pens, pencils, rulers, and notebooks.*

C. A colon may replace a comma before a long quotation, as *Abraham Lincoln said: Fourscore and seven years ago our fathers brought forth on this continent a new nation, conceived in liberty, and dedicated to the proposition that all men are created equal.* (Note: Quotation marks are not used with a long, direct quotation.)

D. A colon is also used after the greeting in a business letter, as *Dear Mr. Franco:*

E. A colon is also used between hours and minutes, as *10:30* A.M. or *2:45* P.M.

F. Insert a colon where it belongs in the following sentences:

1. Here is Zack's problem how to pass his science course.

2. Here is what you should pack for the trip two shirts, one pair of jeans, and three pairs of socks.

3. The article concluded with these words The sort of person you will become is determined by how you live your everyday life and the ways in which you treat your fellow human beings.

4. Remember this rule honesty is the best policy.

5. My shopping list contains the following items milk, bread, apple juice, and cheese.

6. Do these things when you get home eat a snack, walk the dog, and finish your homework.

7. I have four favorite boys' names Bill, Andrew, Colin, and Philip.

8. This is the golden rule do unto others as you would have them do unto you.

*SEE ANSWERS BELOW.

© 2000 by The Center for Applied Research in Education

Answers: A colon should appear after these words: 1. problem: 2. trip: 3. words: 4. rule: 5. items: 6. home: 7. names: 8. rule:

Name _____ Date _____

SEMICOLON SUGGESTIONS
Explanation and Exercises

Think of a semicolon as being stronger than a comma or colon, but not as strong as a period. Here are some rules for using semicolons.

A. Use a semicolon to separate independent clauses not joined by a conjunction.

> **Examples:** *Each clause could stand as a separate sentence; the semicolon brings them closer together.*
> *English class meets at one o'clock; science is at two.*

(Note: In the examples above, each of the clauses on either side of the semicolon could be a complete sentence.)

B. Use a semicolon between independent clauses if they are joined by such words as *however, also, besides, indeed, otherwise, therefore, in fact, meanwhile, furthermore,* and *then.*

> **Examples:** I would like to visit you; however, I have a cold.
> He is not a nice person; besides, he has a bad temper.

(Note: Do not use a colon if the clauses are joined by a conjunction such as *and* or *but,* as *He is not a nice person and he has a bad temper.*

C. Use a semicolon in a series of three or more when commas are used as part of the items.

> **Examples:** *Alex, my brother's friend; Colin, my cousin; and Randy, another cousin are all coming to the party.*
> *She has three pets: Barney, the frog; Marlon, the cat; and Bumbles, the rabbit.*

D. Check the correctly punctuated sentence in each group.

1. ☐ a.   Jenny loves ice cream; her favorite flavor is vanilla.
   ☐ b.   Jenny loves ice cream, her favorite flavor is vanilla.

2. ☐ a.   I like cookies; and I also like cake.
   ☐ b.   I like cookies and I also like cake.

3. ☐ a.   Mr. Adams, the teacher; Ms. Hopkins, the principal; and Mr. Sharp, the superintendent will all be at the meeting.
   ☐ b.   Mr. Adams, the teacher, Ms. Hopkins, the principal, and Mr. Sharp, the superintendent will all be at the meeting.

4. ☐ a.   Susan is ready, however, she is waiting for Elena.
   ☐ b.   Susan is ready; however, she is waiting for Elena.

*SEE ANSWERS BELOW.

© 2000 by The Center for Applied Research in Education

Answers: 1. a   2. b   3. a   4. b

Name _____ Date _____

SEMICOLON SUGGESTIONS
Additional Exercises

Check the correctly punctuated sentence in each group.

1. ☐ a.   It is a long trip, however, I will try to be there.
   ☐ b.   It is a long trip; however, I will try to be there.

2. ☐ a.   Adam, the lawyer, Santiago, the doctor, and Alan, the carpenter belong to
            the same bowling club.
   ☐ b.   Adam, the lawyer; Santiago, the doctor; and Alan, the carpenter belong to
            the same bowling club.

3. ☐ a.   Maria wants to go to the party; and so does Anita.
   ☐ b.   Maria wants to go to the party and so does Anita.

4. ☐ a.   The girl sneezed, then she looked for a tissue.
   ☐ b.   The girl sneezed; then she looked for a tissue.
   ☐ c.   The girl sneezed then she looked for a tissue.

5. ☐ a.   The meeting was attended by Julie, the president; Adam, the vice-president;
            Sam, the secretary; and Joe, the treasurer.
   ☐ b.   The meeting was attended by Julie the president, Adam the vice-president,
            Sam the secretary, and Joe the treasurer.
   ☐ c.   The meeting was attended by Julie, the president, Adam, the vice-president,
            Sam, the secretary, and Joe, the treasurer.

6. ☐ a.   Sheila wants to learn to play the piano, however, she does not have a piano
            in the house.
   ☐ b.   Sheila wants to learn to play the piano; however, she does not have a piano
            in the house.

7. ☐ a.   Tasha is thirsty; she wants a glass of water.
   ☐ b.   Tasha is thirsty, she wants a glass of water.

*SEE ANSWERS BELOW.

© 2000 by The Center for Applied Research in Education

Answers: 1. b   **5.** a
2. b   **6.** b
3. b   **7.** a
4. b

Name _____ Date _____

HYPHEN HELP
Explanation and Exercises

A. RULES FOR USING HYPHENS

1. *Hyphens* are used to divide a word between syllables at the end of a line, as

   When I go to the party, I'll be *care-*
   ful not to tire myself, and not to *over-*
   eat.

   (Note: It is always best *not* to divide a word at the end of a line. When necessary, divide only between syllables. Consult a dictionary if you are not sure of the syllables.)

2. Hyphens are used in compound words before nouns, as in

   Stephen King is a *well-known* writer.

3. Hyphens are used when writing numbers, such as *twenty-one* to *ninety-nine.*

4. Hyphens are used when spelling out fractions, as *one-half.*

5. Hyphens are used when adding *some* prefixes to words, such as *sun-dried* or *non-stop.*

   The prefixes *self-*, *all-*, and *ex-* are almost always followed by a hyphen as in these examples: *self-starting, all-around, ex-marine.*

B. Insert a hyphen where necessary in the following sentences:

1. Last week, my mom turned forty one.
2. My uncle Steve is a well known actor in television.
3. Sheila and I had a fight yesterday, so she is now my ex friend.
4. When I am in my room, my stereo plays non stop music.
5. I admire Tony because he has a lot of self confidence.
6. When I am twenty one, I will get my own apartment.
7. One half of twenty is ten.
8. Sandy is an ex president of our club.
9. My cousin, Joe, is an all around great athlete.

© 2000 by The Center for Applied Research in Education

Answers: 1. forty-one **2.** well-known **3.** ex-friend **4.** non-stop **5.** self-confidence **6.** twenty-one **7.** One-half **8.** ex-president **9.** all-around

Name _____ Date _____

HAPPY PAIRS
Explanation and Exercises

Quotation marks are sociable. They never travel alone, but are always found in pairs: one at the beginning and one at the end.

" _____ "

A. Rules for Using Quotation Marks

→ **RULE 1**   Dialogue—Quotation marks set off words that are spoken.

When the quote comes midway in the sentence, the quotation mark is preceded by a comma, as in *Mark shouted, "Here I come!"*

When the quote comes at the beginning of a sentence, the comma is placed before the closing quotation mark as in *"I'm hungry," said Ed.*

(Note: A question mark or exclamation point can be used instead of the comma, where appropriate, as in *"Where are you?" Megan asked.*)

→ **RULE 2**   Quotation marks are used to set off words that are quoted, as in *Thomas Jefferson wrote, "All men are created equal."*

(Note: Commas are used with quotes the same way as with dialogue.)

B. Copy these sentences on the line below, using quotation marks and commas (or question mark or exclamation point) where necessary.

1. Jeff answered the phone and said Hi.

   _____

2. Hi, it's Phil said the voice at the other end.

   _____

3. I just finished my homework Jeff told him.

   _____

4. Come over and we'll watch t.v. suggested Phil.

   _____

5. Once upon a midnight dreary is from a poem by Poe.

   _____

*ANSWERS ON ACTIVITY SHEET 22B.

© 2000 by The Center for Applied Research in Education

Name _____ Date _____

HAPPY PAIRS
Explanation and Exercises

© 2000 by The Center for Applied Research in Education

A. ANSWERS TO EXERCISE B ON ACTIVITY SHEET 22A:

1. Jeff answered the phone and said, "Hi."
2. "Hi, it's Phil," said the voice at the other end.
3. "I just finished my homework," Jeff told him.
4. "Come over and we'll watch t.v.," suggested Phil.
5. "Once upon a midnight dreary," is from a poem by Poe.

B. WRITING DIALOGUE: When writing dialogue, always begin a new paragraph each time someone else speaks, as

José looked all around the room. He called out, "Where's my brother?"

"Here I am," Luis shouted from the other room.

"Hurry up! Dinner's ready!" José told him.

C. Quotation marks are used around titles of songs, short stories, articles, and poems, as in *"Get Happy" is my favorite song.*

(**Note:** Do not use commas with the quotations marks around titles)

D. Check the sentence in each group that uses quotation marks and related punctuation correctly.

1. ❑ a.   "Hi," said Bobby, opening the door.
   ❑ b.   Hi, said Bobby, opening the door.
   ❑ c.   "Hi" said Bobby, opening the door.

2. ❑ a.   The man standing there asked Is your mother home?
   ❑ b.   The man standing there asked, "Is your mother home?
   ❑ c.   The man standing there asked, "Is your mother home?"

3. ❑ a.   I'll be there soon is Sophie's favorite pop song.
   ❑ b.   "I'll Be There Soon" is Sophie's favorite pop song.
   ❑ c.   "I'll Be There Soon," is Sophie's favorite pop song.

4. ❑ a.   In his essay, Paul wrote "Our generation will be great."
   ❑ b.   In his essay, Paul wrote, "Our generation will be great.
   ❑ c.   In his essay, Paul wrote, "Our generation will be great."

Answers: 1. a   2. c   3. b   4. c

Name _____   Date _____

COOL CONVERSATION
Writing Dialogue—First Draft

A. REVIEW OF RULES FOR WRITING DIALOGUE:

→ 1. Put quotation marks at the beginning and end of each speech.

→ 2. When the quote comes midway in the sentence, the quotation mark is preceded by a comma, as *Matt said to his brother, "Don't come in my room."*

→ 3. When the quote comes at the beginning of a sentence, the comma is placed before the closing quotation mark, as *"You're weird," I told him.*

→ 4. Begin a new paragraph every time someone begins to speak.

B. WRITE SOME COOL CONVERSATION: Below is the beginning of a conversation between Matt and Jonathan. Continue with this dialogue, adding *at least eight* more lines. You can include some action during the dialogue as is done at the beginning. This is just a draft, so concentrate on getting your thoughts down on paper; don't worry about spelling and grammar, except for the use of quotation marks. Indent at the beginning of each paragraph. (Use the back of this paper if you need more room.)

Matt saw Jonathan ahead on his way to school. "Hey, Jonathan," he called. Jonathan stopped to wait. "Hi," he said.

_____

_____

_____

_____

_____

_____

_____

_____

_____

_____

_____

_____

© 2000 by The Center for Applied Research in Education

Name _____ Date _____

COOL CONVERSATION
Writing Dialogue: Revising and Writing a Final Copy

A. REVISE AND EDIT THE DIALOGUE YOU WROTE IN ACTIVITY 22C, USING THE FOLLOWING QUESTIONS AS GUIDELINES:

1. Did you add at least eight more lines? Can you think of more interesting conversation to add?
2. Do you begin a new paragraph and indent each time someone begins to speak?
3. Are there quotation marks at the beginning and end of each speech?
4. Are commas placed where they belong? (Check rules in Activity 22B)
5. Are there any words you are not sure how to spell? Consult a dictionary.

B. When your dialogue is as good as you can make it, write your final copy below.

_____

_____

_____

_____

_____

_____

_____

_____

_____

_____

_____

_____

_____

_____

_____

_____

_____

_____

© 2000 by The Center for Applied Research in Education

Name _____ Date _____

VARIETY SHOW
Explanation and Rules

Here are some additional punctuation marks and directions for using them correctly.

A. ELLIPSIS—An ellipsis, three dots (. . .) is used inside a quote to show that you have omitted some words, as in this example:

> In his letter, Jake wrote, "I'm having a great time here. Yesterday, I saw a movie . . . and stayed up late."

B. SLASH—A slash (/) shows a choice between two words or phrases, as in this example:

> Every student should write his/her name at the top of the paper.

C. PARENTHESES

1. Parentheses ( ) are placed around a word or group of words to show that something is extra or explanatory to the main subject, as in these examples:

   I'll come one day next week (Tuesday or Wednesday) to clean your house.
   Read Chapter 4 (pages 20–27) for homework.

2. When a sentence is used in parentheses inside another sentence, do not use capital letters or periods, as in

   Martha Harmon (you met her last week) will be at the party.

3. When a sentence is used in parentheses after a complete sentence, capitalize the first letter and use a period, question mark, or exclamation point, as in

   Don't forget to bring the supplies. (You know the ones I mean!)

4. Use parentheses around the abbreviation of an organization after its full name, as in

   Where is the Society for the Prevention of Cruelty to Animals (SPCA)?

5. Use parentheses to enclose numbers or letters that show divisions, as in

   Our topics today are (a) election of officers, (b) naming committees, and (c) setting a date for the next meeting.

*CONTINUED ON ACTIVITY SHEET 23B.

© 2000 by The Center for Applied Research in Education

Name _____   Date _____

VARIETY SHOW
Exercises

> Refer to the rules on exercise sheet 23A when doing these exercises.

A. Insert parentheses where they belong in the following sentences:

1. This map I am certain it is accurate will lead to the treasure.

2. I want the following items from the market: a rice, b milk, c bread, d soda.

3. Anita and Lea wherever they are would be interested in this.

4. My Uncle Max works for the National Aeronautics and Space Administration NASA.

5. Turn to Section Two in the book pages 50–60.

6. Alan he's my cousin is going to your camp this summer.

7. Our toll-free number 1-800-222-JUMP is easy to reach.

*ANSWERS AT THE BOTTOM OF THIS PAPER

B. 1. On the lines below, write two sentences using the ellipsis.

  _____

  _____

2. On the lines below, write two sentences using the slash.

  _____

  _____

© 2000 by The Center for Applied Research in Education

Answers to Exercise A—Parentheses should be inserted around:
1. (I am certain it is accurate),   2. (a), (b), (c), (d),   3. (wherever they are),   4. (NASA),
5. (pages 50–60),   6. (he's my cousin),   7. (1-800-222-JUMP)

Name _____ Date _____

STOP!
Explanation and Exercises

The *period,* the *question mark,* and the *exclamation point* are like STOP signs on a highway. They tell the reader to come to a halt.

A. The *period* marks the end of a declarative sentence. Every sentence that is a statement should end with a period, as in

> Alissa is having a Halloween party.
> The Logan family moved to Maryland.
> Hold the dog's leash tightly.

B. The *question mark* marks the end of an interrogative sentence (a sentence that asks a question), as in

> Where is your school?
> Does Jeff like to play basketball?

C. The *exclamation point* marks the end of a sentence that expresses strong feelings or forceful commands, as in

> What a great student you are!
> Hurry up!

D. TRY IT OUT: Insert the correct punctuation mark at the end of each of the following sentences:

1. What grade are you in now

2. Jonathan will be in Little League next year

3. The pool opened for the summer

4. Get out of here right now

5. Look at my new watch

6. What did you get for your birthday

7. Ouch That hurts

8. Stop fighting

9. Did you raise your hand in class

10. Vicki just got a new computer

*Answers on Activity Sheet 24B.

© 2000 by The Center for Applied Research in Education

Name _____ Date _____

STOP!
Exercises—Paragraphs

A. ANSWERS TO EXERCISE ON ACTIVITY 24A: THE PUNCTUATION AT THE END OF EACH SENTENCE SHOULD BE AS FOLLOWS:

1. ?	5. !	8. !
2. .	6. ?	9. ?
3. .	7. ! !	10. .
4. !		

B. Punctuate the following paragraph. Insert periods, question marks, and exclamation points where needed.

> Wow I thought it would be hard to write a paragraph Now I know that it is not hard at all Do you ever have trouble writing paragraphs Don't worry Just do it You'll find it's easy after a little practice

*ANSWER ON ACTIVITY SHEET 24C.

C. The next paragraph is a little more difficult. There are no capital letters to show you where each sentence begins. Rewrite the complete paragraph on the lines below. Capitalize the beginning of each new sentence. Put a period, question mark, or exclamation point at the end of each sentence.

> Do you know that I play first base on my Little League team my team is called the Panthers we won eight games this season and only lost two what a great team this is I'm so proud to be a Panther.

_____

_____

_____

_____

_____

*ANSWERS ON ACTIVITY SHEET 24C.

© 2000 by The Center for Applied Research in Education

Name _____ Date _____

STOP!
Additional Exercises

> **A. ANSWER TO ACTIVITY B ON ACTIVITY SHEET 24B:**
>
> Wow! I thought it would be hard to write a paragraph. Now I know that it is not hard at all. Do you ever have trouble writing paragraphs? Don't worry! Just do it! You'll find it's easy after a little practice.
>
> **B. ANSWER TO ACTIVITY C ON ACTIVITY SHEET 24B:**
>
> Do you know that I play first base on my Little League team? My team is called the Panthers. We won eight games this season and only lost two. What a great team this is! I'm so proud to be a Panther!

C. Write three sentences that end with a period.

_____

_____

_____

D. Write three sentences that end with a question mark.

_____

_____

_____

E. Write three sentences that end with an exclamation point.

_____

_____

_____

© 2000 by The Center for Applied Research in Education

Name _____ Date _____

PUNCTUATION EXPERT
Review

A. Each of these sentences contains at least one error in punctuation. Rewrite each sentence on the line below with the correct punctuation.

1. There will be three boy's at the party.

   _____

2. I had chicken, peas, and french fries, for dinner.

   _____

3. Mrs. Caputo, my mom's best friend came to visit yesterday.

   _____

4. Mike said I'll see you later

   _____

5. Marla laughed, then she apologized.

   _____

6. Pat finished three quarters of the race.

   _____

7. The horse swished it's tail.

   _____

8. Carlos didnt finish his homework.

   _____

9. Hooray. Im finished at last.

   _____

10. Is Michaels brother sick today.

    _____

11. Get home by six. I mean it.

    _____

12. When I finish eating Ill take a nap.

    _____

*Answers on Activity Sheet 25B.

© 2000 by The Center for Applied Research in Education

Name _____ Date _____

PUNCTUATION EXPERT
Review

A. ANSWERS TO EXERCISES ON ACTIVITY 25A:

1. There will be three boys at the party.
2. I had chicken, peas, and french fries for dinner.
3. Mrs. Caputo, my mom's best friend, came to visit yesterday.
4. Mike said, "I'll see you later."
5. Marla laughed; then she apologized.
6. Pat finished three-quarters of the race.
7. The horse swished its tail.
8. Carlos didn't finish his homework.
9. Hooray! I'm finished at last!
10. Is Michael's brother sick today?
11. Get home by six. I mean it!
12. When I finish eating, I'll take a nap.

B. Check the correctly punctuated sentence in each group.

1. ❑ a. Rubbing her eyes Samantha said "Im tired.
   ❑ b. Rubbing her eyes, Samantha said, "I'm tired."
   ❑ c. Rubbing her eyes, Samantha said, "I'm tired"

2. ❑ a. "Goodbye," said Joe waving his hand.
   ❑ b. "Goodbye" said Joe, waving his hand.
   ❑ c. "Goodbye," said Joe, waving his hand.

3. ❑ a. Where would you like to go tomorrow, Pete?
   ❑ b. Where would you like to go tomorrow Pete?
   ❑ c. Where would you like to go tomorrow, Pete.

4. ❑ a. I'll ask my sister (she's a brain) for the answers?
   ❑ b. I'll ask my sister (shes a brain) for the answers.
   ❑ c. I'll ask my sister (she's a brain) for the answers.

5. ❑ a. Oh no. We missed the bus.
   ❑ b. Oh no? We missed the bus!
   ❑ c. Oh no! We missed the bus!

6. ❑ a. Hurry up. It's almost time to leave.
   ❑ b. Hurry up! It's almost time to leave.
   ❑ c. Hurry up! Its almost time to leave.

7. ❑ a. "For You" is my favorite song on Chana's new tape.
   ❑ b. "For You," is my favorite song on Chana's new tape.
   ❑ c. "For You" is my favorite song on Chanas new tape.

*SEE ANSWERS BELOW.

© 2000 by The Center for Applied Research in Education

Answers: 1. b 2. c 3. a 4. c 5. c 6. b 7. a

Name _____ Date _____

FIND THE LOST PUNCTUATION
Review

It's terrible when punctuation is misplaced. Sentences become unclear. In these exercises, it will be up to you to find the lost punctuation.

A. WANDERING COMMAS: Each sentence below contains one or more commas that have wandered off and ended up in the wrong spot. Rewrite each sentence on the lines below, putting the commas where they belong.

1. My, friend Sarah Romano, went to visit her aunt in, Dallas Texas.

_____

2. When you feel tired always, stop to rest.

_____

3. July, 4 1776 an important, date in history is remembered, each year.

_____

4. Theo's dad is, smart handsome and, successful.

_____

5. Jeff called "Let's get, going!"

_____

*Answers on Activity Sheet 26B.

B. The following sentences are in even worse shape. They have lost *all* their punctuation. Rewrite each sentence below with all necessary marks of punctuation.

1. Were going to have twenty five people at the party

_____

2. Stop Sallys teacher want to talk to you

_____

3. Andys cousin said I really like this movie

_____

4. Here take your brothers pencil and sharpen it

_____

*Answers on Activity Sheet 26B.

© 2000 by The Center for Applied Research in Education

Name _____ Date _____

THE PUNCTUATION EXPERT
Review

A. ANSWERS TO EXERCISES ON ACTIVITY SHEET 26A:

Exercise A:

1. My friend, Sarah Romano, went to visit her aunt in Dallas, Texas.
2. When you feel tired, always stop to rest.
3. July 4, 1776, an important date in history, is remembered each year.
4. Theo's dad is smart, handsome, and successful.
5. Jeff called, "Let's get going!"

Exercise B:

1. We're going to have twenty-five people at the party.
2. Stop! Sally's teacher wants to talk to you.
3. Andy's cousin said, "I really like this movie."
4. Here, take your brother's pencil and sharpen it.

B. Write two sentences that are followed by a question mark.

1. _____

2. _____

C. Write two sentences that are followed by an exclamation point.

1. _____

2. _____

D. Write one sentence that uses a colon.

_____

E. Write one sentence that uses a semicolon.

_____

F. Write one sentence that uses a dash.

_____

G. Write two sentences that use quotation marks.

1. _____

2. _____

H. Write one sentence that uses parentheses.

_____

I. Write one sentence that uses a hyphen.

_____

© 2000 by The Center for Applied Research in Education

Section Three

SPELLING HELP

TEACHER'S GUIDE—
ALPHABETICAL LISTING OF SPELLING PROBLEMS
AND THEIR ACTIVITY NUMBERS

Section Three provides remedial help with the following spelling problems:

SPELLING PROBLEM	ACTIVITY NUMBER
abbreviations	43A, B
capitalization	35A, B, C
commonly misspelled words	36A, B, 37A, B, C
compound words	42
homonyms	27A, B, C, 28A, B, 29A, B, 30A, B
plurals	32A, B, 33A, B, 34A, B
prefixes	41A, B, C
spelling review	44A, B
suffixes	39A, B, C, D
suffixes (ful/fully)	40
words containing ie or ei	31A, B, C
writing two words as one	38

Name _____ Date _____

I HEAR WITH MY EAR
Explanation and Exercises

> **Tell everyone *here***
> **You *hear* with your ear.**

Homonyms are words that sound alike but have different meanings. They are often spelled differently, too. There are tricks you can learn to remember which one to use.

The verse above shows you one such trick. Just think of how *ear* is spelled, and you will always know when to use *hear*.

Here are some more ways to remember homonyms:

Principal means "chief" or "head," like the *principal* of your school. Is your principal a *pal?* Well, even if he isn't, you can think of the word *pal* whenever you want to spell it. The other *principle* means "rule" or "law," as in "Correct spelling is an important *principle* of good writing."

Made is the past tense of *make,* meaning to construct or produce, as in "The chocolate factory *made* lots of candy."

Maid is someone who helps out in a house, as in "A *maid* came to clean the house." Remember, the *maid* will *aid* with the housekeeping.

Sea means "ocean," as in "There were high waves in the *sea.*"

See means "look at," as in: "Do you *see* that clown?" There are two *e's* in the word *eye* and two e's in the *see* that you do with your eyes.

Knot is something that is tied, as in "I tied a *knot* with a shoelace."

Not means "no," as in "She would *not* stop laughing." Just think of the letters *no* when you want to spell *not*.

| hear, here | made, maid | knot, not | principal, principle | sea, see |

A. Fill in the blank spaces with the correct word from the above list.

1. My mom _____ a chocolate cake for my birthday.

2. Mike hit a kid and was sent to the office of the _____.

3. Mike said that he did _____ do it.

4. Did anyone _____ what Mike did?

5. Did you _____ about the big storm yesterday?

6. The _____ is in the kitchen cooking dinner.

7. _____ is a gift for your birthday.

ANSWERS ON ACTIVITY SHEET 27B.

© 2000 by The Center for Applied Research in Education

Name _____ Date _____

I HEAR WITH MY EAR
More Homonyms

A. ANSWERS TO ACTIVITY 27A

1. made	3. not	5. hear	7. Here
2. principal	4. see	6. maid	

B. MORE HOMONYMS

Are there tricks for remembering all homonyms? No, some have to be memorized. Study the homonyms below. Perhaps you can think of your own special ways of remembering them.

One: a number, as in "I had only *one* pen."
Won: past tense of "win," as in "Our team *won* the game."

Pain: something that hurts, as in "I had a *pain* in my foot."
Pane: part of a window, as in "There was a glass *pane* in the window."

Days: part of a week, as in "There are seven *days* in a week."
Daze: a confused state, as in "I was in a *daze* after banging my head."

Tale: a story, as in "Do you like to read a fairy *tale?*"
Tail: part of an animal, as in "The squirrel has a bushy *tail.*"

Wait: to expect, as in "We have to *wait* for the doctor."
Weight: heaviness, as in "The *weight* of the bananas was two pounds."

Rowed: propelled a boat, as in "They *rowed* down the river."
Road: a street, as in "The car sped down the *road.*"

Right: correct, as in "Do you know the *right* answer?"
Write: put down letters or words, as in *"Write* a story about ghosts."

C. Fill in the correct word in the blank space.

1. I'll be home late, so don't _____ up for me.   (weight or wait)

2. Are you in _____ from the headache?   (pane or pain)

3. The _____ ahead has four lanes.   (road or rowed)

4. How many _____ are there in February?   (daze or days)

5. Have you heard the _____ about Peter Rabbit?   (tale or tail)

6. My mom wants to lose _____.   (weight or wait)

7. The game was _____ by only _____ team.   (won or one)

8. It's always _____ to tell the truth.   (right or write)

*ANSWERS ON ACTIVITY SHEET 27C.

© 2000 by The Center for Applied Research in Education

Name _____ Date _____

I HEAR WITH MY EAR
Using Homonyms in a Paragraph

© 2000 by The Center for Applied Research in Education

A. ANSWERS TO EXERCISE IN ACTIVITY 27B

1. wait	4. days	7. won, one
2. pain	5. tale	8. right
3. road	6. weight	

Here are more fun homonyms:

Peace: opposite of war, as in "Everyone wants *peace* in the world."
Piece: part of something, as in "Luke wants a big *piece* of cake."

Fair: even-handed, as in "The umpire's call was not *fair.*"
Fare: transportation cost, as in "How much is the bus *fare* to Ohio?"

Hare: a rabbit, as in "I saw a big, brown *hare* in the woods."
Hair: growth on body, as in "Rena has long, blonde *hair.*"

New: not old, as in "My dad bought a *new* car."
Knew: past tense of know, as in "I *knew* every answer on the test."

Break: smash, as in "Be careful not to *break* the new glass."
Brake: part of a car, as in "Step on the *brake* to stop the car."

Blew: past tense of blow, as in "The strong wind *blew* down the tree."
Blue: a color, as in "The sky is *blue.*"

C. PARAGRAPH: Every sentence in the following paragraph contains at least one incorrect homonym. Write the paragraph correctly on the lines below.

We had an accident the first time my mom drove our knew car. It was only two daze old. We could hardly weight to try it out. As soon as we started, I new that something was going to happen. I could here a funny noise in the engine. We road to the end of the block. Mom tried to stop, but the break didn't work. We hit a big, blew truck. My head hit the windshield and I felt as though I was in a days. I could hardly sea straight. I had a pane in my neck, too. But I felt all write the next day.

_____

_____

_____

_____

_____

_____

Name _____ Date _____

A PAIR OF PEARS
Explanation and Exercises

A. More Homonyms: Do you ever mix up these homonyms?

Pear is a tasty fruit, as in My, what a juicy *pear!*
Pair is a set of two, as in Alison's parents are a jolly *pair.*
Pare means "to cut off the peel," as Use that knife to *pare* the apple.

Meat is flesh food, as in Steak is my favorite cut of *meat.*
Meet means "to encounter," as in Did you *meet* Arthur on the street?

Sale is the selling of goods, as in There is a holiday *sale* at the market.
Sail is the canvas on a sailboat. *Sail* is also a verb that means to travel by
    boat, as in The ocean liner will *sail* tomorrow.

Role is a part in a play or film, as in She wants the starring role.
Roll is a list of names. A *roll* is also a kind of bread. *Roll* is also a verb
    meaning to turn over and over, as in The cook must *roll* the dough to
    make a tasty *roll.*

Deer is an animal, as in Bambi was a young *deer.*
Dear means loved or liked, as in My parents are very *dear* to me.
Dear is also part of the salutation on a letter, as in *Dear* Mr. Jones

pear, pair, pare	**meat, meet**
sale, sail	**role, roll**
deer, dear	

B. Fill in the blank spaces with the correct word from the above list.

1. My mom bought me a _____ of sneakers.

2. The letter began, " _____ Friend".

3. Vegetarians never eat _____.

4. I bought a _____; it was on _____ at the market.

5. Do you like your sandwich on rye bread or on a _____?

6. Come and _____ my friend, Orlando.

7. I want to play the _____ of Juliet in the school play.

*Answers on Activity 28B.

© 2000 by The Center for Applied Research in Education

Name _____ Date _____

A PAIR OF PEARS
Explanation and Exercises

A. ANSWERS TO EXERCISE B ON ACTIVITY 28A:

1. pair   2. Dear   3. meat   4. roll, sale
5. roll   6. meet   7. role

© 2000 by The Center for Applied Research in Education

B. There are many homonyms in the English language. Here are some more.

Stair is a step, as in Don't trip on that *stair*.
Stare means "to keep looking at," as in You should not *stare* at people.

Aloud means "out loud," as in The teacher read the story *aloud*.
Allowed means permitted, as in We are not *allowed* to go into that room.

A *bear* is a big, furry animal, as in The toddler held a teddy *bear*.
Bear is also a verb meaning "to stand for," as I cannot *bear* her crying.
Bare means naked, as in He is *bare* in the shower.

The *sun* is the star of a solar system, as The *sun* shines in the sky.
A *son* is a male child, as in The mother kissed her *son*.

Hole is an opening, as in Dig a *hole* in the ground with your spade.
Whole means "all or complete," as in The *whole* class passed the test.

C. Check the correct sentence in each group.

1. ☐ a.   She cannot bare to look at the sick bear.
   ☐ b.   She cannot bear to look at the sick bear.
   ☐ c.   She cannot bear to look at the sick bare.

2. ☐ a.   The earth revolves around the son.
   ☐ b.   The earth revolves around the sun.

3. ☐ a.   That boy has a hole in his socks.
   ☐ b.   That boy has a whole in his socks.

4. ☐ a.   Are you aloud to speak aloud in class?
   ☐ b.   Are you allowed to speak allowed in class?
   ☐ c.   Are you allowed to speak aloud in class?

5. ☐ a.   Do not stand on the stair and stare at the people below.
   ☐ b.   Do not stand on the stare and stare at the people below.
   ☐ c.   Do not stand on the stair and stair at the people below.

6. ☐ a.   Are you aloud to speak to Mr. Petty's sun?
   ☐ b.   Are you allowed to speak to Mr. Petty's son?
   ☐ c.   Are you allowed to speak to Mr. Petty's sun?

*SEE ANSWERS BELOW.

Answers to Exercise C: 1. b,   2. b,   3. a,   4. c,   5. a,   6. b

Name _____ Date _____

THEY SOUND THE SAME
Simple Common Homonyms

> I wouldn't like to be
> A buzzy little bee!

A. What two words sound exactly alike in this poem? If you said be and bee, you are right! *Homonyms* are words that sound the same but are spelled differently.

B. Do you know these homonyms?

HOMONYMS	SENTENCES
be	I want to *be* a doctor.
bee	The *bee* buzzed around the flower.
buy	You can *buy* food in the market.
by	I can do it *by* myself.
close	*Close* the door when you go out.
clothes	We bought new *clothes* for school.
for	Here is a present *for* you.
four	There are *four* rooms in my house.
our	*Our* house is very big.
hour	I will go to bed in one *hour*.

C. Fill in the blank spaces with the correct word.

1. Get into the car and _____ the door.   (close or clothes)

2. The family next door has _____ children.   (for or four)

3. I will be home _____ three o'clock.   (by or buy)

4. When will you _____ home?   (be or bee)

5. Mom will be back in one _____.   (our or hour)

6. When can we go shopping for new _____?   (close or clothes)

7. That candy is _____ me   (for or four)

*ANSWERS ON ACTIVITY SHEET 29B.

© 2000 by The Center for Applied Research in Education

Name _____ Date _____

THEY SOUND THE SAME
Simple Common Homonyms

A. ANSWERS TO EXERCISE C ON ACTIVITY 29A:

1. close	4. be	6. clothes
2. four	5. hour	7. for
3. by		

© 2000 by The Center for Applied Research in Education

B. Here are more words that sound the same but are spelled differently.

HOMONYMS	SENTENCES
no	*No,* I don't want that book.
know	Do you *know* how to skate?
so	I was tired, *so* I went to bed.
sew	I can *sew* with a needle and thread.
plain	He was wearing a *plain* shirt.
plane	Did you ever fly in a *plane?*
week	There are seven days in a *week.*
weak	I felt *weak* when I was sick.
would	I *would* like to go to the movies.
wood	Some houses are built of *wood.*

C. Fill in the blank space with the correct word.

1. My mom can _____ the hem of that skirt.   (so or sew)

2. There is an important holiday next _____.   (week or weak)

3. _____ you like ice cream for dessert?   (Would or Wood)

4. Mike will travel by _____ to New York.   (plain or plane)

5. There are _____ bad marks on my report card.   (no or know)

6. My wrist felt _____ after I sprained it.   (week or weak)

7. Do you _____ why Billy is absent today?   (no or know)

SEE ANSWERS BELOW.

Answers to Exercise C: 1. sew   4. plane   6. weak   2. week   5. no   7. know   3. Would

Name _____ Date _____

SAME SOUND, DIFFERENT MEANING
Paragraph—First Draft

A. FIND THE MISTAKES: What a mixup!! The following paragraph contains ten homonyms that are spelled wrong. Circle each of these. Then write the correct homonyms on the lines below.

> Did you here about the trouble at the Johnson's yesterday? Mr. Johnson's sun, Tommy, had a pane in his foot. The doctor found a whole in Tommy's left toe. Weight till you sea the big bandage on Tommy's foot! He won't be aloud to walk without crutches for five daze. Tommy hates that because he can't bare to have people stair at him.

1. _____ 3. _____ 5. _____ 7. _____ 9. _____

2. _____ 4. _____ 6. _____ 8. _____ 10. _____

*ANSWERS ON ACTIVITY SHEET 30B.

B. Write your own paragraph about an event in your neighborhood or in your school.

Your paragraph should contain at least *four sentences.*
The *first sentence* should introduce the topic.
The next *three or four sentences* should tell more about the topic.
The *last sentence* should provide an ending or sum up the topic.
Include *at least five* of the homonyms from Exercise A.

Write a *first draft* of your paragraph below. This is only a rough copy, so don't be concerned about punctuation or spelling (except for the homonyms, of course)! Just concentrate on getting your thoughts down. (Always indent at the beginning of a paragraph.)

© 2000 by The Center for Applied Research in Education

Name _____ Date _____

SAME SOUND, DIFFERENT MEANING
Paragraph—Revising and Writing a Final Copy

A. ANSWERS TO EXERCISE A ON ACTIVITY SHEET 30A:

1. hear,   2. son,   3. pain,   4. hole,   5. Wait,   6. see,
7. allowed,   8. days,   9. bear,   10. stare

B. Edit and review the paragraph you wrote on activity sheet 30A, using the following questions as guidelines:

1. Did you use *at least five* homonyms in your paragraph? Are they spelled correctly?

2. Does your first sentence introduce the topic?

3. Does the last sentence provide an ending or sum up the topic?

4. Does each sentence begin with a capital letter?

5. Are all your sentences complete? Do subjects and verbs agree?

6. Does each sentence end with a period, question mark, or exclamation point?

7. Is your punctuation correct? Do you use commas where necessary to make the meaning clear?

8. Do you indent at the beginning of the paragraph?

C. Is your paragraph as perfect as you can make it? Write your final copy on the lines below.

© 2000 by The Center for Applied Research in Education

Name _____ Date _____

IE OR EI?
Explanation and Exercises

A. RULES: Did you know that there are about 1,000 common words that contain ei or ie? Do you often wonder which to use?

Everyone has heard this verse:

> Write *i* before *e*
> except after *c*
> Or when sounded like *a*
> As in *neighbor* and *weigh*

Memorizing this rhyme will help you decide whether to use *ie* or *ei*. Here is what it means:

→ *ie* is used most often, as in *piece, lie, believe, chief,* and *thief.*

→ After *c*, use *ei*, as in *receive, ceiling, conceited,* and *receipt.*

→ Use *ei* when it is pronounced *a*, as in *sleigh, weigh, eight,* and *chow mein.*

B. Insert the correct words in these sentences. (Read the rules again before you decide.)

1. Get on the scale and see what you _____. (weigh or wiegh)

2. That toddler always gets into _____. (mischeif or mischief)

3. I like to watch the _____ train go by. (freight or frieght)

4. She has a blue _____. (handkercheif or handkerchief)

5. Mrs. Dow has a _____ on her hat. (veil or viel)

6. The ball teams are on the _____. (feild or field)

7. The teacher didn't _____ Amy's excuse. (beleive or believe)

8. The horse is _____ in the stable. (neighing or nieghing)

9. Santa Claus travels on a _____. (sleigh or sliegh)

10. It is pulled by eight _____. (reindeer or riendeer)

11. There is a spider on the _____. (ceiling or cieling)

12. The salesperson gave Maria a _____. (receipt or reciept)

13. Those apples cost ten cents _____. (apeice or apiece)

*Answers on Activity Sheet 31B.

© 2000 by The Center for Applied Research in Education

Name _____ Date _____

IE OR EI?
Explanation and Exercises

A. ANSWERS TO EXERCISE ON ACTIVITY SHEET 31A:

1. weigh	4. handkerchief	7. believe	10. reindeer
2. mischief	5. veil	8. neighing	11. ceiling
3. freight	6. field	9. sleigh	12. receipt
	13. apiece		

B. EXCEPTIONS: There are exceptions to the rule of

> Write *i* before *e*
> except after *c*
> or when sounding like *a*
> as in *neighbor* and *weigh*

Here are some words that break the rule:

ancient	forfeit	seize
caffeine	height	sheik
counterfeit	heir	sleight
efficient	leisure	their
financier	neither	weird
foreign	protein	

C. Insert an appropriate word from the above list in each sentence.

1. Coffee contains _____.

2. In his _____ time, Ed likes to play baseball.

3. The magician is skilled at _____ of hand.

4. The _____ to Mr. Rollo's estate will inherit a lot of money.

5. Alison and Harry are going to visit _____ Aunt Helen.

6. _____ Sharon nor Jessica want to eat dinner yet.

7. Have you ever traveled in _____ lands?

8. I just read a _____ ghost story.

9. Do you know the _____ of that tall mountain?

10. If you don't follow the rules, you may _____ the game.

*ANSWERS ON ACTIVITY SHEET 31C.

© 2000 by The Center for Applied Research in Education

Name _____ Date _____

IE OR EI?
Review Exercises

A. ANSWERS TO EXERCISE ON ACTIVITY SHEET 31B:

1. caffeine	4. heir	7. foreign
2. leisure	5. their	8. weird
3. sleight	6. neither	9. height
	10. forfeit	

B. REVIEW EXERCISE USING EI AND IE: Check the correct spelling in each group.

1. ❒ a. cheif
 ❒ b. chief

2. ❒ a. protein
 ❒ b. protien

3. ❒ a. sheild
 ❒ b. shield

4. ❒ a. theif
 ❒ b. thief

5. ❒ a. financeir
 ❒ b. financier

6. ❒ a. yeild
 ❒ b. yield

7. ❒ a. weigh
 ❒ b. wiegh

8. ❒ a. beleif
 ❒ b. belief

9. ❒ a. fronteir
 ❒ b. frontier

10. ❒ a. breif
 ❒ b. brief

*ANSWERS AT THE BOTTOM OF THIS PAGE.

C. Circle the words that are spelled incorrectly in the following paragraph:

Anita and Sophie like to shop in thier leisure time. Yesterday, at the mall, Anita bought two handkercheifs that cost three dollars apeice. She gave the money to the cashier and asked for a reciept. The cashier was very wierd. She seized the money and threw the reciept at Anita. The girls were releived when they left the mall.

Answers: Exercise B: 1. b, 2. a, 3. b, 4. b, 5. b, 6. b, 7. a, 8. b, 9. b, 10. b

Exercise C: The following misspelled words should be circled: thier (should be *their*), handkercheifs (should be *handkerchiefs*), apeice (should be *apiece*), reciept (should be *receipt*), wierd (should be *weird*), reciept (should be *receipt*), releived (should be *relieved*)

© 2000 by The Center for Applied Research in Education

Name _____ Date _____

FROM ONE TO MANY
Explanation and Exercises

Singular means one, as *one book*.
Plural means more than one, as *three books*.

A. RULES FOR PLURALS

1. A *plural* is usually formed by adding *s*, as *hands, heads, computers, clocks, friends, elephants, houses,* and *teams.*

2. Nouns ending with *ch, sh, s, x,* or *z* form their plurals by adding *es*, as

brush, brushes	watch, watches	fox, foxes
glass, glasses	box, boxes	buzz, buzzes

3. Add *s* to most nouns ending in *o*, as *radios, rodeos, cameos, pianos, patios, shampoos, trios, banjos, solos, zeros.*

4. Some nouns ending in *o* form plurals by adding *es*, as

buffalo, buffaloes	echo, echoes	tomato, tomatoes
potato, potatoes	hero, heroes	mosquito, mosquitoes
volcano, volcanoes	veto, vetoes	cargo, cargoes

B. Complete the sentences that call for plurals.

1. Cut a tomato into the salad.

   Cut two _____ into the salad.

2. Does your watch keep accurate time?

   Do your _____ keep accurate time?

3. Fill her glass to the top with milk.

   Fill their _____ to the top with milk.

4. There is a chair in the living room.

   There are three _____ in the living room.

5. His office sent out one fax today.

   His office sent out four _____ today.

6. Dad planted a rose bush in the garden.

   Dad planted several rose _____ in the garden.

7. The soprano sang a solo at the concert.

   The soprano sang two _____ at the concert.

8. The bird is sitting in its perch on the tree.

   The birds are sitting in their _____ on the trees.

*ANSWERS ON ACTIVITY SHEET 32B.

© 2000 by The Center for Applied Research in Education

Name _____ Date _____

FROM ONE TO MANY
Additional Exercises

A. ANSWERS TO EXERCISE ON ACTIVITY SHEET 32A:

1. tomatoes	4. chairs	7. solos
2. watches	5. faxes	8. perches
3. glasses	6. bushes	

B. On the lines below, write a sentence using the plural of each of the following words:

1. banjo	4. box	7. actor
2. computer	5. potato	8. mess
3. game	6. tax	9. exercise

Are you unsure about any of these plurals? Consult a dictionary!

1. (banjo) _____

2. (computer) _____

3. (game) _____

4. (box) _____

5. (potato) _____

6. (tax) _____

7. (actor) _____

8. (mess) _____

9. (exercise) _____

*ANSWERS AT THE BOTTOM OF THIS PAGE.

C. On the list next to each word, write the plural.

1. hat _____   4. loss _____

2. hero _____   5. piano _____

3. echo _____

*SEE ANSWERS BELOW.

Exercise C: 1. hats, 2. heroes, 3. echoes, 5. losses, 5. pianos
6. taxes, 7. actors, 8. messes, 9. exercises
Answers: Exercise B: 1. banjos, 2. computers, 3. games, 4. boxes, 5. potatoes,

---

© 2000 by The Center for Applied Research in Education

Name _____ Date _____

PLURALS WITH Y
Explanation and Exercises

A. RULES: Many words end with the letter y. Here are the rules for forming plurals of nouns ending in y.

1. If the letter in front of the *y* is a *vowel* (a, e, i, o, u), add *s*, as in

alley, alleys	monkey, monkeys	turkey, turkeys
valley, valleys	attorney, attorneys	way, ways
chimney, chimneys	highway, highways	key, keys
birthday, birthdays	stay, stays	boy, boys
journey, journeys	essay, essays	joy, joys

2. If the letter before the *y* is a *consonant,* change the *y* to *ie* before adding the *s,* as in

baby, babies	activity, activities	cry, cries
city, cities	library, libraries	fry, fries
fly, flies	dictionary, dictionaries	jury, juries
try, tries	country, countries	story, stories
diary, diaries	jelly, jellies	pastry, pastries

B. One word is underlined in each of the following sentences. On the line below, write another sentence using the plural of the underlined words.

    Example: The teacher said that Harry's <u>essay</u> was excellent.
                 We have to write three essays a semester in social studies.

1. What <u>country</u> would you like to visit?

_____

2. The Johnsons have one <u>baby.</u>

_____

3. I like to read books that tell an exciting <u>story.</u>

_____

4. Leah hopes that she gets a watch for her <u>birthday.</u>

_____

5. Alex borrowed a book from the <u>library.</u>

_____

*ANSWERS ON ACTIVITY SHEET 33B.

© 2000 by The Center for Applied Research in Education

Name _____ Date _____

PLURALS WITH Y
Additional Exercises

A. ANSWERS TO EXERCISE ON ACTIVITY SHEET 33A:

1. countries,   2. babies,   3. stories,   4. birthdays,   5. libraries

---

B. Write the plural of each of the following words:

1. strawberry   _____

2. attorney   _____

3. highway   _____

4. dictionary   _____

5. blackberry   _____

6. journey   _____

7. discovery   _____

8. copy   _____

9. bay   _____

10. laboratory   _____

*ANSWERS AT THE BOTTOM OF THIS PAGE.

C. Circle the misspelled plurals in the following paragraph:

There are three librarys in my town. We have to travel on two highways to get to the one I like best. Two of the librarians there are ladys, and one is a man. I like to look at the mysterys and the dictionaries. One of the ladys is very nice. She always trys to help me find the storys I like best. On the way home, we sometimes stop for burgers and fries.

*SEE ANSWERS BELOW.

© 2000 by The Center for Applied Research in Education

Answers: Exercise B: 1. strawberries,   **2.** attorneys,   **3.** highways,   **4.** dictionaries,   **5.** blackberries,   **6.** journeys,   **7.** discoveries,   **8.** copies,   **9.** bays,   **10.** laboratories

Exercise C: *The misspelled words are* librarys, ladys, mysterys, ladys, trys, storys.

Name _____ Date _____

CHIEFS AND THIEVES
Explanation and Exercises

A. When a word ends with a single *f,* the plural is usually formed by changing the *f* to *v* and adding *es,* as in:

SINGULAR	PLURAL
thief	thieves
shelf	shelves
scarf	scarves
half	halves
calf	calves
elf	elves
hoof	hooves
loaf	loaves
leaf	leaves
sheaf	sheaves

B. Sometimes we just add s to make the plural, as in

SINGULAR	PLURAL
chief	chiefs
handkerchief	handkerchiefs
roof	roofs
reef	reefs

C. Rewrite each sentence on the line below, changing the underlined word to a plural form. (Also make whatever other changes are necessary.)

Example: Give me a <u>loaf</u> of bread.   Give me two <u>loaves</u> of bread.

1. Mom keeps a <u>handkerchief</u> in her purse.

   _____

2. The <u>shelf</u> in my closet is wide.

   _____

3. Santa's <u>elf</u> is busy in December.

   _____

4. Pick one <u>leaf</u> from each tree.

   _____

*CHECK YOUR SPELLING WITH THE LISTS AT THE TOP OF THE PAGE.

© 2000 by The Center for Applied Research in Education

Name _____ Date _____

CHIEFS AND THIEVES
Additional Exercises

A. Fill in the blank spaces with the plural form of the word in parentheses.

1. All the houses on the block have white _____. (roof)

2. There are many brave Native American _____. (chief)

3. Two _____ broke into the house last night. (thief)

4. A whole is composed of two _____. (half)

5. All the girls wore flowered _____ to the party. (scarf)

6. A horse has four _____. (hoof)

7. Those _____ are dangerous for boats. (reef)

8. The cow in the barn has two _____. (calf)

*ANSWERS ON THE BOTTOM OF THE PAGE.

B. Write a sentence with the plural form of each word in parentheses below.

1. (shelf) _____

2. (roof) _____

3. (thief) _____

4. (loaf) _____

5. (elf) _____

6. (handkerchief) _____

7. (scarf) _____

© 2000 by The Center for Applied Research in Education

Answers to Exercise A:
1. roofs, 2. chiefs, 3. thieves, 4. halves, 5. scarves, 6. hooves, 7. reefs, 8. calves

Name _____ Date _____

ALWAYS BEGIN BIG!
Rules and Exercises

A. Do you sometimes wonder when to use capital letters? The best way to be sure is to consult a dictionary, but here are some rules that will help.

A. Always capitalize the first word in a sentence, as in
The first word in this sentence begins with a capital letter.

B. Capitalize the first word of a direct quotation, as in
Andy said, "*Please* pass the potatoes."

C. Always capitalize the pronoun I, as in
Where should *I* put these things?

D. Always capitalize proper nouns, such as names of people, as
Give the ball to *Melanie*.

E. Capitalize proper nouns and adjectives used for geographic areas, such as countries, states, rivers, mountains, etc., as in
The *Hudson River* is in *New York State*.
Rene is a *French* name.

F. Always capitalize names of religions and religious groups, as
Jesse is *Catholic*, but his cousin is *Presbyterian*.

G. Always capitalize national and local holidays, as in
My favorite holidays are *Halloween* and *Thanksgiving*.

H. Always capitalize the *main* words in a title, such as
The *War* of the *Worlds*

I. Always capitalize days of the week and months of the year, as
Sunday, *Monday*, *January*, *February*, etc.

Do not capitalize the seasons: spring, summer, fall, winter

B. Rewrite these sentences on the lines below with correct capitalization.

1. Amy and her family are going hiking in montana on thursday.

_____

2. Did you read the article, "never too late," in this magazine?

_____

3. In august, we are going across the atlantic ocean to europe.

_____

4. What time will i eat breakfast in england?

_____

*ANSWERS ON ACTIVITY SHEET 35B.

© 2000 by The Center for Applied Research in Education

Name _____ Date _____

ALWAYS BEGIN BIG!
Additional Rules and Exercises

A. ANSWERS TO EXERCISE ON ACTIVITY SHEET 35A:

1. Amy and her family are going hiking in *Montana* on *Thursday.*
2. Did you read the article, *"Never Too Late,"* in this magazine?
3. In *August,* we are going across the *Atlantic Ocean* to *Europe.*
4. What time will *I* eat breakfast in *England?*

B. ADDITIONAL CAPITALIZATION RULES:

J. Capitalize the first word in the greeting of a letter, as
Dear friend, *My* dear Melissa,

K. Capitalize the first word in the closing of a letter, as
Yours truly, *Very* truly yours, *Sincerely* yours, *Your* friend,

L. Capitalize titles or positions of people when they refer to specific persons, as in
General Lee and *General* Grant fought in the Civil War.
Tell *Dad* that *Dr.* Smith is on the phone.

But do not capitalize these titles when they are used in general or are preceded by a possessive pronoun, as in
How many *c*aptains are there in the army?
My *f*ather is a *d*octor.

M. Capitalize names of schools and colleges, such as
Franklin High School, Harvard University

But do not capitalize these words when they are not used with a specific name as
the *h*igh *s*chool I attended, or a fine *c*ollege

N. Capitalize directions when they refer to specific areas, as
The American *West,*   The Middle *East*

But do not capitalize directions when they do not refer to these specific areas, as
Go *e*ast on Route 13. or Chicago is *w*est of Pittsburgh.

C. Circle the words that are capitalized incorrectly in these sentences.

1. How old will you be when you graduate from High School?
2. Last spring, general Marco traveled to the middle east.
3. My Grandfather was in a car traveling North.
4. Ellie's Great-Grandmother was spanish.
5. Marty is a student at greenville high school.

*See Answers Below.

Answers: 1. high school, **2.** General, Middle East, **3.** grandfather, north
4. great-grandmother, Spanish, **5.** Greenville High School

© 2000 by The Center for Applied Research in Education

Name _____ Date _____

ALWAYS BEGIN BIG!
Review and Exercises

A. CAPITALIZATION REVIEW

The most important rules to remember about capitalization are

→ 1. Capitalize proper nouns and adjectives including names of people, places, holidays, historical events, months and days of the week (but not seasons!), and the pronoun I.

→ 2. Capitalize the first word of a sentence, the first word of a direct quote, and all the main words of a title.

→ 3. In a letter, capitalize the first word in the greeting and the first word of the closing.

B. Memorize these rules and the others on Activity Sheets 35A and 35B. Then, check the correct sentence in each of the groups below. (If in doubt, consult the dictionary.)

1. ❑ a. The Middle School Principal spoke to Dr. Adams.
   ❑ b. The Middle School principal spoke to Dr. Adams.
   ❑ c. The middle school principal spoke to dr. Adams.
   ❑ d. The middle school principal spoke to Dr. Adams,

2. ❑ a. Roses bloom in the spring during the month of june.
   ❑ b. Roses bloom in the spring during the month of June.
   ❑ c. Roses bloom in the Spring during the month of June.

3. ❑ a. The Star Theater is showing a film about the Civil War.
   ❑ b. The Star theater is showing a film about the Civil War.
   ❑ c. The Star Theater is showing a film about the civil war.

4. ❑ a. He walked North along Maple street.
   ❑ b. He walked north along maple street.
   ❑ c. He walked north along Maple Street.

5. ❑ a. The empire state building is in New York city.
   ❑ b. The Empire State Building is in New York City.
   ❑ c. The Empire State building is in New York City.

6. ❑ a. Jenna said to her mother, "here I come!"
   ❑ b. Jenna said to her Mother, "Here I come!"
   ❑ c. Jenna said to her mother, "Here I come!"

7. ❑ a. I love grandma. She lives in Florida.
   ❑ b. I love Grandma. she lives in Florida.
   ❑ c. I love Grandma. She lives in Florida.
   ❑ d. I love grandma. She lives in florida.

© 2000 by The Center for Applied Research in Education

Answers: 1. d, 2. b, 3. a, 4. c, 5. b, 6. c, 7. c

Name _____

Date _____

THE WORD GARDEN—1

A. Here is a word garden. Each of the flowers contains one word that is often misspelled.

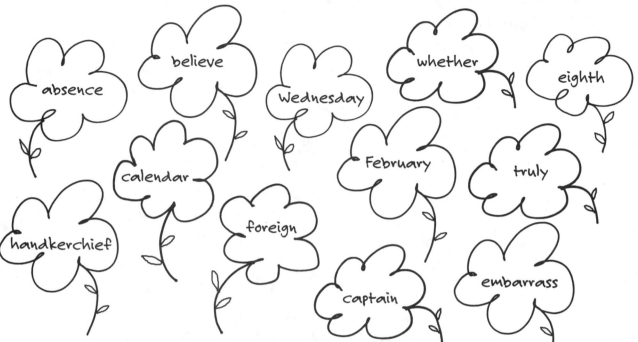

absence · believe · Wednesday · whether · eighth · calendar · February · truly · handkerchief · foreign · captain · embarrass

© 2000 by The Center for Applied Research in Education

B. Can you pluck the correct word from each flower and write it where it belongs in the sentences below? (Be sure to copy the correct spelling!)

1. The ship's _____ wore a blue uniform.

2. Yesterday, I was sick. It was my first _____ from school.

3. Don't _____ me by shouting my name in public.

4. Don't _____ everything you read in the newspaper.

5. Maggie doesn't know _____ or not she will go to the party.

6. Valentine's Day occurs in _____.

7. Nowadays, most people use tissues instead of a _____.

8. Is today Tuesday or _____?

9. Tomorrow is my little brother's _____ birthday.

10. Look at the _____ and tell me today's date.

11. Germany is a _____ country.

12. Do you _____ mean what you say?

Answers: 1. captain **2.** absence **3.** embarrass **4.** believe **5.** whether **6.** February **7.** handkerchief **8.** Wednesday **9.** eighth **10.** calendar **11.** foreign **12.** truly

Name _____ Date _____

THE WORD GARDEN—2

A. Here is another garden of words that are often misspelled.

© 2000 by The Center for Applied Research in Education

B. Pluck the correct word from each flower and write it where it belongs in the sentence below. Be sure to copy the correct spelling!

1. My favorite meal is _____ and meatballs.

2. We're planning a _____ party for my parent's anniversary.

3. Every week, I borrow two books from the _____.

4. _____ are handy for cutting paper.

5. I want to get good marks so I don't _____ my parents.

6. I will _____ go to camp this summer.

7. Jim can't draw a _____ line without a ruler.

8. My father is a geologist and my mother is a _____.

9. I pretended to be happy, but I _____ felt sad inside.

10. Did it ever _____ to you that you could be wrong?

Answers: 1. spaghetti   **2.** surprise   **3.** library   **4.** scissors   **5.** disappoint   **6.** probably   **7.** straight   **8.** lawyer   **9.** really   **10.** occur

Name _____ Date _____

SPELLING DEMONS—1
List and Exercises

A. Can you battle the spelling demons? Here is a list of words that are often misspelled.

abbreviate	believe	disappear
accidentally	benefit	disappoint
achieve	bicycle	familiar
address	business	finally
anxious	career	government
appearance	committed	grief

B. Complete the sentences below by filling in a word from the list. Be sure to copy the correct spelling!

1. Josh plans to follow a _____ in politics after college.

2. I always feel very _____ before a test.

3. Allison wept with _____ when her beloved puppy died.

4. He is in jail because he _____ a serious crime.

5. The magician made the rabbit _____.

6. Joe always rides his _____ to school.

7. I'm not sure of his name, but his face looks _____.

8. At last, I _____ found the video I wanted.

9. Spelling practice will _____ your writing greatly.

10. Can you _____ the names of all the states?

11. I am working hard to _____ all my goals in life.

12. Send the letter to Mr. Brown's home _____.

13. Kevin's uncle is in the construction _____.

14. You can't know a person's character from his _____.

15. Matthew _____ ran his bike into the fence.

16. The federal _____ is in Washington, D.C.

© 2000 by The Center for Applied Research in Education

Name _____ Date _____

SPELLING DEMONS—2
List and Exercises

A. Are you winning the battle against your spelling demons? Here are some more words that are often misspelled.

irresistible	possess	restaurant
library	prejudice	rhythm
lightning	probably	seize
marriage	physician	surprise
mathematics	receipt	suspicious
medicine	receive	twelfth
parallel	recommend	weird

B. Complete the sentences below by filling in a word from the list. Be sure to copy the correct spelling!

1. Dr. Craig is a primary care _____.

2. Everyone loves Amy because she has an _____ manner.

3. Alan plays the drums in a _____ band.

4. The horror film I saw yesterday was _____ and scary.

5. Good people have no _____ against those who are different.

6. Lines that go in the same direction are _____.

7. Can you _____ a good book for me to read?

8. There is a saying that it is better to give than to _____.

9. I heard claps of thunder and saw flashes of _____.

10. The chances are that I will _____ go to a local college.

11. Larry's friends made him a _____ birthday party at a fine _____.

12. The shifty-eyed fellow behind a bush looked _____.

13. It is wise to get a _____ when you make a purchase.

14. The cough _____ is cherry-flavored.

15. Next year, Ally will go into the _____ grade.

© 2000 by The Center for Applied Research in Education

Name _____ Date _____

SPELLING DEMONS—3
A Search for Misspelled Words

A. Are you winning the battle with your spelling demons? If you are, you should be able to find the seventeen misspelled words in the following paragraph. Circle the words that are spelled wrong. (Hint: One misspelled word appears twice.)

> You might not beleive it, but it is possible to have a wierd adventure right in the local libary. I was there last Wenesday looking for a book about goverment that my teacher had reccommended. A man with a foregn accent spoke to me. He asked me to lend him a hanker-chief. I reached in my pocket for a tissue and accidently dropped my keys. They made a realy loud noise. Everyone looked straigt at me. I was embarassed, but the guy was trully nice. He said he was a sea captian and suprised me with some great stories about his life. That was one trip to the libary that didn't dissappoint me!

B. Were you able to find all seventeen spelling errors? If not, study it again and check with your lists of spelling demons. Then, copy the paragraph on the lines below, correcting all the spelling errors.

_____

_____

_____

_____

_____

_____

_____

_____

_____

_____

*SEE ACTIVITY 38 FOR THE CORRECT SOLUTION.

© 2000 by The Center for Applied Research in Education

Name _____ Date _____

DON'T PUT US TOGETHER!

A. Here is the paragraph that appeared on Activity 37C, with all words spelled correctly.

> You might not believe it, but it is possible to have a weird adventure right in the local library. I was there last Wednesday looking for a book about government that my teacher had recommended. A man with a foreign accent spoke to me. He asked me to lend him a handkerchief. I reached in my pocket for a tissue and accidentally dropped my keys. They made a really loud noise. Everyone looked straight at me. I was embarrassed, but the guy was truly nice. He said he was a sea captain, and surprised me with some great stories about his life. That was one trip to the library that didn't disappoint me!

B. WRITING TWO WORDS AS ONE: Some commonly used phrases are often, mistakenly, put together as one. The following should always be written as two words:

a lot,	as in	I like to play basketball *a lot.*
in fact,	as in	I am not tired. *In fact,* I am wide awake!
all right,	as in	The doctor said my brother will be *all right* soon.
high school,	as in	Grades nine through twelve are in our *high school.*
ice cream,	as in	*Ice cream* is my favorite dessert.

C. Complete the following sentences by filling in the blanks with the right words from the above list. Be sure to copy the spelling correctly!

1. Jennifer does not eat hamburgers. _____, she doesn't eat meat at all.

2. Marcy is so conceited she thinks all the boys like her _____.

3. In the summertime, a ringing bell announces the arrival of the _____ truck on our block.

4. After middle school, I will go into _____.

5. "_____," Terry agreed, "I'll go to the movies with you."

© 2000 by The Center for Applied Research in Education

Answers to Exercise C: 1. In fact, **2.** a lot, **3.** ice cream, **4.** high school, **5.** All right

Name _____ Date _____

HAPPY ENDINGS
Rules and Exercises

Here are some rules to follow when adding suffixes.

A. Drop the second *l* when adding *full* to a word.

Examples:		
	playful	(play + full)
	peaceful	(peace + full)
	wonderful	(wonder + full)
	mouthful	(mouth + full)
	forgetful	(forget + full)
	powerful	(power + full)
	helpful	(help + full)

(There are exceptions to this rule, so always check with the dictionary if you are not certain.)

Complete these sentences with a word that has the suffix "ful":

1. My Uncle Jack is so _____ that he sometimes goes shopping without taking money along.

2. Girl Scouts and Boy Scouts are supposed to be _____.

3. Andy couldn't talk because he had a huge _____ of potatoes.

4. A good pitcher must have a _____ arm.

5. The baby looks so _____ when he is sleeping.

B. With a word that ends with a silent *e* (like *scare* or *love*), drop the *e* before adding a suffix that begins with a vowel (like *ing* or *able*).

Examples:		
	lovable	(love + able)
	believable	(believe + able)
	relating	(relate + ing)
	having	(have + ing)
	scary	(scare + y)
	wavy	(wave + y)
	tamest	(tame + est)

(There are exceptions to this rule, so always check with a dictionary if you are not sure.)

Creating words with suffixes (Write the word correctly on the line):

Add	*ing*	to	*dare*	_____
Add	*able*	to	*endure*	_____
Add	*able*	to	*like*	_____
Add	*ing*	to	*judge*	_____
Add	*ible*	to	*reverse*	_____

Did you remember to drop the final *e* before adding the suffix?

© 2000 by The Center for Applied Research in Education

Name _____ Date _____

HAPPY ENDINGS
Rules and Exercises

A. Do not drop the final *e* when adding a suffix beginning with a vowel to words ending *ce* or *ge*.

Examples:	courageous	courage + ous
	changeable	change + able
	marriageable	marriage + able
	noticeable	notice + able
	serviceable	service + able

(There are exceptions to this rule, such as *noticing* and *changing,* so consult a dictionary whenever you are not sure.)

1. My sister's moods are very _____.

2. His bright red pants are quite _____ in the crowd.

3. Our car is old but still _____.

4. The _____ soldier received a medal.

B. Do not drop the final *e* when adding a suffix beginning with a consonant.

Examples:	hateful	hate + ful
	arrangement	arrange + ment
	careless	care + less
	excitement	excite + ment

(There are exceptions to this rule, such as *argument, truly, judgment, and probably,* so check with the dictionary when you are not certain.)

Circle the misspelled words in the following paragraph:

Last week, I made a carless mistake. I was in my room changeing my clothes when I heard a loud noise. I ran to the window and saw a wonderfull sight. The hatful kid next door was having an arguement with a bigger kid. In all the excitment I ran downstairs without putting on my shoes. Everyone was stareing at me. That was surly an embarrassing moment for me.

© 2000 by The Center for Applied Research in Education

Answers: You should have circled: *carless, changeing, wonderfull, hatful, arguement, excitment, stareing, surly.* These should have been spelled *careless, changing, wonderful, hateful, argument, excitement, staring, surely.*

Name _____ Date _____

HAPPY ENDINGS
Examples and Exercises

A. There are many rules for adding suffixes. Sometimes it is easiest to just memorize some of the words with suffixes that are often misspelled, as in the following lists:

Words with *able* or *ible:*

acceptable	excitable	admissible	forcible
available	likable	collapsible	inflexible
believable	lovable	digestible	indigestible
breakable	peaceable	eligible	irresistible
dependable	profitable	flexible	legible

Words with *ance* or *ence:*

attendance	balance	absence	excellence
admittance	distance	audience	existence
allowance	entrance	coincidence	experience
ambulance	guidance	confidence	influence
appearance	insurance	conscience	patience

B. Fill in the sentences below with the correct word.

1. The food in that restaurant is completely _____.
   (indigestible or indigestable)

2. The movie star made a grand _____ into the ballroom.
   (entrance or entrence)

3. The sailor saw land in the _____. (distance or distence)

4. Harry asked for an increase in his _____.   (allowence or allowance)

5. Your excuse is not _____.   (acceptible or acceptable)

6. The _____ applauded wildly.   (audiance or audience)

7. My dog, Shadow, is a _____ pet.   (lovable or lovible)

8. My school strives for _____ in education.   (excellence or excellance)

9. Marla had _____ that she would do well on the test.
   (confidance or confidence)

10. The _____ took the injured man to the hospital.
    (ambulence or ambulance)

CHECK YOUR ANSWERS CAREFULLY WITH THE LISTS ABOVE.

© 2000 by The Center for Applied Research in Education

Name _____ Date _____

HAPPY ENDINGS
Lists and Exercises

A. Here are some more words with suffixes that are often misspelled.

Words with *ar, er, or:*					
beggar	particular	announcer	lawyer	director	minor
burglar	popular	beginner	passenger	elevator	motor
calendar	regular	consumer	traveler	author	neighbor
cellar	similar	employer	actor	escalator	professor
grammar	vinegar	jeweler	counselor	governor	senator

B. Complete these sentences by filling in the correct word from the list above.

1. Mrs. March was a _____ customer at the market.

2. Mr. March woke up and thought he heard a _____ downstairs.

3. Take the _____ to the tenth floor.

4. The chef put oil and _____ into the salad.

5. Sarah wished that she could be more _____ at school.

6. They bought a diamond ring from the _____.

7. Do you know the name of the _____ of your state?

8. You should have a _____ to represent you in court.

9. The radio _____ gave the six o'clock news.

*ANSWERS AT THE BOTTOM OF THE PAGE.

C. The following paragraph contains thirteen misspelled words. Circle them, and rewrite the paragraph correctly on the other side of this page.

Yesterday, I was stuck in an elevater at the mall. The only other passengar was my friend, Larry, who is very exciteable. "This is unbelievible!" he complained. "We should have taken the escalater." I told him it was probably just a minar problem. "This is a reguler thing," I said. "It happened to my neighber, Professer Benson, last week." Larry had no patiance at all. After we finaly got out, Larry pretended he had confidance all along, but I knew better. It was a scary experiance.

© 2000 by The Center for Applied Research in Education

Misspelled Words in Paragraph: elevator, passenger, excitable, unbelievable, escalator, minor, regular, neighbor, Professor, patience, finally, confidence, experience

Answers to Sentences: 1. regular, 2. burglar, 3. elevator, 4. **vinegar,** 5. popular, 6. jeweler, 7. governor (or senator), 8. lawyer, 9. announcer

Name _____ Date _____

BE CAREFUL, DO IT CAREFULLY!
Explanation and Exercises

A. The suffix *ful* is used to make an *adjective* (modifies a noun). It is spelled with one *l*, as in *careful* or *playful*.

   The suffix *fully* is used to make an *adverb* (modifies a verb). it is spelled with two *l*'s, as in *carefully* or *playfully*.

B. Here are some more common examples.

beautiful	That is a beautiful flower.
beautifully	She dances beautifully.
fearful	The baby is fearful of loud noises.
fearfully	I entered the spooky house fearfully.
joyful	The bride was joyful.
joyfully	The choir sang joyfully.
painful	It is not painful to go to the dentist.
painfully	She moved her broken leg painfully.
hopeful	Jesse was hopeful that his team would win.
hopefully	The doctor spoke hopefully about his patient.
hateful	Hitler was a hateful person.
hatefully	He spoke hatefully about other people.

© 2000 by The Center for Applied Research in Education

C. Write a sentence containing each of the words below.

1. careful _____

2. fearfully _____

3. hopefully _____

4. playful _____

5. painful _____

6. fearful _____

7. carefully _____

8. beautifully _____

9. hateful _____

10. playfully _____

Name _____ Date _____

AT THE BEGINNING
Explanation and Exercises

A. A *prefix* is placed in front of a word to change its meaning. Here are some common prefixes and what they often (but not always) mean.

anti means against or opposite, as antibiotic (against bacteria), and antifreeze (against freezing).

con or *com* means with, as contest (test with), combination (together with), and conclude (finish with).

de means down or away, as depress (press down), depart (go away), and descend (climb down).

dis means not or separate, as discount (not count), displease (not please), and disconnected (not connected).

ex means former or out of, as exclude (leave out), and express (speak out).

in means into or not, as invalid (not valid), income (something coming in), and inappropriate (not appropriate).

inter means between, as interfere (come between), interstate (between states), and intercede (come between).

mis means wrong or bad, as misdeed (bad act), mistake (wrong), misread (read wrongly), and mismatch (bad or wrong match).

pre means before, as preview (see before), predict (tell before), and prefix (a syllable that comes before).

re means again or back, as repel (push back), repeat (say or do again), and repay (pay back).

sub means under, as submarine (under water) and subterranean (under the earth).

B. Sometimes, prefixes are followed by hyphens, as ex-soldier, self-confidence, re-examine.

C. Write four sentences on the lines below. Each sentence should contain at least one word that has a prefix. (You may select from the words on this page, or choose others of your own.)

1. _____

2. _____

3. _____

4. _____

© 2000 by The Center for Applied Research in Education

Name _____ Date _____

AT THE BEGINNING
More Prefixes

A. Here are additional prefixes that can be placed in front of words to form new words.

extra means more or above, as extraordinary (more than ordinary), and extrasensory (more than the senses)

micro means small, as microchip (small chip), and microscope (small scope)

mid means center, as midtown (center of town), midstream (center of stream), and midlife (center of a life span)

post means after, as postwar (after the war), and postscript (after the body of the letter)

over means too much, as overload (loaded too much), overcome (win over), over-stressed (too tense), overanxious (too anxious), and overworked (worked too hard)

trans means across, as transfer (send across), transatlantic (across the Atlantic), and transport (carry across)

B. Write six sentences. Each sentence should contain at least one word with one of the above prefixes.

1. _____

2. _____

3. _____

4. _____

5. _____

6. _____

© 2000 by The Center for Applied Research in Education

Name _____ Date _____

AT THE BEGINNING
Doubling Consonants with Prefixes

A. RULE: What happens when a prefix ends with a consonant, and the attached word begins with the same consonant? Both letters are written, as in the following words:

misstep (mis + step)	**misspeak** (mis + speak)
dissimilar (dis + similar)	**commit** (com + mit)
misspell (mis + spell)	**dissolve** (dis + solve)
dissatisfy (dis + satisfy)	**unnatural** (un + natural)
unnoticed (un + noticed)	**dissect** (dis + sect)

B. Write ten sentences below. Each sentence should contain one of the words listed above.

1. _____

2. _____

3. _____

4. _____

5. _____

6. _____

7. _____

8. _____

9. _____

10. _____

C. In the paragraph below, underline every word that begins with a prefix.

Did you ever make a mistake? I did! Are you interested in hearing about it? I'm going to confide in you. I borrowed some money from a friend and forgot to repay it. My friend was very unhappy. I will never commit such a bad act again.

See Answers Below.

Answers to Exercise C: The following words should be underlined: mistake, interested, confide, repay, unhappy, commit

© 2000 by The Center for Applied Research in Education

Name _____ Date _____

PUT THEM TOGETHER
Explanation and Exercises

A. COMPOUND WORDS: A compound word is made up of more than one word. There are three kinds of compound words.

Closed—Words are blended together as one, as notebook (note + book), makeup (make + up), softball (soft + ball), firefly (fire + fly), keyboard (key + board), and bookcase (book + case)

Hyphenated—Examples are mother-in-law, six-pack, and over-the-counter

Open—The compound word is written as two or more words, as real estate, post office, vice president, half sister, blood bank, department store, fire truck, police station

→ **Note:** Words should usually be hyphenated when modifying a noun to avoid confusion.

For example, *An old car salesman greeted us.* is an unclear sentence. As written, it indicates that the salesman is old. If you mean to say that he is selling old cars, it should be hyphenated: *An old-car salesman greeted us.* Here are some more examples:

She worked in the store part time.
She was a part-time worker in the store.

My sister is nine years old.
I have a nine-year-old sister.

This car can travel at a high speed.
This is a high-speed car.

B. Check the correctly spelled sentence in each group. (Always consult a dictionary when you are not sure how to spell a compound word!)

1. ❏ a.　　Tom is my half brother.
　 ❏ b.　　Tom is my half-brother.

2. ❏ a.　　Maria wants to get a full time job.
　 ❏ b.　　Maria wants to get a full-time job.

3. ❏ a.　　My note book is almost filled up.
　 ❏ b.　　My note-book is almost filled up.
　 ❏ c.　　My notebook is almost filled up.

4. ❏ a.　　My mom bought stamps at the post-office.
　 ❏ b.　　My mom bought stamps at the post office.

5. ❏ a.　　Joe put on scary makeup for Halloween.
　 ❏ b.　　Joe put on scary make up for Halloween.

Answers: 1. a, 2. b, 3. c, 4. b, 5. a

© 2000 by The Center for Applied Research in Education

Name _____ Date _____

MAKE IT SHORT
Rules and Exercises

A. Abbreviations are always followed by a period. Here are some common abbreviations.

1. Titles *before* names:

Mr.	our neighbor, Mr. Smith
Mrs.	my mother, Mrs. Fielding
Ms.	my teacher, Ms. Fargo

(**Note:** Miss is not an abbreviation)

Prof.	stands for Professor, as Prof. Jones
Dr.	stands for Doctor, as Dr. Santos
Drs.	stands for more than one doctor, as Drs. Smith and Jones
St.	stands for Saint, as St. Valentine
Gen.	stands for General, as General Patton
Lt.	stands for Lieutenant, as Lt. Sam Albano

2. Titles *after* names

Sr.	stands for Senior, as James Gonzalez, Sr.
Jr.	stands for Junior, as James Gonzalez, Jr.
M.D.	stands for doctor of medicine, as Amy Martin, M.D.
D.D.S.	stands for doctor of dental surgery (dentist), as Ellen Grant, D.D.S.
Ph.D.	stands for doctor of philosophy, as Joe Finch, Ph.D.
M.A.	stands for master of arts, as Alan Gates, M.A.

(**Note:** never use titles before and after a name. Write either Dr. Amy Martin or Amy Martin, M.D. not Dr. Amy Martin, M.D.)

B. Write a sentence for each abbreviation below. (Note: These abbreviations are used only before or after names.)

1. Prof. _____

2. Drs. _____

3. D.D.S. _____

4. Jr. _____

5. Mrs. _____

6. M.D. _____

7. Gen. _____

8. St. _____

© 2000 by The Center for Applied Research in Education

Name _____ Date _____

MAKE IT SHORT
Explanation and Exercises

A. Do you know these common abbreviations?

1. *Days of the week:* Sun., Mon., Tues., Wed., Thurs., Fri., Sat.

2. *Months:* Jan., Feb., Mar., Apr., (May, June, and July are not abbreviated.) Aug., Sept., Oct., Nov., Dec.

3. *States of the U.S.:* Your post office can provide you with the correct postal abbreviations for each state. Here are a few of them:

Alabama	AL	California	CA	Florida	FL
Alaska	AK	Colorado	CO	Georgia	GA
Arizona	AZ	Connecticut	CT	Hawaii	HI
Arkansas	AR	Delaware	DE	Idaho	ID

(**Note:** These abbreviations are used on letters and envelopes. Do not abbreviate when referring to the state in a sentence. It should be, "I visited New York in April." NOT "I visited NY in April.")

4. Here are some more abbreviations:

adjective	adj.	dozen	doz.	miscellaneous	misc.
and others	etc.	example	ex.	ounce	oz.
assistant	asst.	foot or feet	ft.	pound	lb.
avenue	ave.	gallon	gal.	page	p.
street	st.	hour	hr.	pages	pp.
road	rd.	minute	min.	telephone	tel.
company	co.	second	sec.	singular	sing.
corporation	corp.	month	mo.	plural	pl.
department	dept.	year	yr.	population	pop.
building	bldg.	number	no.	miles per hour	m.p.h.

B. In the following letter, circle ten errors in abbreviation

39 Main Str.
Sunshine, FLOR 03459
Novem. 16, 1999

Wilson and Comp.
2500 Salem Aven.
Northport, Conn 06023

Dear Sirs:

On Septem. 5, 1999, I ordered 2 do. pairs of socks from pg. 52 of your winter catalog, item num. H350. That was two months ago and I have not received these socks. Please send them immediately.

Yours truly,
Arthur Rodriguez

Answer: You should have circled these incorrect abbreviations: Str. (St.), FLOR (FL), Novem. (Nov.), Comp. (Co.), Aven. (Ave.) Conn. (CT), Septem. (Sept.), do. (doz.), pg. (p.), num (no.)

© 2000 by The Center for Applied Research in Education

Name _____ Date _____

SPELL CHECK!
Exercises

Some computers have a spell check program to find words that have been spelled wrong. You can be your own spell checker. Complete this exercise and find out how good a spell checker you are!!

A. Each of these sentences contains at least one misspelled word. Write each sentence correctly on the line below.

1. Did you here the tail about the tortoise and the hair?

_____

2. Our school principle gained a lot of wait last summer.

_____

3. Ellen said, "i have a pane in my stomach."

_____

4. Ellen went to sea Dr. Fred Magli, M.D.

_____

5. I canot beleive that wierd story about the police chief.

_____

6. How many potatos did the babys eat?

_____

7. We're going to california on the first wenesday in Febuary.

_____

8. Did you beleive everything that foriegn captian said?

_____

9. Mrs Smith lost her hankercheif at the post-office on tuesday.

_____

10. The police cheif said that a crime had been comitted.

_____

*Answers on Activity Sheet 44B.

© 2000 by The Center for Applied Research in Education

Name _____ Date _____

SPELL CHECK
Exercises

A. ANSWERS TO EXERCISE ON ACTIVITY 44A:

1. Did you *hear* the *tale* about the tortoise and the *hare?*
2. Our school *principal* gained a lot of *weight* last summer.
3. Ellen said, "*I* have a *pain* in my stomach."
4. Ellen went to *see Dr. Fred Magli.* (or *Fred Magli, M.D.)*
5. I *cannot believe* that *weird* story about the police chief.
6. How many *potatoes* did the *babies* eat?
7. We're going to *California* on the first *Wednesday* in *February.*
8. Did you *believe* everything that *foreign captain* said?
9. *Mrs.* Smith lost her handkerchief at the *post office* on *Tuesday.*
10. The police *chief* said that a crime had been *committed.*

B. Circle the spelling errors in the following paragraph. If you can find them all, then you are an excellent spell checker!

David was called to the scool office on Thrusday. The principle, mr. mackay, wanted to no why David had so many absens-
es this semestre. David was embarassed to tell the reason.
Finaly, he admited that he had been spending alot of time in
the public libary because he was ashamed of the cloths his
mother maid him wear. At frist, the principal didn't beleive
David. Finaly, he called David's mother and perswaded her to
by the boy new clothes. After that, David was realy happy and
proud of his apearance.

*CHECK YOUR ANSWER BELOW.

© 2000 by The Center for Applied Research in Education

Answer: Here is the correct spelling of the words you should have circled in the paragraph:
school, Thursday, principal, Mr. Mackay, know, absences, semester, Finally, admit-
ted, a lot, library, clothes, made, first, believe, Finally, persuaded, buy, really, appearance

Section Four

GRAMMAR HELP

TEACHER'S GUIDE—
ALPHABETICAL LISTING OF GRAMMAR PROBLEMS
AND THEIR ACTIVITY NUMBERS

Here is a list of the grammar problems addressed in this section and the relevant exercises.

GRAMMAR PROBLEM	ACTIVITY NUMBER
Adjectives	54A
Adjectives, Proper	54B
Adjectives, Comparison	54C
Adverbs	55A, B
Adverbs vs. Adjectives	56A, B, C
Modifiers, Misplaced	57A, B, C
Prepositions, Misused	58A, B
Pronouns, Agreement with Antecedent	45A, B, C, D
Pronouns, In Combination	48A, B
Pronouns, Indefinite	46A, B, C
Pronouns, Possessive	47A, B
Pronouns, Them vs. Those	50
Pronouns, Who vs. Whom	49A, B
Verbs, Linking	52A, B
Verbs, Person	53A, B
Verbs, Tense	51A, B, C, D

Name _____ Date _____

DO YOU AGREE WITH ME?
Explanation and Exercises

A. DEFINITIONS

1. A *pronoun* is a word that is used in place of a noun.

   In place of *this man*, you could say *he*.
       Look at *this man. He* is my father.

   In place of *the horses*, you could say *they*.
       The horses pulled a heavy wagon. *They* are tired.

2. The noun that the pronoun stands for is called its *antecedent*.

   In the examples above, *man* is the antecedent of *he. Horses* is the antecedent of *they.*

B. List the pronouns and their antecedents for each of the following:

1. My computer is not working; it is broken.

   Pronoun _____ Antecedent _____

2. Linda examined the window and saw that it was cracked.

   Pronoun _____ Antecedent _____

3. Carlos is sad because he lost the game.

   Pronoun _____ Antecedent _____

4. Maria was driving the car at its top speed.

   Pronoun _____ Antecedent _____

5. All the people in the audience are clapping their hands.

   Pronoun _____ Antecedent _____

6. The dog has two thorns in its paw.

   Pronoun _____ Antecedent _____

*SEE ANSWERS BELOW.

Answers to Exercise B: 1. pronoun—*it*, antecedent—*computer;* **2.** pronoun—*it*, antecedent—*window;* **3.** pronoun—*he*, antecedent—*Carlos;* **4.** pronoun—*its*, antecedent—*Car;* **5.** pronoun—*their*, antecedent—*people;* **6.** pronoun—*its*, antecedent—*dog*

© 2000 by The Center for Applied Research in Education

Name _____ Date _____

DO YOU AGREE WITH ME?
Explanation and Exercises

A. RULES: A pronoun must always agree with its antecedent. It must always be clear to whom or what that pronoun refers. Here are some rules that will make it easy for you to always remember which pronoun to use.

➤ **RULE 1**   A pronoun must agree with its antecedent in person.

The person (or thing) who is speaking is called *first person,* such as *I* or *we.*
The person (or thing) spoken to is called *second person,* such as *you.*
The person (or thing) spoken about is called *third person,* such as *he, she, it,* or *they.*

Example: Wrong—If all the boys are ready, *you* can begin the race.
➤ Right—If all the boys are ready, *they* can begin the race.

[boys is third person, so a *third person* pronoun *(they)* must be used]

➤ **RULE 2**   A pronoun must agree with its antecedent in number (singular or plural).

Example: Wrong—Every student wants to do well on *their* exam.
➤ Right—Every student wants to do well on *his* exam.

(Every *student* is singular. *Their* is plural. *His* is singular.)

➤ **RULE 3**   A pronoun must agree with its antecedent in gender (male, female, or neuter).

Example: Wrong—Ellie's new house has four windows on *her* third floor.
➤ Right—Ellie's new house has four windows on *its* third floor.

(The *house* is not feminine. It is neuter and takes the pronoun *its.*)

C. EXERCISES: Write the correct pronouns in the following sentence. Be sure they agree in person, number, and gender with their antecedents.

1. Elena thinks that Jack will lose _____ chance to be on the team.

2. Jack's dog has a white spot on _____ tail.

3. Jack and Elena ate _____ breakfast together.

4. Elena dropped _____ glass and _____ shattered on the floor.

5. All the students did well on _____ final exams.

*ANSWERS ON ACTIVITY SHEET 45C.

© 2000 by The Center for Applied Research in Education

Name _____ Date _____

DO YOU AGREE WITH ME?
Additional Exercises

A. ANSWERS TO EXERCISE C IN ACTIVITY 45B:

1. *his* (agrees with *Jack*)
2. *its* (agrees with *dog*)
3. *their* (agrees with *Jack and Elena*)
4. *her* (agrees with *Elena*); *it* (agrees with *glass*)
5. *their* (agrees with *students*)

B. ADDITIONAL EXERCISES: If you practice using pronouns, you will become more skilled in their correct use. Here are some additional exercises that will help. Complete these sentences by filling in the correct pronouns. Be sure the pronouns agree with their antecedents in person, number, and gender.

1. Greg has a new computer in _____ room. _____ is set up on _____ desk.

2. Take this mail to your dad. _____ is in a hurry to get _____.

3. My brother and I can hardly wait to get _____ presents.

4. I tried to open _____ umbrella, but _____ was stuck.

5. Alice said that _____ doll had a hole in _____ head.

6. Jody's essay on elections had a mistake in _____ first sentence.

7. Mike wanted me to give the book to _____ because _____ had _____ name on the cover.

8. The plaque on the door to the doctor's office has _____ name on _____.

9. Anna and her parents are taking along _____ dog when _____ go to the shore this summer.

10. The captain told the passengers to wear caps when _____ sailed in _____ ship.

*SEE ANSWERS BELOW.

© 2000 by The Center for Applied Research in Education

Answers to Exercises Above: 1. his, it, his; 2. he, it; 3. our 4. my, it; 5. her, its; 6. its; 7. him, it, his 8. his, it; 9. their, they; 10. they, his

Name _____ Date _____

DO YOU AGREE WITH ME?
Additional Exercises

A. Check the correct sentence in each group.

1. ☐ a.   Tamar reads mystery books in their spare time.
   ☐ b.   Tamar reads mystery books in its spare time.
   ☐ c.   Tamar reads mystery books in her spare time.

2. ☐ a.   Arthur's parents are going on their vacation in June.
   ☐ b.   Arthur's parents are going on his vacation in June.

3. ☐ a.   The kids laughed when the teacher dropped his pen.
   ☐ b.   The kids laughed when the teacher dropped their pen.

4. ☐ a.   The Johnson's house is ready and you can move in now.
   ☐ b.   The Johnson's house is ready and they can move in now.

5. ☐ a.   Mike hopes to get a good grade in your English class.
   ☐ b.   Mike hopes to get a good grade in his English class.

6. ☐ a.   Try this exercise to test your knowledge of pronouns.
   ☐ b.   Try this exercise to test their knowledge of pronouns.

7. ☐ a.   The teachers at that school are proud of his students.
   ☐ b.   The teachers at that school are proud of their students.

*SEE ANSWERS BELOW.

B. The pronouns in these sentences do not agree with their antecedents. Rewrite each sentence correctly on the line below.

1. These products are outstanding because of its good quality.

   _____

2. Harry's Little League team won most of their games this season.

   _____

3. The twins are taking the dog for their walk this morning.

   _____

4. These exercises will help you improve their writing skill.

   _____

*SEE ANSWERS BELOW.

© 2000 by The Center for Applied Research in Education

Answers: Exercise A: 1. c,   2. a,   3. a,   4. b,   5. b,   6. a,   7. b

Exercise B: 1. their,   2. its,   3. its,   4. your

Name _____ Date _____

ANYONE CAN BE SOMEBODY
Explanation and Exercises

A. DEFINITION: An indefinite pronoun names a person, thing, or amount that is not specified.

Most indefinite pronouns are *singular,* as

anybody, anyone, anything
everybody, everyone, everything
nobody, no one, nothing
somebody, someone, something
another, each, either, little, much, neither, one, other

A few indefinite pronouns are *plural:*

both, few, many, others, several

Examples:	Everyone knows the answer to this question.	(singular)
	Both students know the answer to this question.	(plural)
	Nobody knows the answer to this question.	(singular)
	There are many who know the answer.	(plural)
	No one does his best work.	(singular)
	A few do their best work.	(plural)

B. Fill in the blank space in these sentences.

1. Something weird _____ to me every day.   (happen or happens)

2. They both _____ to school in the morning.   (walk or walks)

3. Anyone _____ welcome at the party.   (is or are)

4. Nobody _____ to play with Alicia.   (want or wants)

5. Neither of the brothers _____ to wait.   (like or likes)

6. Much of the homework _____ easy.   (is or are)

7. Both of the sisters _____ to play ball.   (like or likes)

8. Neither of them _____ the correct answer.   (know or knows)

9. Many of them _____ the correct answer.   (know or knows)

10. Everybody _____ going to the movies.   (is or are)

*ANSWERS ON ACTIVITY SHEET 46B.

© 2000 by The Center for Applied Research in Education

Name _____ Date _____

ANYONE CAN BE SOMEBODY
Explanation and Exercises

A. ANSWERS TO EXERCISE B, ACTIVITY 46A

1. happens,   2. walk,   3. is,   4. wants,   5. likes,   6. is,
7. like,   8. knows,   9. know,   10. is

B. Some indefinite pronouns can be either singular *or* plural. It depends on the rest of the sentence. These indefinite pronouns can be either singular or plural: *all, any, more, most, none, some, enough.*

Examples:

All of the action was exciting. (*action* is singular, so *all* is singular, too.)

All of the actors were running. (*actors* is plural, so *all* is plural, too.)

Most of my life is boring. (*life* is singular, so *most* is singular, too.)

Most of my friends are funny. (*friends* is plural, so *most* is plural, too.)

C. Check the correct sentence in each of these groups.

1. ☐ a.   Any of your friends are welcome here.
   ☐ b.   Any of your friends is welcome here.

2. ☐ a.   Most of the work is complete.
   ☐ b.   Most of the work are complete.

3. ☐ a.   All of the animals is in their cages.
   ☐ b.   All of the animals are in their cages.

4. ☐ a.   None of the questions is easy.
   ☐ b.   None of the questions are easy.

5. ☐ a.   Some of the boys on the team plays well.
   ☐ b.   Some of the boys on the team play well.

6. ☐ a.   More polish is needed on these shoes.
   ☐ b.   More polish are needed on these shoes.

7. ☐ a.   More guests is expected to arrive later.
   ☐ b.   More guests are expected to arrive later.

8. ☐ a.   Most of your answers is right.
   ☐ b.   Most of your answers are right.

9. ☐ a.   All of the ice cream is gone.
   ☐ b.   All of the ice cream are gone.

SEE ACTIVITY 46C FOR ANSWERS.

© 2000 by The Center for Applied Research in Education

Name _____ Date _____

ANYONE CAN BE SOMEBODY
Additional Exercises

A. ANSWERS TO EXERCISE C ON ACTIVITY 46B

1. a,   2. a,   3. b,   4. b,   5. b,   6. a,   7. b,   8. b,   9. a

---

B. Write a sentence containing each of the following indefinite pronouns:

1. someone _____

2. all _____

3. everybody _____

4. anyone _____

5. both _____

6. nobody _____

7. nothing _____

8. most _____

9. each _____

10. any _____

C. Fill in the blank spaces in these sentences.

1. Another train _____ arriving soon.   (is or are)

2. Everybody _____ to win the race.   (want or wants)

3. None of your friends _____ here.   (is or are)

4. Most of the seats _____ taken.   (is or are)

5. Nobody important ever _____ here.   (come or comes)

6. Most of this building _____ empty.   (is or are)

7. I hope nothing bad _____ to them.   (happen or happens)

8. All of the students _____ hard.   (work or works)

*SEE ANSWERS BELOW.

Answers to Exercise C: 1. is,   2. wants,   3. are,   4. are,   5. comes,   6. is,   7. happens,   8. work

---

© 2000 by The Center for Applied Research in Education

Name _____ Date _____

YOURS AND MINE
Explanation and Exercises

A. A personal possessive pronoun shows possession, as *my book, your coat, his ball*. The personal possessive pronouns are

his, her, hers, its	their, theirs
my, mine	your, yours
our, ours	

Never add an apostrophe and *s* to a personal pronoun, since it already shows possession!

WRONG: This jacket is her's.
→ **RIGHT:** *This jacket is hers.*

WRONG: The dog wagged it's tail.
→ **RIGHT:** *The dog wagged its tail.*

Note: *It's* always stands for *it is*.

B. Fill in the blank spaces with a personal possessive pronoun from the list above.

1. This is not Ashana's coat. It's _____.

2. The angry cat arched _____ back.

3. Brad grabbed _____ coat and ran out.

4. The team won _____ final game.

5. The students handed in _____ test papers.

6. Look at this glove and tell me if it's _____.

7. The neighbors say the rose bush is in _____ yard, but it is really in _____.

8. The store closes _____ doors at 9 P.M.

9. Margo insisted that the book was _____.

10. All the students opened _____ books.

11. Don't take anything that is not _____.

*ANSWERS ON ACTIVITY SHEET 47B.

© 2000 by The Center for Applied Research in Education

Name _____ Date _____

YOURS AND MINE
Additional Exercises

A. ANSWERS TO EXERCISE B ON ACTIVITY 47A:

1. yours, hers, his, or mine;   2. its;   3. his;   4. its;   5. their;   6. yours;
7. their, ours;   8. its;   9. hers;   10. their;   11. yours

---

B. Fill in the blank spaces in the following paragraph with the correct personal possessive pronoun from the list below.

> his, her, hers, its   their, theirs
> my, mine   your, yours
> our, ours

    I saw my sister, Rosa, writing in a notebook. It looked just like _____.
"That's my notebook!" I shouted. "It's not _____." She ignored me and took
the notebook into _____ room. I complained to _____ mother. "Are you sure that
notebook is _____?" she asked. I nodded. Then she pointed to something on the
kitchen table. "What is that?" she asked. It was _____ notebook. The one Rosa was
using was _____.

*SEE ANSWERS BELOW.

C. Write five sentences on these lines. Each sentence should contain at least one pronoun from the list above.

1. _____

2. _____

3. _____

4. _____

5. _____

Answers to Exercise B (paragraph): mine, yours, her, our, yours, my, hers

© 2000 by The Center for Applied Research in Education

Name _____ Date _____

I OR ME?
Explanation and Exercises

A. Do not change the form of a pronoun when it is combined with other words.

    WRONG: The ice cream is for Ahmed and I.
→ **RIGHT:** *The ice cream is for Ahmed and me.*
    (Think: The ice cream is for *me*.)

    WRONG: Dolores and me went to the movies.
→ **RIGHT:** *Dolores and I went to the movies.*
    (Think: *I* went to the movies.)

B. Write the correct pronoun in the spaces below.

1. The prize winners were Frank and _____. (I or me)

2. Lola said that _____ and her brother had a fight. (she or her)

3. Give the tickets to my friend and _____. (I or me)

4. Joe said that his sister and _____ are going to Maine. (he or him)

5. Wait for Alma and _____ outside. (I or me)

6. Alma and _____ will be there soon. (I or me)

7. Two of my friends and _____ were late to school. (I or me)

8. Alma said that spot is where her friend and _____ will wait. (she or her)

9. This house belongs to my parents and _____. (I or me)

10. My friend and _____ are going to the party. (I or me)

*SEE ANSWERS BELOW.

© 2000 by The Center for Applied Research in Education

Answers: 1. me, **2.** she, **3.** me, **4.** he, **5.** me, **6.** I, **7.** I, **8.** she, **9.** me, **10.** I

Name _____   Date _____

I OR ME?
Additional Exercises

A. *Remember the Rule!* Do not change the form of a pronoun when it is combined with other words. Always use the pronoun that would be appropriate if those other words were not there.

Examples: **WRONG:**   Dad gave the money to Manny and *she.*
→ **RIGHT:**   Dad gave the money to Manny and *her.*

(Think: Dad gave the money to *her.)*

WRONG: My brother and *me* have brown eyes.
→ **RIGHT:**   My brother and *I* have brown eyes.

(Think: I have brown eyes.)*

B. Check the correct sentence in each group.

1. ☐ a.   Rita said that she and her mother are going shopping.
   ☐ b.   Rita said that her and her mother are going shopping.

2. ☐ a.   Bruno and me both play outfield on the Little League team.
   ☐ b.   Bruno and I both play outfield on the Little League team.

3. ☐ a.   The teacher asked Jon and I to erase the chalkboard.
   ☐ b.   The teacher asked Jon and me to erase the chalkboard.

4. ☐ a.   My sister and I rode in the back seat of the car.
   ☐ b.   My sister and me rode in the back seat of the car.

5. ☐ a.   The Raiders and the Tigers won championships in their league.
   ☐ b.   The Raiders and the Tigers won championships in its league.

6. ☐ a.   My father blamed my brother and me for being late.
   ☐ b.   My father blamed my brother and I for being late.

7. ☐ a.   Bart's mother made lunch for Greg and he.
   ☐ b.   Bart's mother made lunch for Greg and him.

8. ☐ a.   I'm glad that Rhonda and I got good marks in English.
   ☐ b.   I'm glad that Rhonda and me got good marks in English.

*SEE ANSWERS BELOW.

Answers: 1. a, 2. b, 3. b, 4. a, 5. a, 6. a, 7. b, 8. a

© 2000 by The Center for Applied Research in Education

Name _____ Date _____

WHO GAVE WHAT TO WHOM?
Explanation and Exercises

A. *Interrogative Pronouns* are pronouns that ask questions. There are five interrogative pronouns:

> **what, which, who, whom, whose**

Examples:	*What* is the name of this book?
	Which book do you want?
	Who wants the book?
	To *whom* does the book belong?
	Whose book is this?

B. THE WHO/WHOM PROBLEM: *What, which,* and *whose* are easy to use, but sometimes writers have problems deciding between *who* and *whom.*

Here is how you can decide which form to use. Just remember that *who* is a subject. It usually refers to *he, she,* or *they,* as in

> *Who* is responsible? (Is *he* responsible?)
> *Who* will attend the meeting? (Will *they* attend the meeting?)
> *Who* came to the party? (Did *they* or *he* come?)

But *whom* is used as an object, like *him, her,* or *them,* as in

> *Whom* shall we invite to the party? (Shall we invite *them* to the party?)
> To *whom* is the letter addressed? (Is it addressed to *him?*)
> That is the girl *whom* I met yesterday. (I met *her* yesterday.)

C. Fill in the blank spaces with *who* or *whom.* In each case ask yourself if it is a subject like he, she, or they *(who),* or if it is an object like him, her, or them *(whom)*

1. To _____ are you speaking?

2. The person _____ hit my car should pay for the damage.

3. _____ did well on the test?

4. The students _____ pass the final will also pass the course.

5. _____ did the police blame for the accident?

6. To _____ did you mention the accident?

*Answers on Activity Sheet 49B.

© 2000 by The Center for Applied Research in Education

Name _____ Date _____

WHO DID WHAT TO WHOM?
Additional Exercises

© 2000 by The Center for Applied Research in Education

A. ANSWERS TO EXERCISE C ON ACTIVITY 49A:

1. whom,   2. who,   3. who,   4. who,   5. whom,   6. whom

B. Check the correct sentence in each group below.

1. ❑ a.   We gave the prize to the person whom is most qualified.
   ❑ b.   We gave the prize to the person who is most qualified.

2. ❑ a.   That is the family whom we met at Disney World in July.
   ❑ b.   That is the family who we met at Disney World in July.

3. ❑ a.   Whom did you want to invite?
   ❑ b.   Who did you want to invite?

4. ❑ a.   Whom do you think will be elected?
   ❑ b.   Who do you think will be elected?

5. ❑ a.   To whom do I owe the money?
   ❑ b.   To who do I owe the money?

6. ❑ a.   Whom is at the door?
   ❑ b.   Who is at the door?

*SEE ANSWERS BELOW.

C. Write four sentences using the word *who*.

1. _____

2. _____

3. _____

4. _____

D. Write four sentences using the word *whom*.

1. _____

2. _____

3. _____

4. _____

Answers to Exercise B: 1. b,   2. a,   3. a,   4. b,   5. a,   6. b

Name _____ Date _____

DON'T OVERWORK THEM
Explanation and Exercises

A. EXPLANATION: *Them* means *those people* or *those things,* as The dogs were hungry, so I gave *them* food. *Them* is always the object of a verb.

Never use *them* to modify a noun! Use *those, these,* or *the.*

WRONG:	Them dogs are hungry.
➤ **RIGHT:**	These dogs are hungry.
WRONG:	I want a pound of them apples.
➤ **RIGHT:**	I want a pound of those apples.
WRONG:	Look at them racers go!
➤ **RIGHT:**	Look at the racers go!

B. Check the correct sentences in each of these groups.

1. ❏ a.   I'll call in the girls and give them dinner.
   ❏ b.   I'll call in the girls and give these dinner.

2. ❏ a.   You should be more careful with them knives.
   ❏ b.   You should be more careful with those knives.

3. ❏ a.   These are the stores I like.
   ❏ b.   Them are the stores I like.

4. ❏ a.   Look at those shiny bicycles!
   ❏ b.   Look at them shiny bicycles!

5. ❏ a.   I like to read these ghost stories.
   ❏ b.   I like to read them ghost stories.

*ANSWERS AT THE BOTTOM OF THIS PAGE.

C. Fill in the blank spaces with *them* or *those.*

1. The boy said, "I want _____ toys for my birthday."

2. The twins want to know what you are giving _____ for dinner.

3. Put _____ books back on the shelf.

4. _____ children like to play in the park.

5. The nails were loose so I tightened _____.

© 2000 by The Center for Applied Research in Education

Answers to Exercise C: 1. Those,   2. them,   3. those,   4. those,   5. them

Answers to Exercise B: 1. a,   2. b,   3. a,   4. a,   5. a.

Name _____ Date _____

DON'T GET TENSE ABOUT TENSES
Explanation and Exercises

A. DEFINITION: A verb shows action or being.
Verbs can be really active, like *leap, hop, chase, climb,* or *scream.* They can also show quiet action or a state of being, like *hear, believe, dream, think,* or *is.*

B. VERB TENSES: The tense of a verb tells when the action occurs.

Present Tense means right now, as *I see you now.*

Past Tense means before now, as *I saw you yesterday.*

Future Tense means any time after now, as *I will see you tomorrow.*

Present Perfect Tense means began in the past and is still continuing (or only recently finished), as *I have seen you five times this week.*

Past Perfect Tense means finished before another past action, as *I had seen you twice before you went away.*

Future Perfect Tense means action starts and ends in the future, as *I will have seen you twice before you leave next week.*

C. PRESENT AND PAST: The most commonly used verb tenses are present and past. The *past tense* is usually made by adding *d* or *ed* to the *present tense*. These are called regular verbs.

Examples: Present: I *like* the book I am reading.
                Past: I *liked* the book I was reading yesterday.

                Present: I *use* a spoon to eat ice cream.
                Past: Yesterday, I *used* a spoon to eat ice cream.

D. EXERCISE: The regular verbs in the sentences below are present tense. Rewrite each sentence on the line below, changing the verbs to past tense by adding *d* or *ed*.

1. I walk to school.

    _____

2. The teachers look at the class.

    _____

3. Our neighbors knock on our door.

    _____

4. The dogs bark in the back yard.

    _____

5. The pitchers hurl the balls.

    _____

*SEE ACTIVITY 51B FOR ANSWERS.

© 2000 by The Center for Applied Research in Education

Name _____ Date _____

DON'T GET TENSE ABOUT TENSES
Explanation and Exercises

A. ANSWERS TO EXERCISE ON ACTIVITY 51A:

1. I walked to school.
2. The teachers looked at the class.
3. Our neighbors knocked on our door.
4. The dogs barked in the back yard.
5. The pitchers hurled the balls.

B. IRREGULAR VERBS: Sometimes the past tense of verbs are formed in ways other than adding d or ed. These are called irregular verbs, and they must be memorized. Here are some common irregular verbs:

PRESENT	PAST		PRESENT	PAST
awake	awoke		get	got
begin	began		give	gave
bite	bit		grow	grew
blow	blew		go	went
break	broke		hide	hid
buy	bought		hold	held
catch	caught		keep	kept
choose	chose		know	knew
come	came		leave	left
dig	dug		lose	lost
do	did		meet	met
draw	drew		pay	paid
fall	fell		ride	rode
fight	fought		sing	sang
fly	flew		sit	sat
forget	forgot		write	wrote

(There are many more irregular verbs. Always look in a dictionary when you are not sure.)

C. EXERCISE: Write a sentence using the past tense of each verb below. (You can find the correct word on the list above.)

1. (break) _____

2. (sing) _____

3. (blow) _____

4. (choose) _____

5. (forget) _____

6. (hide) _____

7. (write) _____

© 2000 by The Center for Applied Research in Education

Name _____ Date _____

DON'T GET TENSE ABOUT TENSES
Irregular Verbs—Exercises

Use the list of irregular verbs on Activity 51B for these exercises.

A. Rewrite the sentences on the line below, using the past tense.

1. Mrs. Gomez sits in the front row at plays.

   _____

2. Mr. Jackson always pays his bills at the end of the month.

   _____

3. Those two boys fight every day.

   _____

4. Shanna chooses to eat only vegetables.

   _____

5. I hold a pen in my right hand.

   _____

*SEE ANSWERS AT THE BOTTOM OF THE PAGE.

B. Write a sentence using the past tense of each verb below.

1. (begin) _____

2. (grow) _____

3. (bite) _____

4. (catch) _____

5. (know) _____

6. (dig) _____

7. (buy) _____

*SEE ANSWERS AT THE BOTTOM OF THE PAGE.

© 2000 by The Center for Applied Research in Education

Answers: Exercise A: 1. sat, 2. paid, 3. fought, 4. chose, 5. held
Exercise B: 1. began, 2. grew, 3. bit, 4. caught, 5. knew, 6. dug, 7. bought

Name _____ Date _____

DON'T GET TENSE ABOUT TENSES
Additional Exercises

A. Rewrite the following sentences using the future tense.

1. Antonia saw an alligator in the lake.

   _____

2. Julio put five dollars in his pocket.

   _____

3. Rebecca says that she works hard in school.

   _____

4. I am so happy to have a ten-speed bike.

   _____

5. Frank did well on the final test in science.

   _____

*SEE ANSWERS AT THE BOTTOM OF THIS PAGE.

B. Rewrite the following sentences using the past tense.

1. The first baseman throws the ball to the pitcher.

   _____

2. I want to see my cousins in Los Angeles.

   _____

3. The moving van will arrive at the new house late.

   _____

4. The doctor knows what medicine to prescribe.

   _____

5. Ellen's friend lives in New York City.

   _____

*SEE ANSWERS AT BOTTOM OF THE PAGE.

© 2000 by The Center for Applied Research in Education

Answers: Exercise A: 1. will see, 2. will put, 3. will work, 4. will be, 5. will do
Exercise B: 1. threw, 2. wanted, 3. arrived, 4. knew, 5. lived

Name _____ Date _____

TO BE OR NOT TO BE!
Explanation and Exercises

A. DEFINITION: The most common verb in English is *to be*. This verb does not show action. It shows something is, was, or will be. This is called a linking verb because it connects the subject to the rest of the sentence without really showing action.

B. PRESENT TENSE: When used in the present tense, the parts of *to be* are

> *am,* as in I *am* happy.
> *is,* as in He *is* here. She *is* here. It *is* here.
> *are,* as in You *are* sad. We *are* sad. They *are* sad.

C. PAST TENSE: The past tense of *to be* is as follows:

> *was,* as in I *was* happy. He *was* happy. She *was* happy. It *was* happy.
> *were,* as in You *were* there. We *were* there. They *were* there.

D. FUTURE TENSE: The future tense of *to be* is always *will be*, as in I *will be* happy. You *will be* happy. He *will be* happy. She *will be* happy. It *will be* happy. We *will be* happy. They *will be* happy.

E. PRESENT PERFECT TENSE: The present perfect tense uses the words *have* or *has* combined with *been*, as in I *have been*, you *have been*, we *have been*, they *have been*, but he, she, or it *has been*.

F. Check the correct sentence in each group below.

1. ☐ a.   The boys was late to school yesterday.
   ☐ b.   The boys were late to school yesterday.

2. ☐ a.   We know you were in that store.
   ☐ b.   We know you was in that store.

3. ☐ a.   I am going to see you after school.
   ☐ b.   I is going to see you after school.

4. ☐ a.   The girls was sad when their uncle died.
   ☐ b.   The girls were sad when their uncle died.

5. ☐ a.   The family be happy in their new house next year.
   ☐ b.   The family will be happy in their new house next year.

6. ☐ a.   I have been in that store recently.
   ☐ b.   I has been in that store recently.

7. ☐ a.   He have been very sad this week.
   ☐ b.   He has been very sad this week.

*ANSWERS ON ACTIVITY SHEET 52B.

© 2000 by The Center for Applied Research in Education

Name _____ Date _____

TO BE OR NOT TO BE!
Explanation and Exercises

A. ANSWERS TO EXERCISE F ON ACTIVITY SHEET 52A:

1. b,   2. a,   3. a,   4. b,   5. b,   6. a,   7. b

B. Past Perfect Tense: The past perfect tense of *to be* is always *had been,* as I *had been* work-ing too hard. He (She or It) *had been* swimming too long. You *had been* sleeping too much. We *had been* best friends once. They *had been* hiking in the woods.

C. Fill the blanks with the correct form of *to be.*

1. They were tired last February because they _____ mountain climbing the day before.

2. I _____ feeling sick all last year until the end of November.

3. We _____ happy to be here today.

4. You _____ lucky to have such good friends.

5. We _____ at our aunt's house tomorrow.

6. The teacher _____ grumpy, but cheered up after vacation.

7. Wang's grandmother _____ very old.

8. Our family _____ together every Thanksgiving until Grandma died.

9. The family _____ together next summer.

*SEE ANSWERS AT THE BOTTOM OF THIS PAGE.

D. Write a sentence for each form of *to be* listed below.

1. have been   _____

2. are   _____

3. were   _____

4. will be   _____

5. is   _____

6. was   _____

© 2000 by The Center for Applied Research in Education

Answers to Exercise C: 1. had been,   2. had been,   3. are,   4. are,   5. will be,   6. had been,   7. is,   8. had been,   9. will be

Name _____ Date _____

A PROPER PERSON
Explanation and Exercises

© 2000 by The Center for Applied Research in Education

A. EXPLANATIONS:

1. The *person* of a verb means who or what is speaking or doing. A verb is used for one of three persons:

   First Person: I *am*
   Second Person: you *are*
   Third Person: he, she, it (or any noun) *is*

   These examples are all singular (one person or thing).

   There is also plural person for a verb, as

   First Person (Plural): We *are*
   Second Person (Plural): You *are*
   Third Person (Plural): they (or any noun) *are*

2. For most regular verbs, each person uses the basic verb form, except third person singular, which adds an s, as in these examples.

	SINGULAR	PLURAL	SINGULAR	PLURAL
First Person:	I *play*	we *play*	I *see*	we *see*
Second Person:	you *play*	you *play*	you *see*	you *see*
Third Person:	he, she, it *plays*	they *play*	he, she, it *sees*	they *see*

3. Some verbs are irregular, such as

	SINGULAR	PLURAL	SINGULAR	PLURAL
First Person:	I *am*	we *are*	I *have*	we *have*
Second Person:	you *are*	you *are*	you *have*	you *have*
Third Person:	he, she, it *is*	they *are*	he, she, it *has*	they *have*

B. Check the correct sentence in each group.

1. ❐ a.   Carla's dog eat his food.
   ❐ b.   Carla's dog eats his food.

2. ❐ a.   John's father has a good job.
   ❐ b.   John's father have a good job.

3. ❐ a.   The team usually plays well.
   ❐ b.   The team usually play well.

4. ❐ a.   Greg and Jimmy is going to the party.
   ❐ b.   Greg and Jimmy are going to the party.

5. ❐ a.   Linda do not like any kind of meat.
   ❐ b.   Linda does not like any kind of meat.

6. ❐ a.   They are going to be late to class.
   ❐ b.   They is going to be late to class.

*SEE ACTIVITY SHEET 53B FOR ANSWERS.

Name _____ Date _____

A PROPER PERSON
Explanation and Exercises

A. ANSWERS TO EXERCISE B ON ACTIVITY 53A:

1. b,   2. a,   3. a,   4. b,   5. b,   6. a

B. A singular verb is usually used with a collective noun.

A collective noun stands for a group. It is usually used with a third-person singular verb, as in these examples:

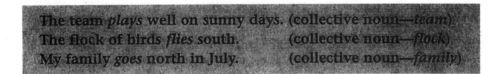

The team *plays* well on sunny days. (collective noun—*team*)
The flock of birds *flies* south.   (collective noun—*flock*)
My family *goes* north in July.   (collective noun—*family*)

C. Check the correct sentence in each group.

1. ☐ a.   The rock band play the songs I like.
   ☐ b.   The rock band plays the songs I like.

2. ☐ a.   That bunch of grapes is not ripe enough to eat.
   ☐ b.   That bunch of grapes are not ripe enough to eat.

3. ☐ a.   Sometimes a jury finds an innocent person guilty.
   ☐ b.   Sometimes a jury find an innocent person guilty.

4. ☐ a.   Ali's family are very nice.
   ☐ b.   Ali's family is very nice.

*ANSWERS AT THE BOTTOM OF THE PAGE.

D. Fill in the blanks with the correct verb.

1. Joe and Sally _____ in the marching band. (play, plays)

2. Babies _____ not like loud voices. (do, does)

3. Marty _____ not get good grades in school. (do, does)

4. The herd of cattle _____ being moved south. (is, are)

5. I _____ to hang out with my friends. (like, likes)

6. That little girl _____ her mother. (want, wants)

7. The alien from outer space _____ two heads. (have, has)

8. The teacher _____ I did well on the test. (say, says)

*SEE ANSWERS BELOW.

Answers to Exercise D: 1. play, 2. do, 3. does, 4. is, 5. like, 6. wants, 7. has, 8. says
Answers to Exercise C: 1. b, 2. a, 3. a, 4. b

© 2000 by The Center for Applied Research in Education

Name _____ Date _____

DYNAMIC DESCRIPTIONS
Explanation and Exercises

> She is a girl.
> Harry rode his bike.

Aren't these sentences dull? Wouldn't they be more dynamic like this?

> **She is a beautiful, red-haired girl.**
> **Harry rode his shiny, new, ten-speed bike.**

In these sentences, *beautiful, red-haired, shiny, new,* and *ten-speed* are all adjectives. We use adjectives every day in our speech and writing to communicate clearer images.

A. DEFINITION: An adjective modifies or describes a noun or pronoun. In the sentences above, the nouns are *girl* and *bike.*

An adjective answers one of these questions: *what kind, how many,* or *which one.*

> Examples: a *beautiful* girl   (what kind)
> *several* weeks   (how many)
> *that* boy   (which one)

(**Note:** *That* is a *demonstrative adjective.* Other demonstrative adjectives are *this, these* and *those.* They always answer the question, which one?

B. Placement of Adjectives: Adjectives usually appear before the noun they modify, as in the examples above. They can also be placed after the noun, separated from it by commas, as

> **The runners, tired but happy, reached their goal.**
> **Rita's grandmother, old and frail, was in a wheelchair.**

C. After each sentence, list the adjective (or adjectives) and the noun it modifies.

1. She was a graceful dancer.   (Adjective: _____ Noun: _____)

2. Do you want this ball?   (Adjective: _____ Noun: _____)

3. The red van is here.   (Adjective: _____ Noun: _____)

4. Give him six dollars.   (Adjective: _____ Noun: _____)

5. Every person, rich or poor, is important. (Adjectives: _____ Noun: _____)

*ANSWERS ON ACTIVITY SHEET 54B.

© 2000 by The Center for Applied Research in Education

Name _____ Date _____

DYNAMIC DESCRIPTIONS
Explanation and Exercises

A. ANSWERS TO EXERCISE C ON ACTIVITY 54A:

	ADJECTIVE	NOUN
1.	graceful	dancer
2.	this	ball
3.	red	van
4.	six	dollars
5.	rich, poor	person

B. A proper adjective is always capitalized, as in these examples.

> The Spanish rice was delicious.
> April showers bring May flowers.

C. Adjectives usually come before the noun. Sometimes they come later and are linked to the noun by a verb, as in these examples.

> The fruit is ripe. (*adjective*—ripe; *noun*—fruit)
> Alex is handsome. (*adjective*—handsome; *noun*—Alex)
> The ocean water felt cold. (*adjectives*—ocean, cold; *noun*—water)

D. Underline each adjective and circle each noun in these sentences.

1. My New England friends like to dine at seafood restaurants.

2. The bracelet, shiny and golden, was expensive.

3. The Martian spacecraft was enormous.

4. Her best friend could not come to the birthday party.

5. This haunted house is scary.

*ANSWERS ON ACTIVITY SHEET 54C.

E. Fill in the blank spaces with adjectives.

1. I don't like that _____ creature.

2. The final exam was _____.

3. The _____ woman bought a _____ hat.

4. The _____ rocket landed on a _____ planet.

5. The house, _____ and _____, stood at the top of a _____ hill.

© 2000 by The Center for Applied Research in Education

Name _____ Date _____

DYNAMIC DESCRIPTIONS
Explanation and Exercises

A. ANSWERS TO EXERCISE D, ACTIVITY 54B:

1. My <u>New England</u> (friends) like to dine at <u>seafood</u> (restaurants).
2. The (bracelet), <u>shiny</u> and <u>golden,</u> was <u>expensive.</u>
3. The <u>Martian</u> (spacecraft) was <u>enormous.</u>
4. Her <u>best</u> (friend) could not come to the <u>birthday</u> (party).
5. <u>This haunted</u> (house) is <u>scary.</u>

B. Comparison Adjectives: Most adjectives show comparison by adding *er* (when comparing two things) and *est* (when comparing more than two things.)

Examples:	great,	greater,	greatest
	ugly,	uglier,	ugliest
	sad,	sadder,	saddest

Many other adjectives show comparison with the words *more* (for comparing two things) and *most* (for comparing more than two things).

Examples:	horrible,	more horrible,	most horrible
	colorful,	more colorful,	most colorful

A few comparison adjectives do not follow these rules.

Examples:	good,	better,	best
	bad,	worse,	worst
	many,	more,	most

C. Fill in the blank spaces with a comparison adjective.

1. One medal is good, but two are _____.

2. Brad's answer is bad, but Mike's is even _____.

3. Nancy is happy, Tina is _____, and Alice is the _____ of all.

4. Maria is tall, but her sister is even _____.

*ANSWERS AT BOTTOM OF THE PAGE.

D. Fill in the blank space with an appropriate adjective.

1. My dog is _____ than yours.

2. This is the _____ meal I ever ate.

3. The patient seems _____ today than she was yesterday.

4. Brad is the _____ kid in our class.

Answers to Exercise C: 1. better, **2.** worse, **3.** happier, happiest, **4.** taller

© 2000 by The Center for Applied Research in Education

Name _____ Date _____

HOW? WHERE? WHEN?
Explanation and Exercises

A. DEFINITIONS:

→ 1. An *adverb* tells more about a verb. It usually answers one of three questions: How? When? Where?

        walk *quickly*   (walk how? walk quickly)
        smile *happily*   (smile how? smile happily)
        traveled *yesterday*   (traveled when? traveled yesterday)
        play *outside*   (play where? play outside)

      [Note: Adverbs that tell *how* usually (not always) end with *ly*, (such as *angrily, badly, easily, really, happily, quickly, quietly, roughly, sadly*). Some adverbs that do not end *ly* are *quite, very, well.***]**

→ 2. An adverb can also modify an adjective.

        a *really* good play   (*really* modifies the adjective *good*)
        He is *too* tall.   (*too* modifies the adjective *tall*)
        She is *quite* sad.   (*quite* modifies the adjective *sad*)

→ 3. An adverb can also modify another adverb.

        walk *very* quickly   (*very* modifies the adverb *quickly*)
        eat *too* slowly   (*too* modifies the adverb *slowly*)

B. Rewrite these sentences, adding an adverb to modify the verb.

     Example: Fred ate the hamburger.   *Fred ate the hamburger quickly.*

  1. Jennifer walked down the street.

    _____

  2. The train came into the station.

    _____

  3. The bird sang.

    _____

  4. The waiter poured the coffee.

    _____

C. Rewrite these sentences, adding an adverb to modify the adjective.

     Example: The train was slow.   *The train was quite slow.*

  1. I finished my homework quickly.

    _____

  2. Carla is smart.

    _____

  3. The baby smiled happily.

    _____

© 2000 by The Center for Applied Research in Education

Name _____ Date _____

HOW? WHERE? WHEN?
Exercises

A. Adverbs modify verbs, adjectives, or other adverbs. They usually tell how, where, or when (and can also answer the questions: *How often?* or *How long?* Adverbs often (but not always) end in *ly*.

B. Identify the adverb and the word it modifies in these sentences.

1. The mother looked at her child lovingly.

   Adverb _____ What does it modify? _____

2. We go to the movies often.

   Adverb _____ What does it modify? _____

3. Are you quite certain your answer is right?

   Adverb _____ What does it modify? _____

4. He ran swiftly to the playground.

   Adverb _____ What does it modify? _____

5. Sophie came to the party late.

   Adverb _____ What does it modify? _____

6. Let's go to the movies tomorrow.

   Adverb _____ What does it modify? _____

*ANSWERS AT THE BOTTOM OF THIS PAGE.

C. Fill in the blank spaces with adverbs.

1. Always chew your food _____.

2. He waited _____ in the doctor's office.

3. Joe always comes _____ to parties.

4. The dad looked at his son _____.

5. The storekeeper spoke _____.

6. Pat picked up the bat _____.

Answers to Exercise B: 1. Adverb: *lovingly,* Modifies: *looked;*   2. Adverb: *often,* Modifies: *go;*   3. Adverb: *quite,* Modifies: *certain;*   4. Adverb: *swiftly,* Modifies: *ran;*   5. Adverb: *late,* Modifies: *came;*   6. Adverb: *tomorrow,* Modifies: *go.*

© 2000 by The Center for Applied Research in Education

Name _____ Date _____

ADVERBS vs. ADJECTIVES
Explanation and Exercises

A. EXPLANATION: *Bad or Badly?*

Do you sometimes have trouble deciding whether to use an adverb or an adjective? Here are some hints that will make this decision easier.

1. Do not use an adjective to modify a verb.

   The boy is bad. The adjective *bad* describes the *boy* (noun).
   But *The boy did badly on the test.* The adverb *badly* modifies the verb and tells how the boy did.

   Here are some other examples.

   Here comes the beautiful girl. (Adjective *beautiful* describes noun *girl.*)
   But *The girl dances beautifully.* (Adverb *beautifully* modifies verb *dances* and tells how.)

   The lamp is bright. (Adjective *bright* describes the noun *lamp.*)
   But *The lamp shone brightly.* (Adverb *brightly* tells how the lamp *shone* (verb).

2. Do not use an adjective to modify another adjective.

WRONG:	Jimmy is a real fine catcher.
➙ **RIGHT:**	Jimmy is a really fine catcher. (Adverb *really* modifies adjective *fine.*)
WRONG:	That is an awful big portion.
➙ **RIGHT:**	That is an awfully big portion. (adverb *awfully* modifies adjective *big.*)

B. Check the correct sentence in each of the following groups:

1. ❑ a.   She played the piano bad.
   ❑ b.   She played the piano badly.

2. ❑ a.   The train is moving slowly.
   ❑ b.   The train is moving slow.

3. ❑ a.   The mother sang soft to her baby.
   ❑ b.   The mother sang softly to her baby.

4. ❑ a.   This fabric feels softly.
   ❑ b.   This fabric feels soft.

5. ❑ a.   His voice is awfully loud.
   ❑ b.   His voice is awful loud.

6. ❑ a.   José got to first base quick.
   ❑ b.   José got to first base quickly.

*ANSWERS ON ACTIVITY SHEET 56B.

© 2000 by The Center for Applied Research in Education

Name _____ Date _____

ADVERBS vs. ADJECTIVES
Explanation and Exercises

A. ANSWERS TO EXERCISE B ON ACTIVITY 56A:
1. b,   2. a,   3. b,   4. b,   5. a,   6. b

© 2000 by The Center for Applied Research in Education

B. GOOD or WELL

These two words are sometimes confused.

→ *Good* is an adjective, as in

Carlos is a good athlete.	(modifies noun *athlete*)
My dog, Rex, is good.	(modifies noun *dog*)
That is good work.	(modifies noun *work*)

→ *Well* is an adverb, as in

Carlos plays basketball well.	(modifies verb *plays*)
My dog, Rex, sleeps well.	(modifies verb *sleeps*)
That printer works well.	(modifies verb *works*)

[Note: *Well* can sometimes be used as an adjective when it means *in good health*, as in The patient feels *well* today. (*Well* describes the noun *patient;* therefore, it is used as an adjective here.)]

C. SURE OR SURELY

→ *Sure* is an adjective, as in

It is a sure thing.	(modifies noun *thing*)
I am sure.	(describes pronoun *I*)
This game is a sure win.	(describes *win*, which is used as a noun here)

→ *Surely* is an adverb, as in

I am surely going.	(modifies verb *going*)
The team will surely win this game.	(modifies *win*, which is used here as a verb)

D. Fill in the blank spaces with the correct word.

1. I am _____ going to enjoy this game.   (sure or surely)

2. Did you do _____ in your interview?   (good or well)

3. I don't feel _____ with this headache.   (good or well)

4. Maria feels _____ about herself.   (good or well)

5. Are you _____ about that answer?   (sure or surely)

6. This party is going _____.   (good or well)

*ANSWERS ON ACTIVITY SHEET 56C.

Name _____ Date _____

ADVERBS vs. ADJECTIVES
Additional Exercises

A. ANSWERS TO EXERCISE D ON ACTIVITY 56B

1. surely,   2. well,   3. well,   4. good,   5. sure,   6. well

---

B. Check the correct sentence in each of these groups.

1. ☐ a.   The pitcher threw the ball slow.
   ☐ b.   The pitcher threw the ball slowly.

2. ☐ a.   Carla stayed home because she didn't feel well.
   ☐ b.   Carla stayed home because she didn't feel good.

3. ☐ a.   The actor sure is good-looking.
   ☐ b.   The actor surely is good-looking.

4. ☐ a.   That beast is awfully ugly.
   ☐ b.   That beast is awful ugly.

5. ☐ a.   The teacher spoke loud to the class.
   ☐ b.   The teacher spoke loudly to the class.

6. ☐ a.   Her hands were softly.
   ☐ b.   Her hands were soft.

7. ☐ a.   The coffee tastes good.
   ☐ b.   The coffee tastes well.

8. ☐ a.   She dances good.
   ☐ b.   She dances well.

9. ☐ a.   Julie is a real good painter.
   ☐ b.   Julie is a really good painter.

*ANSWERS AT THE BOTTOM OF THIS PAGE.

C. Fill in each blank space with an adjective or an adverb.

1. My brother eats his food _____ quickly.

2. Sammy always rides his bike _____.

3. That woman speaks with a _____ accent.

4. Elena is _____ than Patty.

5. Everyone knows that Mike is _____ .

6. The woman looked at her baby _____.

Answers to Exercise B: 1. b,   2. a,   3. b,   4. a,   5. b,   6. b,   7. a,   8. b,   9. b.

© 2000 by The Center for Applied Research in Education

Name _____ Date _____

MISPLACED MODIFIERS
Explanation and Exercises

A. DEFINITIONS:

1. A modifier is a word that tells something about another word. The modifier must be in the right place in the sentence to show which word it is modifying. Otherwise, it can seem to be attaching itself to a different word. That can give the sentence a completely different meaning.

   Examples:

   The teacher only gave Dave the book.
   (The only thing the teacher did was give the book to Dave.)

   The teacher gave only Dave the book.
   (The only person the teacher gave the book to was Dave.)

   The teacher gave Dave only the book.
   (The book was the only thing the teacher gave to Dave.)

   I almost saw the whole game.
   (I came close to seeing the game, but did not do so.)

   I saw almost the whole game.
   (I saw most of the game, but not the whole thing.)

2. A modifier can also be a phrase. It can be confusing if misplaced in the sentence.

   Examples:

   She hung the jacket on a hanger so it wouldn't get creased.
   (So the hanger wouldn't get creased? This sentence can be fixed as follows: "So as not to crease the jacket, she hung it on a hanger.")

   I went to see the team play with my father.
   (Did the team really play with your father? It should say, "I went with my father to see the team play.")

B. Rewrite each sentence on the line below. Place the modifier where it belongs in the sentence.

1. (Modifier: nearly)   Patrick was able to stay for the whole party.

   _____

2. (Modifier: just)   Matthew has enough money to buy a sled.

   _____

3. (Modifier: even)   It was too late to finish half the work.

   _____

4. (Modifier: to visitors)   The museum is closed for alterations.

   _____

*SEE ACTIVITY SHEET 57B FOR ANSWERS.

© 2000 by The Center for Applied Research in Education

Name _____ Date _____

MISPLACED MODIFIERS
Explanation and Exercises

> **A. ANSWERS TO EXERCISE B ON ACTIVITY SHEET 57A:**
> 1. Patrick was able to stay for nearly the whole party.
> 2. Matthew has just enough money to buy a sled.
> 3. It was too late to finish even half the work.
> 4. The museum is closed to visitors for alterations.

B. DANGLING MODIFIERS: Here are some more examples of misplaced modifiers.

 1. *While talking to a neighbor, the dog ran off.*
   (Was the dog really talking to a neighbor? This sentence should be "While talking to a neighbor, I saw the dog run off.")

 2. *Walking down the aisle, the stage looked empty.*
   (Can a stage walk down an aisle? This sentence should be "Walking down the aisle, I looked at the empty stage.")

A misplaced modifier at the beginning of the sentence is called a dangling modifier. It can cause confusion, especially if the modifier is a clause containing a word that ends in *ing*, as in the examples above. The word following the clause should be the word that is modified. Here are some more examples of misplaced dangling modifiers.

 1. *Running to second base, the ball was caught by the shortstop.*
   (The runner, not the ball, was running, so the sentence should read, "Running to second base, I stopped when the shortstop caught the ball.")

 2. *Hunting with a bow and arrow, the deer fled.*
   (The deer was not hunting, was it? This sentence can only be fixed by turning it around. You could say, "The deer fled from the hunter who had a bow and arrow.")

C. Rewrite each sentence correctly on the line below.

 1. Hanging on the wall, I examined the calendar.

   _____

 2. Talking to my friend, the dog jumped up on me.

   _____

 3. Driving down the street, the car got a flat tire.

   _____

 4. Turning on the light, the bulb exploded.

   _____

*ANSWERS ON ACTIVITY SHEET 57C.

© 2000 by The Center for Applied Research in Education

Name _____ Date _____

MISPLACED MODIFIERS
Additional Exercises

A. ANSWERS TO EXERCISE C ON ACTIVITY SHEET 57B:

1. I examined the calendar that was hanging on the wall.
2. The dog jumped on me while I was talking to my friend.
3. As I was driving down the street, the car got a flat tire.
4. When I turned on the light, the bulb exploded.

B. MISPLACED MODIFIERS: A modifier should always be placed so it is clear which word is modified. If the modifier is misplaced, the sentence will mean something different from what the writer intends.

C. Check the correct sentence in each of these groups.

1. ❒ a. As Sara walked to the side of the house, a light went on.
   ❒ b. Walking to the side of the house, a light went on.

2. ❒ a. Getting A's on tests, the teacher gave a good grade.
   ❒ b. Getting A's on tests, Tom got a good grade from the teacher.

3. ❒ a. Walking through the zoo, many animals look fierce.
   ❒ b. Many animals look fierce when you walk through the zoo.

4. ❒ a. Clanging and whistling, the fire truck sped to the blaze.
   ❒ b. Clanging and whistling, the firemen sped to the blaze.

5. ❒ a. Licking my hand, I petted the dog.
   ❒ b. I petted the dog as he licked my hand.

*ANSWERS ON THE BOTTOM OF THIS PAGE.

D. Rewrite each sentence correctly on the line below.

1. While working yesterday morning, the power went off.

   _____

2. I visited the town where I was born with my son.

   _____

3. When taking a picture, the sun should be behind you.

   _____

4. At the age of 90, Mrs. Santo's family found her cooking a turkey.

   _____

*ANSWERS AT THE BOTTOM OF THIS PAGE.

Answers to Exercise C: 1. a, 2. b, 3. b, 4. a, 5. b.
Answers to Exercise D: 1. While I was working yesterday morning, the power went off; 2. My son and I visited the town where I was born; 3. When you take a picture, the sun should be behind you. 4. When Mrs. Santo was 90, her family found her cooking a turkey.

© 2000 by The Center for Applied Research in Education

Name _____ Date _____

DON'T FLY OVER!
Explanation and Exercises

A. DEFINITION: A preposition is a word that shows how a noun or pronoun is connected to another word in the sentence in place, time, or direction. Here are some common prepositions.

> above, after, around, at, away, before, behind,
> by, from, in, into, on, over, through, under

B. Here are some prepositions that are often used incorrectly.

1. *By* means *past* or *by way of.* NEVER use *by* in place of *at.*

   WRONG: Billy stopped *by* my house on the way to school.
   → **RIGHT:** Billy stopped *at* my house on the way to school.
   → **RIGHT:** Billy walked *by* my house on the way to school.

2. *Beside* means *next to. Besides* means *in addition to.*

   WRONG: Sara has no one to play with *beside* her brother.
   → **RIGHT:** Sara has no one to play with *besides* her brother.
   → **RIGHT:** Sara sat *beside* her brother in the car.

3. You cannot go *over* a place without wings. You can go *to* that place.

   WRONG: I went *over* my friend's house after school.
   → **RIGHT:** I went *to* my friend's house after school.
   → **RIGHT:** The plane flew *over* my friend's house.

4. Do not use *off* when you mean *from.*

   WRONG: I bought this notebook *off* my friend.
   → **RIGHT:** I bought this notebook *from* my friend.
   → **RIGHT:** I got *off* the train and saw my cousin.

C. Check the correct sentence in each of the following groups.

1. ❑ a.   I am going over the record store this afternoon.
   ❑ b.   I am going to the record store this afternoon.

2. ❑ a.   Andy got that bike from his friend.
   ❑ b.   Andy got that bike off his friend.

3. ❑ a.   Joe stopped by my house to see my brother.
   ❑ b.   Joe stopped at my house to see my brother.

4. ❑ a.   Maria has no homework today beside English.
   ❑ b.   Maria has no homework today besides English.

5. ❑ a.   I like to sit beside my dad when he drives.
   ❑ b.   I like to sit besides my dad when he drives.

*ANSWERS ON ACTIVITY SHEET 58B.

© 2000 by The Center for Applied Research in Education

Name _____ Date _____

DON'T FLY OVER!
Additional Exercises

A. ANSWERS TO EXERCISE C ON ACTIVITY SHEET 58A

1. b,   2. a,   3. b,   4. b,   5. a

© 2000 by The Center for Applied Research in Education

B. Some prepositions that are often used incorrectly are

By means *past* or *by way of.* NEVER use *by* in place of *at.*
Beside means *next to. Besides* means *in addition to.*
Over means *above.* It is never used in place of *to.*
Do not use *off* when you mean *from.*

C. Check the correct sentence in each of the following groups:

1. ☐ a.   I got the homework assignment off my friend.
   ☐ b.   I got the homework assignment from my friend.

2. ☐ a.   Maria went to her aunt's house yesterday.
   ☐ b.   Maria went over her aunt's house yesterday.

3. ☐ a.   I will stop at the market on the way home.
   ☐ b.   I will stop by the market on the way home.

4. ☐ a.   Greg has two other friends beside Mike.
   ☐ b.   Greg has two other friends besides Mike.

5. ☐ a.   Greg sat besides Mike on the bus.
   ☐ b.   Greg sat beside Mike on the bus.

*SEE ANSWERS AT THE BOTTOM OF THE PAGE.

D. Fill in the blank spaces with the correct words.

1. Let's go _____ Lee's house to watch tv. (over or to)

2. I saw you walking _____ Linda. (beside or besides)

3. No one _____ me has seen the new movie. (beside or besides)

4. I stopped _____ the Conti's house to see their dog. (by or at)

5. I got an extra worksheet _____ the teacher. (off or from)

*SEE ANSWERS BELOW.

Answers: Exercise C: 1. b,   2. a,   3. a,   4. b,   5. b
Exercise D: 1. to,   2. beside,   3. besides,   4. at,   5. from

Section Five

SENTENCE WRITING HELP

TEACHER'S GUIDE—
ALPHABETICAL LIST OF SENTENCE WRITING
PROBLEMS AND ACTIVITY NUMBERS

Here is a list of the sentence problems addressed in this section and the relevant exercises.

SENTENCE PROBLEM	ACTIVITY NUMBER
Agreement of Subject and Verb	63A, B, C
Confusing Blends	71
Confusing Comparisons	66A, B
Cutting Superfluous Phrases	68A, B
Inconsistencies in Tense and Number	70A, B
Leaving Out Necessary Verbs	64A, B
Misuse of Dependent Clauses	69A, B
Redundancies	67A, B, C, D
Recognizing a Complete Sentence	59A, B, C
Run-on Sentences	62A, B, C, D
Sentence Fragments	60A, B, C, D
Sentence Fragments: Simple Exercises	61
Split Verb Phrases	65A, B

Name _____ Date _____

PUTTING IT TOGETHER
Explanation and Exercises

A. A complete thought—that is the definition of a *sentence*. A complete thought always contains a *subject* (who or what) and a *predicate* (the rest of the thought).

Steve is laughing.	(Subject: Steve;	Predicate: is laughing)
The dog barked loudly.	(Subject: dog;	Predicate: barked loudly)

B. The subject is always a noun (person, place or thing).
The predicate always contains a verb (action or being).

In the first sentence above, the subject noun is *Steve,* and the predicate verb is *is laughing.* (The verb tells what the subject is doing, thinking or feeling)
In the second sentence, the subject noun is *dog,* and the predicate verb is *barked.*

C. Circle the subject noun and <u>underline</u> the verb in these sentences.

1. The band played in the parade.

2. Mina eats fruit and vegetables.

3. My neighbor was mowing his lawn.

4. The old man walks slowly.

*Answers on Activity Sheet 59B.

D. There can be more than one subject in a sentence.

My brother and sister went to the movies.
(Subject: *brother and sister*)

The actors and actresses performed on stage.
(Subject: *actors and actresses*)

E. There can be more than one verb in the predicate.

The people in the chorus sang and danced.
(Predicate Verbs: *sang* and *danced*)

Frieda skipped and jumped all the way to school.
(Predicate Verbs: *skipped* and *jumped*)

F. Circle the subjects and <u>underline</u> the verbs in these sentences.

1. Mom and her sisters talked and laughed.

2. Jamie and his brother tossed and kicked the ball.

3. Johnny and I are watching and waiting for the mailman.

*Answers on Activity Sheet 59B.

© 2000 by The Center for Applied Research in Education

Name _____ Date _____

PUTTING IT TOGETHER
Explanation and Exercises

> **A. ANSWERS TO EXERCISE C ON ACTIVITY SHEET 59A:**
> 1. The (band) played in the parade.
> 2. (Mina) eats fruits and vegetables.
> 3. My (neighbor) was mowing his lawn.
> 4. The old (man) walks slowly.
>
> **ANSWERS TO EXERCISE F ON ACTIVITY SHEET 59A:**
> 1. (Mom and her sisters) talked and laughed.
> 2. (Jamie and his brother) tossed and kicked the ball.
> 3. (Johnny and I) are watching and waiting for the mailman.

B. THE INVISIBLE SUBJECT: In a command, the subject *You* may be omitted. You is still the subject, even if you can't see it.

Come here! (The subject is *you*)
Go to your room! (The subject is *you*)

C. THE TRAVELING SUBJECT: Usually, the subject is at the beginning of the sentence, but sometimes it can come later.

While waiting for the bus, I met my pal, Fred. *(I is the subject)*
Long ago, before the stone age, dinosaurs roamed the earth. *(dinosaurs is the subject)*

D. Identify the subject in these sentences.

1. Yesterday, before going to work, Mom baked a cake.

   Subject: _____

2. Go to the principal's office.

   Subject: _____

3. At two o'clock in the morning, I heard a strange noise in my room.

   Subject: _____

4. Yelling and shouting, the fans rooted for their team.

   Subject: _____

5. Answer these questions right now.

   Subject: _____

6. Confident that she could hit the ball, Wendy stepped up to bat.

   Subject: _____

*ANSWERS ON ACTIVITY SHEET 59C.

© 2000 by The Center for Applied Research in Education

Name _____ Date _____

PUTTING IT TOGETHER
Exercises

A. ANSWERS TO EXERCISE D, ACTIVITY SHEET 59B:

1. Mom,   2. you,   3. I,   4. fans,   5. you,   6. Wendy

B. Can you combine each subject in column A with a predicate from column B to make a complete sentence? Write these sentences on the lines below.

A	**B**
1. Jack and Jill	are sometimes noisy
2. The big black car	tastes delicious
3. The store on the corner	rang loudly
4. My cousin's cat	went up the hill
5. The kids in my class	was licking its fur
6. The telephone	sped down the street
7. This hamburger	sells hardware
8. My best friend	is very easy
9. This test	came to my party.

(Write the complete sentences below.)

1. _____

2. _____

3. _____

4. _____

5. _____

6. _____

7. _____

8. _____

9. _____

*SEE ANSWERS BELOW.

Answers to Exercise B: 1. Jack and Jill went up the hill.   **2.** The big black car sped down the street.   **3.** The store on the corner sells hardware.   **4.** My cousin's cat was licking its fur.   **5.** The kids in my class are sometimes noisy.   **6.** The telephone rang loudly.   **7.** This hamburger tastes delicious.   **8.** My best friend came to my party.   **9.** This test is very easy.

© 2000 by The Center for Applied Research in Education

Name _____ Date _____

BROKEN APART
Explanation and Exercises

It's sad when something gets broken. Did you ever drop a prized possession—maybe an electronic game—and see it smash into pieces? Or the cat knocks over Mom's favorite vase and splinters it into fragments?

That is what we call pieces of broken sentences—*fragments*. These damage your writing, as though you had dropped that sentence and shattered it. Here are some examples of fragmented sentences.

1. *A senior who starred in the annual school production*

2. *Although Jon was happy to have his own room*

3. *Sarah's new white prom dress in the closet*

Can you see what is wrong with these sentences? None of them is a complete thought!
A sentence *must* have a subject *and* a predicate (verb). The first sentence above, "A senior who starred in the annual school production," is the subject. To complete the thought, something must follow that tells what the subject did or said, as

→ *A senior who starred in the annual school production forgot his lines.*

Look at the second sentence. "Although Jon was happy to have a room of his own" is a clause that cannot stand on its own. Try saying it aloud, and you will hear that it is incomplete. Something else must follow, as

→ *Although Jon was happy to have his own room, he missed his brother.*

The third sentence, like the first, contains only a subject—"Sarah's new white prom dress in the closet." There is no verb, no predicate. Here are two possible ways of making it a complete sentence.

→ *Sarah's new white prom dress hung in the closet.*
→ *Sarah's new white prom dress in the closet fell on the floor.*

Here are some fragments. Rewrite them on the lines below, making them complete sentences.

1. An exciting and scary ghost story.

_____

2. An end-of-the-year party at Jeff's house.

_____

3. The camping trip that my family was planning last summer.

_____

4. Standing at home plate and clutching the bat tightly.

_____

*ANSWERS ON ACTIVITY SHEET 60B.

© 2000 by The Center for Applied Research in Education

Name _____ Date _____

BROKEN APART
Exercises

A. ANSWERS TO EXERCISES ON ACTIVITY SHEET 60A:

Here are some possible solutions:

1. I am reading an exciting and scary ghost story.
2. An end-of-the-year party at Jeff's house is planned for June 25.
3. The camping trip that my family was planning last summer was rained out.
4. Standing at home plate and clutching the bat tightly, Mike vowed to hit a home run.

Do your sentences now express complete thoughts? Do they contain both subjects and predicates?

B. Here is another exercise that will help you write complete sentences. The paragraph below contains three sentence fragments. Rewrite the whole paragraph on the lines below, making sure that every sentence is complete.

Steve and Jess standing in front of Steve's house. They were trying to decide what to do. Going to the park to play baseball. That seemed like a good idea. Or they could go downtown to the video arcade. Lots of exciting games there. They decided to ride their bikes downtown.

Now write this paragraph correctly below.

_____

_____

_____

_____

_____

_____

Answer: The three sentence fragments in this paragraph are

Steve and Jess standing in front of Steve's house.
Going to the park to play baseball.
Lots of exciting games there.

Did you find these three fragments and complete them? If you missed any, go back and fix your paragraph now.

© 2000 by The Center for Applied Research in Education

Name _____ Date _____

REPAIR

BROKEN APART
Paragraph—First Draft

Now that you have learned to avoid sentence fragments, it is time to write a paragraph of your own that contains no sentence fragments.

Since we have been examining broken sentences, you're going to write a paragraph about one of the following:

> I Broke Something That Belonged to Me
> I Broke Something That Belonged to Someone Else
> I Got into Trouble for Breaking Something
> Someone Else Broke Something Belonging to Me
> I Know Someone Who Is Always Breaking Things
> Something I Would Like to Break
> One Careless Moment

1. Choose one of these titles and write it on the title line below. (The incident you write about can be true, or you can make it up.)

2. Write a first draft of your paragraph. Be sure to

   a. introduce the subject in the first sentence.
   b. tell what happened with as much detail as possible.
   c. use only complete sentences.
   d. include *at least five* sentences in your paragraph.
   e. conclude the incident in your last sentence.

(This is a *first draft,* so concentrate on getting your thoughts down on paper. Don't be too concerned with spelling or grammar. Just be sure you have no sentence fragments. (Indent at the beginning of the paragraph.)

_____

_____

_____

_____

_____

_____

_____

_____

_____

© 2000 by The Center for Applied Research in Education

Name _____ Date _____

BROKEN APART
Paragraph—Revising and Writing a Final Copy

A. Edit and revise the paragraph you wrote in Activity 60C, using the following questions as guidelines:

1. Did you indent at the beginning of the paragraph?
2. Do you introduce the subject in the first sentence?
3. Do you have *at least five* sentences in your paragraph?
4. Are all your sentences complete? If there are any sentence fragments, correct them.
5. Do your subjects and verbs agree?
6. Can you add any details to make your paragraph more interesting?
7. Do you conclude the story in the last sentence?
8. Are there any words you are not sure how to spell? Consult a dictionary.

B. When your paragraph is as perfect as you can make it, write the final copy below.

_____

_____

_____

_____

_____

_____

_____

_____

_____

_____

_____

_____

_____

_____

_____

© 2000 by The Center for Applied Research in Education

Name _____ Date _____

PUTTING IT TOGETHER
Simple Exercises

A. EXPLANATION: Did you ever see a broken branch on a tree? It just hangs there like half an arm. That's how it is with sentence fragments. They dangle sadly because they have no meaning by themselves.

The broken branch. This fragment doesn't mean anything because it is only a subject and not a complete sentence. It could be fixed as follows:
The broken branch had a raw, jagged edge.

The happy girl in her beautiful new prom dress. This is just a subject. It is incomplete until you tell what the girl did, as
The happy girl in her beautiful new prom dress danced all evening.

B. The fragments in the first column are dangling alone. Find the rest of each sentence in the second column. Then write the complete sentences on the lines below.

1. My neighbor's big dog   looked a lot alike

2. The calendar on the kitchen wall   won the championship

3. Maria, on her way to school   was open to December

4. Patrick and Luke, who were brothers   arrived in the mail

5. A big box filled with presents   met her best friend

6. The best team in the league   barked all night

1. _____

2. _____

3. _____

4. _____

5. _____

6. _____

*ANSWERS AT THE BOTTOM OF THIS PAGE.

Answers: 1. My neighbor's big dog barked all night.   **2.** The calendar on the kitchen wall was open to December.   **3.** Maria, on her way to school, met her best friend.   **4.** Patrick and Luke, who were brothers, looked a lot alike.   **5.** A big box filled with presents arrived in the mail.   **6.** The best team in the league won the championship.

© 2000 by The Center for Applied Research in Education

Name _____ Date _____

RUNNING PAST THE BASE
Explanation and Exercises

A. What happens in baseball when a runner misses a base and keeps on running? There's a good chance the runner will be ruled out.

In order to get a hit, the runner must stop at the base. The base is a signal to the runner—STOP!

The same signal in a sentence is the period. A period means stop. It means that the sentence is complete. If you keep on past the point where a period should be, then you have a *run-on sentence,* as

> *I went to Molly's house, her mother likes me.*

This example has *two* complete thoughts. First thought: I (*subject*) went to Molly's house (*verb and predicate*); Second thought: Her mother (*subject*) likes me (*verb and predicate*). The comma is misplaced. A period should show the end of the first complete thought.

→ *I went to Molly's house. Her mother likes me.*

Here is another example.

> *Eric lives on Maple Street his house is the yellow one on the corner.*

The first complete thought is: Eric (*subject*) lives on Maple Street (*verb and predicate*); Second thought: His house (*subject*) is the yellow one on the corner (*verb and predicate*). This should be two complete sentences with a stop (period) at the end of each.

→ *Eric lives on Maple Street. His house is the yellow one on the corner.*

B. Here are five run-on sentences. Rewrite them on the lines below, placing a stop (period) after each sentence. (Also, be sure to begin each sentence with a capital letter.)

1. The first day of school is exciting I always wear new clothes.

   _____

2. My dad is a great fisherman we are going fishing next Saturday.

   _____

3. Call me any time I'm always home.

   _____

4. Watch out for Bobby he can sometimes act like a bully.

   _____

5. Come with me to the video store there's a good video I want to get.

   _____

*SEE ACTIVITY SHEET 62B FOR ANSWERS.

© 2000 by The Center for Applied Research in Education

Name _____ Date _____

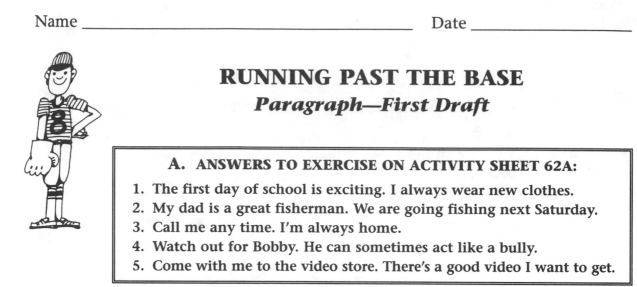

RUNNING PAST THE BASE
Paragraph—First Draft

A. ANSWERS TO EXERCISE ON ACTIVITY SHEET 62A:

1. The first day of school is exciting. I always wear new clothes.
2. My dad is a great fisherman. We are going fishing next Saturday.
3. Call me any time. I'm always home.
4. Watch out for Bobby. He can sometimes act like a bully.
5. Come with me to the video store. There's a good video I want to get.

B. When you write a paragraph, take extra care to avoid sentence fragments and run-on sentences so that your meaning is always clear.

Can you think of a time when running too fast can cause trouble? You are going to write a paragraph describing such an incident. It can be true or imaginary. Here is an example.

> Frank was proud of his ability to run fast. He never thought it would be possible to run too fast, but that is what happened last Thursday morning. Frank was on his way to his school, which was five blocks from his house. He had overslept and was afraid of being late. He began to run, faster and faster. He turned the corner at a lightning pace, too fast to stop, and crashed right into a police officer, almost knocking him down. Frank wondered if he would end up in jail instead of school. But the police officer just brushed himself off and went on his way. What a relief!

Write the first draft of *your* paragraph below. Include *at least five* sentences. Be sure to avoid run-on and fragmented sentences.

_____

_____

_____

_____

_____

_____

_____

_____

_____

© 2000 by The Center for Applied Research in Education

Name _____ Date _____

RUNNING PAST THE BASE
Paragraph—Revising and Writing a Final Copy

A. Revise and edit the paragraph you wrote in activity 62B, using the following questions as guidelines:

1. Did you indent at the beginning of the paragraph?

2. Are all your sentences complete? If there are any sentence fragments, correct them.

3. Are there any run-on sentences? If so, use periods to make two separate sentences.

4. Do your subjects and verbs agree?

5. Are there *at least five* sentences in your paragraph?

6. Can you add any details to make your paragraph more interesting?

B. When your paragraph is as perfect as you can make it, write the final copy below.

_____

_____

_____

_____

_____

_____

_____

_____

_____

_____

_____

_____

_____

_____

_____

_____

© 2000 by The Center for Applied Research in Education

Name _____ Date _____

RUNNING PAST THE BASE
Additional Explanation and Exercises

A. *We are going to the park tomorrow then we'll visit the zoo.*

This is a run-on sentence. There are several ways to correct it.

   1. *Divide it into two sentences:*

      We are going to the park tomorrow. Then we'll visit the zoo.

   2. *Use a comma and a connective word such as "and" or "but:"*

      We are going to the park tomorrow, and then we'll visit the zoo.

B. Each of the following is a run-on sentence. On the first line below, rewrite it correctly as two sentences. On the second line, rewrite it correctly as one sentence with a comma and connective word.

   1. My library book was overdue I brought it back the next day.

      _____

      _____

   2. Mr. Cowley's ranch is huge it is in Oklahoma.

      _____

      _____

   3. I never saw a spaceship I would love to see one.

      _____

      _____

   4. I visited my friend's house yesterday she wasn't home.

      _____

      _____

*ANSWERS AT THE BOTTOM OF THE PAGE.

© 2000 by The Center for Applied Research in Education

Answers: 1. My library book was overdue. I brought it back the next day.
My library book was overdue, but I brought it back the next day.
2. Mr. Cowley's ranch is huge. It is in Oklahoma.
Mr. Cowley's ranch is huge, and it is in Oklahoma.
3. I never saw a spaceship. I would love to see one.
I never saw a spaceship, but I would love to see one.
4. I visited my friend's house yesterday. She wasn't home.
I visited my friend's house yesterday, but she wasn't home.

Name _____ Date _____

WE MUST AGREE!
Explanation and Exercises

A. A complete sentence must contain a subject (noun or pronoun) and a verb (action or being word). The subject and verb must agree to make the meaning clear. A singular subject takes a singular verb. A plural subject takes a plural verb, as in these examples.

Jennifer has a bike.
Subject: *Jennifer* (singular); Verb: *has* (singular)

Jennifer has two bikes.
Don't be confused by "two bikes." The subject, *Jennifer,* is still singular, so the verb must also be singular.

Allergic people sneeze when there is pollen in the air.
Subject: *people* (plural); Verb: *sneeze* (plural)

My cousin, Jake, always sneezes a lot in the summer.
Subject: *Jake* (singular); Verb: *sneezes* (singular)

B. Complete the sentences below by filling in the correct verb form.

1. Jonathan _____ his homework every day.   (finish or finishes)

2. My three dogs _____ at every noise.   (bark or barks)

3. Two calendars _____ on the classroom wall.   (hang or hangs)

4. My calendar _____ that today is Tuesday.   (show or shows)

5. My dad _____ funny jokes.   (tell or tells)

6. TV comedians _____ funny jokes.   (tell or tells)

*See Activity Sheet 63B for Answers.

C. It's easy to make subjects and verbs agree in simple sentences. With complex sentences, this becomes more difficult, as in these examples.

The tourists on the cross-country bus make a lot of noise.
The subject is not *bus* but *tourists* (plural) and takes the verb *make.*

Alan and his friends like chocolate ice cream.
The subject is not *Alan* but *Alan and his friends* (plural).

D. Fill in the correct verb form in the following sentences:

1. The coach and players _____ on the play.   (decide or decides)

2. The ballerina and her partner _____ graceful.   (is or are)

3. Chuck, Alan, and Joe _____ very well.   (swim or swims)

*See Activity Sheet 63B for Answers

© 2000 by The Center for Applied Research in Education

Name _____ Date _____

WE MUST AGREE!
Editing a Paragraph

© 2000 by The Center for Applied Research in Education

A. ANSWERS TO EXERCISES ON ACTIVITY SHEET 63A:

Exercise B: 1. finishes, 2. bark, 3. hang, 4. shows, 5. tells, 6. tell
Exercise D: All these subjects are plural, so the answers are 1. decide, 2. are, 3. swim

---

B. MAKE THEM AGREE: The following paragraph contains errors in agreement of subjects and verbs. Circle the subjects and verbs that do not agree. Then copy the complete paragraph correctly on the lines below.

I like to listen to my CD player. My mom and dad does not like my choice of music. The stuff I play are not so bad. My sister's music sound much louder. I try to keep the sound low. Still, my parents complains. What can you do? A teenager never win.

Write the complete paragraph correctly here.

_____
_____
_____
_____

*SEE ANSWER AT BOTTOM OF PAGE

C. Here is another paragraph with errors in agreement of subject and verb. Circle those that are wrong. Then copy the whole paragraph correctly.

Today is finals day at school. All students takes exams at the same time. I am one person who study hard. Some of the kids doesn't care, but I want to do well. The hardest tests for me is English and Math. My friends, Jackie and Mark, doesn't worry at all. I'll be glad when today ends.

_____
_____
_____
_____

D. Here Are the Correct Paragraphs:

I like to listen to my CD player. My mom and dad do not like my choice of music. The stuff I play is not so bad. My sister's music sounds much louder. I try to keep the sound low. Still, my parents complain. What can you do? A teenager never wins!

Today is finals day at school. All students take exams at the same time. I am one person who studies hard. Some of the kids don't care, but I want to do well. The hardest tests for me are English and Math. My friends, Jackie and Mark, don't worry at all. I'll be glad when today ends.

Name _____ Date _____

WE MUST AGREE!
Explanation and Exercises

A. A *collective noun* names a group of people, animals, or things, such as

> **band, orchestra, crowd, gang, family, chorus, jury, audience, herd, flock, bunch, stack, set, bundle**

A *collective noun* is usually followed by a singular verb because the group acts as one, as in these examples:

> The school orchestra rehearses on Friday afternoons.
> (collective noun: *orchestra;* singular verb: *rehearses)*

> The audience applauds after a fine performance.
> (collective noun: *audience;* singular verb: *applauds)*

> The flock of birds is flying south for the winter.
> (collective noun: *flock;* singular verb: *is flying)*

B. Write the correct verb in the spaces below.

1. My class _____ going on a field trip.   (is, are)

2. The chorus _____ going to perform seasonal songs.   (is, are)

3. The committee _____ made a decision.   (has, have)

4. A stack of test papers _____ on the teacher's desk.   (is, are)

5. A herd of cows _____ gathered in the meadow.   (was, were)

*SEE ANSWERS AT THE BOTTOM OF THE PAGE.

C. Write a sentence containing each of these words.

1. (band) _____

2. (family) _____

3. (gang) _____

4. (bunch) _____

5. (jury) _____

6. (crowd) _____

© 2000 by The Center for Applied Research in Education

Answers to Exercise B: 1. is,   **2.** is,   **3.** has,   **4.** is,   **5.** was

Name _____ Date _____

THE LOST VERB
Explanation and Exercises

A. Sometimes a sentence requires more than one verb. For example:

1. The door is locked, and the keys put away.

   In this sentence, the verb *is* is fine with *door,* but you cannot says "keys *is* put away." It must say, "keys *are* put away." Therefore, this sentence should be written

   ➤ The door is locked, and the keys are put away.

   Here is another example.

2. The flowers have been watered, and the grass mowed.

   This should be written.

   ➤ The flowers have been watered, and the grass has been mowed.

B. Rewrite each sentence correctly on the line below.

1. The dishes have all been washed, and the big pot scrubbed.

   _____

2. Karen works best in the morning, and the boys in the afternoon.

   _____

3. The dog gets fed at 3, and the cats at 5.

   _____

4. A dog has four legs, but people only two.

   _____

5. Maria has grown two inches, but the boys only one inch.

   _____

6. The desk goes in the corner, and the chairs on the other side.

   _____

7. The Smiths have two cats, but Mrs. Santiago only one.

   _____

8. The roast turkey was delicious, and the desserts even better.

   _____

*SEE ACTIVITY SHEET 64B FOR ANSWERS.

© 2000 by The Center for Applied Research in Education

Name _____ Date _____

THE LOST VERB
Additional Exercises

A. ANSWERS TO EXERCISE B ON ACTIVITY SHEET 64A:

1. The dishes have all been washed, and the big pot has been scrubbed.
2. Karen works best in the morning, and the boys work best in the afternoon.
3. The dog gets fed at 3, and the cats get fed at 5.
4. A dog has four legs, but people have only two.
5. Maria has grown two inches, but the boys have grown only one inch.
6. The desk goes in the corner, and the chairs go on the other side.
7. The Smiths have two cats, but Mrs. Santiago has only one.
8. The roast turkey was delicious, and the desserts were even better.

B. Check the correct sentence in each of the following groups.

1. ❏ a. The rug was green, and the walls white.
   ❏ b. The rug was green, and the walls were white.

2. ❏ a. The boys leave for school at 7:30, and Mary leaves at 8.
   ❏ b. The boys leave for school at 7:30, and Mary at 8.

3. ❏ a. Maria likes to eat chicken, but the boys meat.
   ❏ b. Maria likes to eat chicken, but the boys like meat.

4. ❏ a. The chorus members sing together, but the soloist alone.
   ❏ b. The chorus members sing together, but the soloist sings alone.

5. ❏ a. Matthew attends one church, and his grandparents another.
   ❏ b. Matthew attends one church, and his grandparents attend another.

6. ❏ a. Mrs. Geller plants vegetables, but her neighbors plant flowers.
   ❏ b. Mrs. Geller plants vegetables, but her neighbors flowers.

*ANSWERS AT THE BOTTOM OF THIS PAGE.

© 2000 by The Center for Applied Research in Education

Answers: 1. b,   2. a,   3. b,   4. b,   5. b,   6. a

Name _____ Date _____

DON'T SPLIT MY VERB
Explanation and Exercises

A. A *Verb Phrase* is a verb that contains more than one word, usually a main verb and an auxiliary (helping) verb.

Some examples of verb phrases are *had been, has walked, have eaten,* and *am going.*

Verb phrases are like married people—they hate to be separated from each other. If you place other words between them, they make an awkward sentence, such as

Arthur had, it's hard to believe, visited two countries in one day.
Helen has, much to my surprise, finished all her homework.

Here is how these sentences should look.

→ *It's hard to believe that Arthur had visited two countries in one day.*
→ *Helen has finished all her homework, much to my surprise.*

B. The following sentences contain split verb phrases. Rewrite each sentence on the line below.

1. Maya had, much to her relief, passed all her courses.

_____

2. I am, if at all possible, coming to your birthday party.

_____

3. Joe has, though he was told not to, turned on the tv.

_____

4. That dog was, I had no doubt, going to bite the mailman.

_____

5. She has, for no good reason, gone away.

_____

6. Greg was, if he could get ready early, planning to eat breakfast.

_____

*SEE ACTIVITY SHEET 65B FOR ANSWERS.

© 2000 by The Center for Applied Research in Education

Name _____ Date _____

DON'T SPLIT MY VERB
Additional Exercises

A. ANSWERS TO EXERCISE B ON ACTIVITY SHEET 65A:

1. Much to her relief, Maya had passed all her courses.
2. I am coming to your birthday party if at all possible.
3. Though he was told not to, Joe has turned on the tv.
4. I had no doubt that dog was going to bite the mailman.
5. She has gone away for no good reason.
6. Greg was planning to eat breakfast if he could get ready early.

B. Can you find four split verb phrases in the following paragraph? Circle them and rewrite the paragraph correctly on the lines below.

> Ed was, while his mind was on something else, riding his bike through the park. At first, he did not notice the child who was, tears running down her face, crouched near the bushes. Ed stopped and got off the bike. "What has," he asked the crying child, "happened to you?" The child took one look at Ed and went flying down the path, screaming. Ed shrugged and got back on his bike. I guess I haven't, he thought to himself, helped her at all.

_____

_____

_____

_____

_____

_____

_____

_____

*ANSWER AT BOTTOM OF PAGE.

© 2000 by The Center for Applied Research in Education

Here is the Corrected Paragraph: Ed was riding his bike through the park while his mind was on something else. At first, he did not notice the child who was crouched near the bushes, tears running down her face. Ed stopped and got off the bike. "What has happened to you?" he asked the crying child. The child took one look at Ed and went flying down the path, screaming. Ed shrugged and got back on his bike. I guess I haven't helped her at all, he thought to himself.

Name _____ Date _____

LONGER THAN WHAT?
Explanation and Exercises

A. CONFUSING COMPARISONS:

> *Rita's hair is longer than any girl in her class.*

This sentence makes no sense at all! Rita's hair must trail along the ground behind her if it is longer than the length of a girl!

What the writer meant to say is, *Rita's hair is longer than that of any girl in her class.* This compares *hair* to *hair,* not *hair* to *girl.*

A comparison must make clear exactly what is being compared to what.

Here is another example of a confusing comparison.

> *The singer's act was the greatest success.*

Greatest is a comparison word. The singer's *act* is being compared to something, but this sentence doesn't say to what. It should read, *"The singer's act was the greatest success of any act on stage that night."*

B. The following sentences contain confusing comparisons. Rewrite each sentence correctly on the line below.

1. Matt's grades are the best.

   _____

2. My dog, Freddie, is smarter than anyone's.

   _____

3. My hamster is bigger than all my friends.

   _____

4. My dad is the greatest.

   _____

5. Darla's family is bigger than the rest of the school.

   _____

*SEE ACTIVITY SHEET 66B FOR ANSWERS.

© 2000 by The Center for Applied Research in Education

Name _____ Date _____

LONGER THAN WHAT?
Explanation and Exercises

© 2000 by The Center for Applied Research in Education

> **A. ANSWERS TO EXERCISE B ON ACTIVITY SHEET 66A:**
>
> 1. Matt's grades are the best grades in the class.
> 2. My dog, Freddie, is smarter than anyone else's dog.
> 3. My hamster is bigger than all my friends' hamsters.
> 4. My dad is the greatest of all dads.
> 5. Darla's family is bigger than any family in the rest of the school.

B. Never use *double* comparatives on superlatives.

WRONG:	My aunt is the most saddest lady I know.
➝ **RIGHT:**	My aunt is the saddest lady I know.
WRONG:	She seems a bit more happier today.
➝ **RIGHT:**	She seems a bit happier today.
WRONG:	My dog, Monty, is more noisier than the one we had before.
➝ **RIGHT:**	My dog, Monty, is noisier than the one we had before. OR
➝ **RIGHT:**	My dog, Monty, is more noisy than the one we had before.

C. The sentences below contain double comparatives or superlatives. Rewrite each sentence correctly on the line below.

1. Fifth grade is more harder than fourth grade.

_____

2. Mrs. Harrison is the most kindest teacher in the school.

_____

3. Harry is the most best pitcher on the team.

_____

4. The patient is feeling a lot more better today.

_____

5. Mr. Adams is the most grumpiest man on our block.

_____

*Answers at the Bottom of This Page.

Answers to Exercise C:

1. Fifth grade is harder than fourth grade.
2. Mrs. Harrison is the kindest teacher in the school.
3. Harry is the best pitcher on the team.
4. The patient is feeling a lot better today.
5. Mr. Adams is the grumpiest man on our block.

Name _____ Date _____

YOU SAID THAT ALREADY!
Explanation and Exercises

A. REDUNDANCIES: A sentence can get too wordy and confusing if it says the same thing twice.

> **REDUNDANT:** Max woke up at 12 midnight.
> → **BETTER:** Max woke up at midnight. (*Midnight* means 12.)

> **REDUNDANT:** I read a biography about the life of John F. Kennedy.
> → **BETTER:** I read a biography about John F. Kennedy. (*Biography* means "about the life." You don't need to say it twice!)

> **REDUNDANT:** Let us cooperate together to complete the project.
> → **BETTER:** Let us cooperate to complete the project. (*Cooperate* means doing something together.)

B. Here are other common redundancies:

REDUNDANCY	THE BETTER WAY
12 noon	noon
4 A.M. in the morning	4 A.M.
a total of 15 boxes	15 boxes
each and every	each
final end	end
free gift	gift
period of three months	three months
refer back	refer
personally, I think	I think
repeat again	repeat
revert back	revert

C. Check the correct sentence in each group.

1. ❑ a. The new store gave free gifts on opening day.
   ❑ b. The new store gave gifts on opening day.

2. ❑ a. The teacher said, "Don't make me repeat that."
   ❑ b. The teacher said, "Don't make me repeat that again."

3. ❑ a. I had a bad dream at 3 A.M.
   ❑ b. I had a bad dream at 3 A.M. in the morning.

4. ❑ a. When his punishment ended, he reverted back to his old ways.
   ❑ b. When his punishment ended, he reverted to his old ways.

5. ❑ a. The building was closed for three months.
   ❑ b. The building was closed for a period of three months.

6 ❑ a. The last thing Mary did was the end of our friendship.
   ❑ b. The last thing Mary did was the final end of our friendship.

*ANSWERS ON ACTIVITY SHEET 67B.

© 2000 by The Center for Applied Research in Education

Name _____ Date _____

YOU SAID THAT ALREADY!
Explanation and Exercises

A. ANSWERS TO EXERCISE C ON ACTIVITY SHEET 67A:

1. b, 2. a, 3. a, 4. b, 5. a, 6. a

B. Here are other common redundancies.

REDUNDANCY	BETTER WAY
surrounded on all sides	surrounded
square in shape	square
round in shape	round
small (or large) in size	small (or large)
return again	return
ATM machine	ATM (The M stands for machine)
the future to come	the future
he is a person who	he
personal opinion	opinion
ac/dc current	ac/dc (c stands for current)

C. Copy each sentence on the line below, taking out the redundancy.

1. An island is surrounded on all sides by water.

   _____

2. In the future to come, everyone will own a computer.

   _____

3. Raul wanted to return again to the house where he was born.

   _____

4. Mrs. Sanchez got the money she needed from the ATM machine.

   _____

5. What is your personal opinion about this school?

   _____

6. This machine will only fit in a box that is square in shape.

   _____

7. Matthew is a person who likes to play basketball.

   _____

*ANSWERS ON ACTIVITY SHEET 67C.

© 2000 by The Center for Applied Research in Education

Name _____ Date _____

YOU SAID THAT ALREADY!
Explanation and Exercises

A. ANSWERS TO EXERCISE C ON ACTIVITY SHEET 67B:

1. An island is surrounded by water.
2. In the future, everyone will own a computer.
3. Raul wanted to return to the house where he was born.
4. Mrs. Sanchez got the money she needed from the ATM.
5. What is your opinion about this school?
6. This machine will only fit in a box that is square.
7. Matthew likes to play basketball.

B. MORE COMMON REDUNDANCIES

REDUNDANCY	BETTER WAY
circle around	circle
in the event that	if
new innovation	innovation (innovation means new)
one and the same	the same
shorter in length	shorter
longer in length	longer
shorter in height	shorter
taller in height	taller

C. Can you find the six redundancies in the following paragraph? Underline these redundancies. Then rewrite the paragraph correctly on the lines below.

Jamie was a passenger on the first space ship to Mars. It was the one and the same ship that had made a journey to the moon the previous year and had spent a period of three months there. An addition had been built on to the ship that made it taller in height and rounder in shape. There was also a new innovation in the engine that sent an automatic message back to Earth in the event there was a problem.

_____

_____

_____

_____

_____

Answer to Exercise C: Jamie was a passenger on the first space ship to Mars. It was the *same* ship that had made a journey to the moon the previous year and had spent *three months* there. An addition had been built on to the ship that made it *taller* and *rounder*. There was also an *innovation* in the engine that sent an automatic message back to Earth *if* there was a problem.

© 2000 by The Center for Applied Research in Education

Name _____ Date _____

YOU SAID THAT ALREADY!
Explanation and Exercises

A. REDUNDANCIES: Don't say the same thing twice! Here are other common redundancies.

REDUNDANCY	THE BETTER WAY
absolutely essential	essential
around about that time	around that time
combine together	combine
cooperate together	cooperate
most unkindest	unkindest
rise up	rise
many in number	many
completely unanimous	unanimous
first beginnings	beginnings

B. Copy each sentence on the line below, taking out the redundancies.

1. Mr. Hill is the most unkindest man I ever met.

   _____

2. Let's cooperate together to get the job done.

   _____

3. Look at the smoke rising up from the chimney!

   _____

4. The vote for class president was completely unanimous.

   _____

5. Carl's friends are many in number.

   _____

6. Do you know how our government had its first beginnings?

   _____

7. I can combine together all these ingredients to make a cake.

   _____

*SEE ANSWERS BELOW.

Answers to Exercise B: 1. Mr. Hill is the unkindest man I ever met. **2.** Let's cooperate to get the job done. **3.** Look at the smoke rising from the chimney. **4.** The vote for class president was unanimous. **5.** Carl's friends are many. **6.** Do you know how our government had its beginnings? **7.** I can combine all these ingredients to make a cake.

© 2000 by The Center for Applied Research in Education

Name _____ Date _____

CUT THAT FAT!
Explanation and Exercises

A. You don't want extra fat on your body. Sentences, too, are stronger and clearer without a lot of extra words that add nothing to the meaning. Here are some examples.

> **TOO MUCH FAT:** All things considered, I liked sixth grade a lot.
> → **BETTER:** I liked sixth grade a lot.
>
> **TOO MUCH FAT:** For the most part, Luke does well in school.
> → **BETTER:** Luke does well in school.
>
> **TOO MUCH FAT:** In a manner of speaking, Colleen is nicer than Amy.
> → **BETTER:** Colleen is nicer than Amy.

B. Here are other phrases that are unnecessary and should be cut or shortened.

> **as far as I'm concerned**
> **at this point in time**
> **as a matter of fact**
> **due to the fact that** (just say *because*)

C. Can you cut out the fat in the following sentences? Write each sentence correctly on the line below.

1. I like dogs better than cats for the most part.

   _____

2. Jennifer is not prepared for the test at this point in time.

   _____

3. I am tired due to the fact that I went to bed late last night.

   _____

4. As a matter of fact, Matt and Jimmy are both coming to the party.

   _____

5. All things considered, I think I'll stay home today.

   _____

6. In a manner of speaking, I prefer history to science.

   _____

*SEE ACTIVITY SHEET 68B FOR ANSWERS.

© 2000 by The Center for Applied Research in Education

Name _____ Date _____

CUT THAT FAT!
Explanation and Exercises

A. ANSWERS TO EXERCISE C ON ACTIVITY SHEET 68A:

1. I like dogs better than cats.
2. Jennifer is not prepared for the test.
3. I am tired because I went to bed late last night.
4. Matt and Jimmy are both coming to the party.
5. I think I'll stay home today.
6. I prefer history to science.

B. Here are other words and phrases that should usually be cut from a sentence.

> so to speak
> one of the reasons that
> in my opinion
> more or less
> so very
> basically

C. Can you cut the fat from these sentences? Write each sentence correctly on the line below.

1. One of the reasons that Max went to New York was to see his aunt.

   _____

2. In my opinion, our team needs a better coach.

   _____

3. I was so very afraid to go into the haunted house.

   _____

4. Jimmy is more or less thankful to have passed all his courses.

   _____

5. The Alonsos live in a good neighborhood, so to speak.

   _____

6. Basically, he is a good person.

   _____

Answers to Exercise C: 1. Max went to New York to see his aunt.   2. Our team needs a better coach.   3. I was afraid to go into the haunted house.   4. Jimmy is thankful to have passed all his courses.   5. The Alonsos live in a good neighborhood.   6. He is a good person.

© 2000 by The Center for Applied Research in Education

Name _____ Date _____

A CLAUSE IS NOT SANTA
Explanation and Exercises

A. DEFINITION: A *clause* is a group of words containing a subject and a predicate.

B. Some clauses can stand alone as sentences.

→ *Mike stayed home from school today.*

C. Other clauses cannot stand alone as sentences. These are called dependent or subordinate clauses.

Because he was sick. This has a subject and a verb, but it is not a sentence. The word *because* at the beginning makes it a dependent clause that cannot stand on its own.
There are several ways to fix this.

→ 1. Take out *because: He was sick.*

→ 2. Keep *because* and attach it to the main sentence:
Mike stayed home from school today because he was sick.

D. If a dependent clause is misplaced, a sentence can be confusing.

WRONG: I was sick was the reason why I didn't go to the party.

→ **RIGHT:** I didn't go to the party because I was sick.

(**Note:** "the reason why" and "the reason is because" are often misused and should be reworded.)

E. Rewrite each sentence correctly on the line below.

1. I was not prepared was the reason I failed the test.

   _____

2. Maria bought a new dress. Because she was going to a party.

   _____

3. I like children is the reason why I want to be a teacher.

   _____

4. The reason why I'm not ready is because I woke up late.

   _____

*ANSWERS ON ACTIVITY SHEET 69B.

© 2000 by The Center for Applied Research in Education

Name _____ Date _____

A CLAUSE IS NOT SANTA
Explanation and Exercises

A. ANSWERS TO EXERCISE E ON ACTIVITY SHEET 69A:

1. I failed the test because I was not prepared.
2. Maria bought a new dress because she was going to a party.
3. I want to be a teacher because I like children.
4. I'm not ready because I woke up late.

B. Do not attach dependent clauses to the sentence with words that cause confusion, as in these examples.

WRONG: Although Chita studied hard caused her to fail the test.
→ **RIGHT:** Chita studied hard but she failed the test.

WRONG: Clara's only hope of passing is she will study even harder.
→ **RIGHT:** Clara's only hope of passing is to study even harder.

WRONG: In trying to fix the chair another leg broke.
→ **RIGHT:** When I tried to fix the chair, another leg broke.

C. Check the correct sentence in each of these groups.

1. ❑ a. Although I rushed to get ready, I was late.
   ❑ b. Although I rushed to get ready was why I was late.

2. ❑ a. In doing Mark's homework there were difficult problems.
   ❑ b. There were difficult problems in Mark's homework.

3. ❑ a. I was sick caused me to have a fever.
   ❑ b. I had a fever because I was sick.

4. ❑ a. By using a new ball, our team won the game.
   ❑ b. By using a new ball helped our team win the game.

5. ❑ a. Going to the beach is not a good place at this time of year.
   ❑ b. The beach is not a good place to go at this time of year.

6. ❑ a. My only hope is to pass the test.
   ❑ b. My only hope is I will pass the test.

7. ❑ a. Even though Pete did his best was a surprise to fail the test.
   ❑ b. Even though Pete did his best, he failed the test.

*SEE ANSWERS BELOW.

Answers to Exercise C: 1. a, 2. b, 3. b, 4. a, 5. b, 6. a, 7. b.

© 2000 by The Center for Applied Research in Education

Name _____ Date _____

THE OLD SWITCHEROO
Explanation and Exercises

A. Don't change tense in the middle of a sentence.

     WRONG: I woke up at 7 A.M. and brush my teeth.
→ **RIGHT:**   I woke up at 7 A.M. and brushed my teeth.

     WRONG: Andrea walked down the street and a car almost hits her.
→ **RIGHT:**   Andrea walked down the street and a car almost hit her.

B. Don't change number in the middle of a sentence.

     WRONG: I like to eat candy but they sometimes make me sick.
→ **RIGHT:**   I like to eat candy but it sometimes makes me sick.

     WRONG: If the boys listen to the teacher, she will respect him.
→ **RIGHT:**   If the boys listen to the teacher, she will respect them.

C. Don't change subject in the middle of a sentence.

     WRONG: When you go outside, flowers are in the garden.
→ **RIGHT:**   When you go outside, you will see flowers in the garden.

     WRONG: Luke's mom baked cookies, and cake is delicious, too.
→ **RIGHT:**   Luke's mom baked delicious cookies and cake.

D. Rewrite each sentence correctly on the line below.

1. Pete walked up to the plate and the ball was hit.

_____

2. The dog jumped on Carrie and she screams.

_____

3. I was minding my own business when a strange thing happens.

_____

4. If kids try their best, he will succeed.

_____

5. Eat your food while they are still warm.

_____

*SEE ACTIVITY SHEET 70B FOR ANSWERS.

© 2000 by The Center for Applied Research in Education

Name _____ Date _____

THE OLD SWITCHEROO
Additional Exercises

A. ANSWERS TO EXERCISE D ON ACTIVITY SHEET 70A:

1. Pete walked up to the plate and hit the ball.
2. The dog jumped on Carrie and she screamed.
3. I was minding my own business when a strange thing happened.
4. If kids try their best, they will succeed.
4. Eat your food while it is still warm.

B. CONSISTENCY: Do not change tense, number, or subject in the middle of a sentence.

C. Check the correct sentence in each group.

1. ❑ a.   Jesse went into the room and sees a weird sight.
    ❑ b.   Jesse went into the room and saw a weird sight.

2. ❑ a.   The girls dressed and looked at themselves in the mirror.
    ❑ b.   The girls dressed and looked at herself in the mirror.

3. ❑ a.   I eat cereal and toast for breakfast and it tastes good.
    ❑ b.   I eat cereal and toast for breakfast and they taste good.

4. ❑ a.   As you go into the house you will see three rooms.
    ❑ b.   As you go into the house there are three rooms.

5. ❑ a.   The boys were walking on the beach and turn to look at me.
    ❑ b.   The boys were walking on the beach and turned to look at me.

6. ❑ a.   The band was performing and it played perfectly.
    ❑ b.   The band was performing and they played perfectly.

7. ❑ a.   He ate a banana and threw away the skin.
    ❑ b.   He ate a banana and throws away the skin.

8. ❑ a.   When the passengers boarded the bus, he sat at the back.
    ❑ b.   When the passengers boarded the bus, they sat at the back.

9. ❑ a.   I walked into the room and there was my father.
    ❑ b.   I walked into the room and there's my father.

*ANSWERS AT THE BOTTOM OF THE PAGE.

© 2000 by The Center for Applied Research in Ecucation

Answers to Exercise C: 1. b,   2. a,   3. b,   4. a,   5. b,   6. a,   7. a,   8. b,   9. a

Name _____ Date _____

DON'T PUT ME INTO A BLENDER!
Explanation and Exercises

A. EXPLANATION: Do you ever blend two words or phrases into one word or phrase that is not correct?

Some examples of confusing blends are

irregardless—This is an incorrect blend of *regardless* and *irrespective*.

    WRONG: Irregardless of what you say, I won't go.
→ **RIGHT:**   Regardless of what you say, I won't go.

despite of—This is an incorrect blend of *in spite of* and *despite*.

    WRONG: Mark did not succeed despite of his hard work.
→ **RIGHT:**   Mark did not succeed despite his hard work.

where at—This is an incorrect blend of *where* and *at*.

    WRONG: Where does Amy live at?
→ **RIGHT:**   Where does Amy live?

where in—This is an incorrect blend of *where* and *in*.

    WRONG: This is the town where I live in.
→ **RIGHT:**   This is the town in which I live. OR
    This is the town where I live.

D. Rewrite each sentence correctly on the line below.

1. Despite of what you say, I refuse to go.

    _____

2. That is the hotel where I stay at every summer.

    _____

3. I'm going to tell the truth irregardless of the consequences.

    _____

4. Is that the house where you live in?

    _____

5. We're going away for the weekend despite of the bad weather.

    _____

*SEE ANSWERS BELOW.

Answers to Exercise B: 1. Despite what you say, I refuse to go. **2.** That is the hotel where I stay every summer. **3.** I'm going to tell the truth regardless of the consequences. **4.** Is that the house where you live? **5.** We're going away for the weekend despite the bad weather.

© 2000 by The Center for Applied Research in Education

PARAGRAPH HELP

TEACHER'S GUIDE—
ALPHABETICAL LIST OF PARAGRAPH PROBLEMS
AND RELEVANT EXERCISES

Here is a list of the sentence problems addressed in this section and the relevant exercises.

PARAGRAPH PROBLEM	ACTIVITY NUMBER
Changing the Subject	83A, B
Concluding Sentence	74A, B
Consistency of Tense	76A, B
Consistency of Pronoun	77A, B, C
Irrelevant Details	84A, B, C, D
Organizing a Paragraph	75A, B, C
Sentence Order	72A, B, C
Sentence Variety: Clauses	80A, B, C
Sentence Variety: Questions, Etc.	81A, B, C
Sentence Variety: Too Long	79A, B, C
Sentence Variety: Too Short	78A, B, C
Topic Sentence	73A, B, C
Transitions	82A, B, C

Name _____ Date _____

MIX AND MATCH
Explanation and Exercises

A. A *paragraph* is like a very short story. It has a beginning, middle, and end.

→ The beginning sentence introduces the story and is called the topic sentence.

→ The middle sentences tell the story in logical order.

→ The last sentence brings the story to an end and is called the concluding sentence.

B. SCRAMBLED PARAGRAPH: The six sentences below can be combined into one paragraph. But they are not in the correct order! Can you unscramble them and copy them in the right order into a paragraph? The topic sentence should come first, the concluding sentence last, and the other four sentences in a logical order between them.

---

1. I named the puppy Max, and I know we'll be great friends.
2. I looked inside, and there was a little puppy, wagging its tail.
3. That was one birthday I'll never forget.
4. When I woke up in the morning, I saw a box in the corner of my room.
5. Last week, I had the best birthday ever.
6. It was what I wanted more than anything else.

Write the paragraph on the lines below.

_____

_____

_____

_____

_____

_____

_____

_____

_____

*ANSWER ON ACTIVITY SHEET 72B.

© 2000 by The Center for Applied Research in Education

Name _____ Date _____

SCRAMBLED PARAGRAPHS
Additional Exercises

A. ANSWER TO EXERCISE B ON ACTIVITY SHEET 72A:

Last week, I had the best birthday ever. When I woke up in the morning, I saw a box in the corner of my room. I looked inside, and there was a little puppy, wagging its tail. It was what I wanted more than anything else. I named the puppy Max, and I know we'll be great friends. That was one birthday I'll never forget.

B. ANOTHER SCRAMBLED PARAGRAPH: The six sentences below can be combined into one paragraph. But they are not in the right order! Can you unscramble them and copy them in the right order to form a paragraph? The topic sentence should come first, the concluding sentence last, and the other four sentences in a logical order between them.

1. Mike was chosen for his intelligence, character, and health.
2. Mike was a passenger on the first voyage from Earth to Venus.
3. That trip made Mike famous.
4. They wanted to test the effect of space travel on children.
5. There was a nationwide search that lasted two months.
6. NASA had decided to send one twelve-year-old.

Write the paragraph on the lines below.

_____

_____

_____

_____

_____

_____

_____

_____

*ANSWER ON ACTIVITY SHEET 72C.

© 2000 by The Center for Applied Research in Education

Name _____ Date _____

SCRAMBLED PARAGRAPHS
Another Exercise

A. ANSWER TO EXERCISE B ON ACTIVITY SHEET 72B:

Mike was a passenger on the first voyage from Earth to Venus. NASA had decided to send one twelve-year-old. They wanted to test the effect of space travel on children. There was a nationwide search that lasted two months. Mike was chosen for his intelligence, character, and health. That trip made Mike famous.

B. ANOTHER SCRAMBLED PARAGRAPH: The six sentences below can be combined into one paragraph. But they are not in the right order! Can you unscramble them and copy them in the right order into a paragraph? The topic sentence should come first, the concluding sentence last, and the other four sentences in a logical order between them.

> 1. Then I go out trick-or-treating.
> 2. Halloween is my favorite holiday.
> 3. This year I was a pirate.
> 4. The best part of Halloween is eating all that candy.
> 5. First, I put on my costume.
> 6. It's fun to go from house to house getting treats.

Write the paragraph on the lines below.

_____

_____

_____

_____

_____

_____

*SEE THE ANSWER BELOW.

Answer to Exercise B: Halloween is my favorite holiday. First, I put on my costume. This year I was a pirate. Then I go out trick-or-treating. It's fun to go from house to house getting treats. The best part of Halloween is eating all that candy.

© 2000 by The Center for Applied Research in Education

Name _____ Date _____

WHAT'S IT ALL ABOUT?
Explanation and Exercises

A. DEFINITION: A *topic sentence* tells what the paragraph is about. It is usually the first sentence of a paragraph. The rest of the paragraph develops the theme stated in the topic sentence.

B. PURPOSE: A topic sentence has two purposes.

→ 1. It helps the readers by telling them what the paragraph is about.

→ 2. It helps the writer by focusing attention on the main subject, and keeps the writer from wandering off the topic.

C. FIND THE TOPIC SENTENCE: In the following paragraph, the topic sentence is hidden in the middle of the paragraph. Find the topic sentence and circle it. Then write a paragraph of your own that uses the same topic sentence.

> Last year, I made three New Year's resolutions. I didn't manage to stick to any of them. New Year's resolutions are hard to keep. This year, I plan to make only one. I resolve never to make another New Year's resolution. That should take care of the resolution problem once and for all.

You should have circled *"New Year's resolutions are hard to keep."* The first sentence in this paragraph is *not* the topic sentence because it refers only to last year's resolutions, while the rest of the paragraph goes on to talk about this year, too.

Now, write the same topic sentence—*New Year's resolutions are hard to keep*—below, and write your own paragraph to go with this topic sentence.

_____

_____

_____

_____

_____

_____

_____

_____

© 2000 by The Center for Applied Research in Education

Name _____ Date _____

WHAT'S IT ALL ABOUT?
Additional Exercises and Paragraph Draft

A. Can you find the topic sentence that is hidden inside the following paragraph? Circle the topic sentence and copy it on the lines below. Then write your own paragraph using the same topic sentence.

> Everyone was happy when we won the opening game of the season. The second game was a heart breaker that we lost by just one point. The season that just ended was the worst in our team's history. When our best pitcher broke his arm, we didn't win one more game.

Did you circle *"The season that just ended was the worst in our team's history."* This is the topic sentence. Copy this topic sentence on the lines below. Then write your own paragraph using the same topic sentence.

_____

_____

_____

_____

_____

B. Choose one of the following topic sentences to use in writing a paragraph, and check the box you have chosen.

- ❑ 1. March was the worst month of my life.
- ❑ 2. It's easy to make a healthful salad.
- ❑ 3. There are three things that I always look for in a friend.
- ❑ 4. I really like my English teacher this year.

C. FIRST DRAFT: Write a paragraph below that begins with the topic sentence you have checked. You should have *at least four* additional sentences. This is just a first draft, so don't worry about spelling or grammar. Just concentrate on getting down your ideas.

_____

_____

_____

_____

_____

© 2000 by The Center for Applied Research in Education

Name _____ Date _____

WHAT'S IT ALL ABOUT?
Writing a Paragraph—Final Copy

A. Revise the paragraph draft you wrote for Exercise C on Activity Sheet 73B, using the following guidelines:

1. Does the first sentence introduce the subject? Can you think of any way to make it more interesting?

2. Do the following sentences give facts or details about this topic?

3. Does the last sentence conclude the "story" of the paragraph?

4. Are all your sentences complete? Do subjects and verbs agree?

5. Should any words or phrases be changed to make your writing clearer or more understandable to the reader?

6. Check your spelling with a dictionary.

B. Write a final copy of your paragraph on the lines below. Try to make it as perfect and interesting as you can. (Indent at the beginning.)

_____

_____

_____

_____

_____

_____

_____

_____

_____

_____

_____

_____

© 2000 by The Center for Applied Research in Education

Name _____ Date _____

SUM IT UP!
Explanation and Exercises

A. EXPLANATION: The concluding (last) sentence in a paragraph is often used to sum up the topic, as in the following example:

> Some interesting people live on my street. The Randoses next door have traveled all over the world and tell great stories about the places they have seen. Jake Siscoe, whose parents live down the block, plays pro football. Sometimes Jake stops by to say hello to us when he is visiting. Old Mrs. O'Grady across the street is an author, and I've seen her books in the library. Yes, Malcolm Place is not an ordinary street.

Notice how the concluding sentence, *Yes, Malcolm Place is not an ordinary street,* sums up the topic "Some interesting people live on my street."

B. Add a concluding sentence to each of the following paragraphs:

1. Marla had fun decorating her room in the new house. The bed and dresser are dark oak. There is a big lamp with the figure of a ballet dancer on the table. Marla chose a blue rug for the floor and blue-flowered curtains at the windows.

   _____

   _____

2. Everyone in Ricky's family is talented. His mother and father are musicians. His brother, Sam, sings with a rap group. Rita, his sister, is an actress, and Ricky excels in drawing.

   _____

   _____

*SEE ANSWERS BELOW.

Answers: Here are possible concluding sentences for these paragraphs.
1. Now Marla's room is just the way she wants it.
2. That is really a creative family.

© 2000 by The Center for Applied Research in Education

Name _____ Date _____

SUM IT UP!
Additional Exercises

A. Write a concluding sentence for the following paragraph:

I'd rather have a cat than a dog. Cats are easy to care for. They don't have to be walked. They always keep themselves very clean. They never make a racket barking or jump on guests.

_____

_____

B. Write a paragraph for each of the concluding sentences below. (Each paragraph should contain *at least five* sentences.)

1. _____

_____

_____

_____

_____

That was a trip that I'll never forget!

2. _____

_____

_____

_____

_____

That's why Poppy's is my favorite restaurant.

© 2000 by The Center for Applied Research in Education

Name _____ Date _____

THE PARAGRAPH STORY
Prewriting

A. DEFINITION: What is a paragraph? It is like a story, with a beginning, middle, and end. The first sentence states what the story is about. The sentences that follow tell the details of the story. The last sentence provides an ending to the story.

B. EXAMPLE: Here is an example of how a paragraph can be organized.

→ 1. First Sentence: *If I could change one thing about myself, it would be my size.* This is the beginning of the story. It states the subject.

→ 2. Middle: Three or four sentences follow to tell details. Here are some of the details that could be included. (These are not in sentence form, just briefly noted.)

shortest person in class	lots of friends despite size
always been short	doesn't like to have to look up to everyone

→ 3. Last Sentence: The last sentence should bring the subject to a conclusion, as *Maybe I'll have a growth spurt some day and no longer be a "shorty."*

4. The completed paragraph might look like this:

> If I could change one thing about myself, it would be my size. I'm the shortest person in my class. I've always been short. This does not affect my social life. I have lots of friends, and everyone likes me. It would be nice, however, not having to look up to all the other people in the world. Maybe I'll have a growth spurt some day and no longer be a "shorty."

C. You are going to write a paragraph on the same topic. What is one thing you would like to change about yourself? It will be easy to do if you first complete this brainstorming list.

BRAINSTORMING LIST

1. **Beginning: Introduce the topic in your first sentence. Try to make the beginning as interesting as possible. Write your first sentence below:**

   _____

2. **Middle: List three or four details about your subject. You don't have to put these in sentences yet. Just jot down a short phrase for each.**

   (1) _____

   (2) _____

   (3) _____

3. **End: Write a concluding sentence here to sum up your ideas.**

   _____

© 2000 by The Center for Applied Research in Education

Name _____ Date _____

THE PARAGRAPH STORY
Writing a First Draft

A. You are going to write a paragraph about one thing you'd like to change about yourself. It will be easy to do if you keep handy the brainstorming list you prepared in Activity 75A. You just have to follow these three steps.

→ 1. Beginning: Copy the first sentence you prepared for the brainstorming list. (If you think of a better beginning, you can change it.)

→ 2. Middle: Follow the list you have already prepared. Put each detail into a complete sentence. You might need more than one sentence for some of these details. You should have at least three or four sentences in the middle.

→ 3. End: Copy the concluding sentence from your brainstorming list. You can change it if a better ending has occurred to you.

B. WRITE A PARAGRAPH: Follow the directions above, and write your complete paragraph on the lines below. This is just a first draft, so don't be concerned about spelling or grammar. Just try to get your thoughts down on paper. (Indent at the beginning of the paragraph.)

© 2000 by The Center for Applied Research in Education

Name _____ Date _____

THE PARAGRAPH STORY
Revising and Writing a Final Copy

A. Edit and revise the paragraph you wrote for Activity 75B, using the following guidelines:

1. Does the first sentence introduce the subject? Can you think of any way to make it more interesting?

2. Do you have *at least three or four* middle sentences giving details? Is there any interesting or important fact you would like to add?

3. Does the last sentence conclude the "story" of the paragraph?

4. Are your sentences complete? Do subjects and verbs agree?

5. Should any words or phrases be changed to make your writing clearer or more understandable to the reader?

6. Check your spelling with a dictionary.

B. Write a final copy of your paragraph on the lines below. Try to make it as perfect and as interesting as you can. (Indent at the beginning.)
   (If you wish, you can make up a title, and write it on the first line.)

_____

_____

_____

_____

_____

_____

_____

_____

_____

_____

_____

_____

© 2000 by The Center for Applied Research in Education

Name _____ Date _____

NO SWITCHING ALLOWED
Explanation and Exercises

A. RULE: Do not switch tenses in the middle of a paragraph unless there is a good reason for doing so.

> **WRONG:** Manny likes his science teacher. Mr. McLean is tall and thin, with a neat red beard. He explains lessons clearly. He *was* always calm and patient. Manny thinks that Mr. McLean is the best teacher in the school.

> → **RIGHT:** Manny likes his science teacher. Mr. McLean is tall and thin, with a neat red beard. He explains lessons clearly. He *is* always calm and patient. Manny thinks that Mr. McLean is the best teacher in the school.

B. Each paragraph below switches tenses in the middle. <u>Underline</u> the sentence where this incorrect switch occurs.

1. Last week, I flew in an airplane for the first time. My mom and I had to travel to Atlanta to visit her aunt. I was a little scared when the plane first took off. Once we were in the air, however, I am perfectly calm. It was a great trip.

2. I have a pen pal in England. His name is Jamie, and he lives in a city called Leeds. He is the same age as me. We wrote to each other about three times a year. It's fun to correspond with someone in another country.

3. My best friend is Rosa Gomez. She is very pretty. She has long, curly, black hair and big brown eyes. Rosa and I had a lot in common. We both love music and spend a lot of time listening to our cd's. We like to shop, too. I'm lucky to have a friend like Rosa.

*ANSWERS ON ACTIVITY SHEET 76B.

© 2000 by The Center for Applied Research in Education

Name _____ Date _____

NO SWITCHING ALLOWED
Explanation and Exercises

A. ANSWERS TO EXERCISE B ON ACTIVITY SHEET 76A:

You should have underlined the following sentences in each paragraph:

1. *Once we were in the air, however, I am perfectly calm.*
2. *We wrote to each other about three times a year.*
3. *Rosa and I had a lot in common.*

B. You may switch tenses in the middle of a paragraph if there is a good reason, as in this example:

> I like camp a lot this summer. The counselors are nice and the other kids are fun. Last year, I was not happy because I did not have any friends. This year, I have lots of friends. I guess that's why I like it so much now.

(**Note:** Even though the rest of the paragraph is in the present tense, the third sentence is in the past tense because it talks about a past event.)

C. Both paragraphs below switch tense in the middle.

In each paragraph, underline the sentence that switches tenses. Put a check next to the paragraph that switches tenses correctly.

1. We had an unexpected visitor last night. The doorbell rang at 9 o'clock. It was my Uncle Bill. We had not seen Uncle Bill in two years, but I recognized him right away. He hugged and kissed everybody. He was a welcome sight. I hope we see more of Uncle Bill from now on.

2. I like to go to my grandparent's house. They live in the next town, and we visit them once a week. Grandma always bakes oatmeal raisin cookies and lets me eat as many as I want. Grandpa never got tired of playing card games with me. I wish we could go there every day.

*SEE ANSWERS BELOW.

Answers to Exercise C: You should have checked Paragraph 1, which uses a change of tense correctly. The sentences where the tense is changed are

1. *I hope we see more of Uncle Bill from now on.*
2. *Grandpa never got tired of playing card games with me.*

© 2000 by The Center for Applied Research in Education

Name _____ Date _____

EITHER YOU OR I
Explanation and Exercises

A. RULE: When using pronouns, try to remain consistently in the same case.

Examples:

WRONG:

> The Runaway Dog is one of my favorite books. I usually like stories about animals, but this one is even better than most. You can really understand how this dog thinks and feels. When I came to the end, I was sorry it was over.

(In most of this paragraph, the pronoun "I" is used. In the third sentence, it suddenly becomes "You." This is incorrect. This sentence should be changed to, *"I can really understand how this dog thinks and feels."*)

WRONG:

> Lots of people come into my Dad's jewelry store. Sometimes they want to buy rings or watches. Some people bring things that need to be repaired. You can even come in just to browse.

(This paragraph refers to "people" or "they." "You" is inconsistent and should not be used in the last sentence. This sentence could be changed to, *"They can even come in just to browse."* or *"People can even come in just to browse."*)

B. In each of the following paragraphs, underline the sentence that changes the pronoun case. Then write that sentence correctly on the line below each paragraph.

1.
> I like to go on walks with my cousin, Alfredo. You have fun with Alfredo. He always notices unusual things along the way and points them out to me. I laugh a lot when I'm with Alfredo.

(Rewrite the incorrect sentence here.) _____

_____

2.
> People have fun at our after-school baseball games. You don't have to be an expert player to have a good time. All kids and parents are welcome to come and play or just watch.

(Rewrite the incorrect sentence here.) _____

_____

*ANSWERS ON ACTIVITY SHEET 77B.

© 2000 by The Center for Applied Research in Education

Name _____ Date _____

EITHER YOU OR I
Paragraph—First Draft

> **A. ANSWERS TO EXERCISE B ON ACTIVITY SHEET 77A:**
>
> 1. The incorrect sentence is, "You have fun with Alfredo." It should be changed to, "I have fun with Alfredo." or "Alfredo is fun."
>
> 2. The incorrect sentence is, "You don't have to be an expert player to have a good time." It should be changed to, "They don't have to be expert players to have a good time." or "It is not necessary to be an expert player to have a good time."

B. Choose one of the following subjects for a paragraph. (Check the one you have chosen.)

❑ 1. The Best Friend I Ever Had

❑ 2. Where I'd Like To Be Next Year

❑ 3. My Worst Enemy

❑ 4. Last Month's Worst Moment

C. Write a topic sentence for your paragraph below.

_____

_____

D. Next, write a first draft of the rest of your paragraph. This is just a first draft, so just concentrate on getting down your thoughts. (You should have *at least four* sentences in your paragraph in addition to the topic sentence.) Be sure that your use of pronouns is consistent.

_____

_____

_____

_____

_____

_____

_____

_____

© 2000 by The Center for Applied Research in Education

Name _____ Date _____

EITHER YOU OR I
Paragraph—Writing a Final Copy

A. Read the paragraph you wrote on Activity 77B and think about ways to make it better. Here are some things you can consider to improve it. (Do all your corrections—crossing out, adding words, and so on—right on the first draft.)

---

1. Did your first sentence (topic sentence) tell what the paragraph is about?

2. Can you make that first sentence more interesting so the reader will want to continue?

3. Does the body of the paragraph tell details about the topic? Is there any sentence that is not clear? If so, fix it.

4. Does the final sentence conclude the topic? Perhaps you need an additional sentence to accomplish this—if so, add it now.

5. Are your pronouns consistent throughout the paragraph? If there are any inconsistent pronouns, change them now.

6. Are your sentences all complete? Do subjects and verbs agree?

7. Have you checked the dictionary for the correct spelling of words you may be unsure of?

B. When your paragraph is as perfect as you can make it, write your final copy below.

_____

_____

_____

_____

_____

_____

_____

_____

_____

_____

_____

© 2000 by The Center for Applied Research in Education

Name _____ Date _____

CHOP! CHOP!
Explanation and Exercises

A. WHAT'S WRONG WITH SHORT SENTENCES?

Nothing is wrong with short sentences. They can be clear and snappy and easy to read. All short sentences in a paragraph, however, can make the paragraph seem awkward and choppy.

CHOPPY: Personal computers are good. Every kid should have his own. They are useful for homework. They are good for research. They have e-mail, too. There are many good computer games. Computers are useful. They are fun.

BETTER: Every kid should have his own personal computer. They are useful for homework and research. They have e-mail, too. There are many good computer games. Computers are useful and fun.

There is no variety in the first paragraph. *All* the sentences are short, which makes it choppy and boring. The second paragraph keeps some of these short sentences, but combines others. Now, there are some short sentences and also some long ones. It flows, with no choppiness.

B. The sentences in the following paragraph are too short and choppy. Rewrite the paragraph on the lines below. Combine and rearrange some of the sentences to make the paragraph flow better.

> I admire my Dad. He is the person I admire the most. He is so strong. He can open stuck windows. He can move heavy furniture. He is gentle, too. Our dog, Ruff, loves it when Dad gives him a bath. Dad is honest. He tells the truth. He always has time to help others. That's why I admire him.

_____

_____

_____

_____

_____

_____

_____

*ANSWER ON ACTIVITY SHEET 78B.

© 2000 by The Center for Applied Research in Education

Name _____ Date _____

CHOP! CHOP!
Additional Exercises

A. ANSWER TO EXERCISE B ON ACTIVITY SHEET 78A:

There are several ways you can combine and reword sentences to make this paragraph less choppy. Here is one suggestion:

My Dad is the person I admire the most. He is strong enough to open stuck windows and move heavy furniture. He is gentle, too. Our dog, Ruff, loves it when Dad gives him a bath. Dad is honest and tells the truth. He always has time to help others. That's why I admire him.

B. Here are two more paragraphs with short, choppy sentences. Rewrite each paragraph on the lines below. Combine and rearrange some of the sentences to make the paragraph flow better.

1. My grandparents are coming on Sunday. They will stay for three days. They will have my room. I'll sleep with my brother. I love it when my grandparents come. They always bring presents. They play games with us. They take us on trips, too. I can hardly wait to see them on Sunday!

_____
_____
_____
_____
_____

2. My favorite school subject is art. I am good in art. I like my teacher. His name is Mr. Anthony. He is a great artist. He draws pictures that look like the real thing. He gives good directions. I try to follow his directions. I want to become a good artist. I want to be as good as Mr. Anthony.

_____
_____
_____
_____
_____

*ANSWER ON ACTIVITY SHEET 78C.

© 2000 by The Center for Applied Research in Education

Name _____ Date _____

CHOP! CHOP!
Additional Exercises

A. ANSWER TO EXERCISE B ON ACTIVITY SHEET 78B:

There are several ways you can combine and reword sentences to make these paragraphs less choppy. Here is one suggestion.

1. My grandparents are coming on Sunday and will stay for three days. They will have my room, and I'll sleep with my brother. I love it when my grandparents come! They always bring presents and play games with us. They take us on trips, too. I can hardly wait to see them on Sunday.

2. My favorite school subject is art. I am good in art, and I like my teacher, Mr. Anthony. He is a great artist and draws pictures that look like the real thing. He gives good directions, which I try to follow. I want to become a good artist like Mr. Anthony.

B. Here is another choppy paragraph with too many short sentences. Rewrite the paragraph on the lines below. Combine and rearrange some of the sentences to make the paragraph flow better.

> I always notice people's eyes. My eyes are brown. They are like my Dad's. My sister, Jenna, has blue eyes. My mother has blue eyes, too. My friend, Tom, has brown eyes. Tom's eyes are darker than mine. My other friend, Jamie, has hazel eyes. They sometimes look green. Some people never notice eye color. I always do.

_____

_____

_____

_____

_____

*See Answer Below.

Answer to Exercise B: Here is one way of fixing that choppy paragraph. My eyes are brown like my Dad's. My sister, Jenna, and my mother have blue eyes. My friend, Tom, has brown eyes that are darker than mine. My other friend, Jamie, has hazel eyes. They sometimes look green. Some people never notice eye color, but I always do.

© 2000 by The Center for Applied Research in Education

Name _____ Date _____

DON'T STRETCH IT OUT
Explanation and Exercises

A. Long sentences are fine. However, if every sentence in a paragraph consists of lengthy, complex sentences, the writing can be unclear and dull, as in this example.

> **This is an example of a paragraph that contains only long sentences, with no short ones at all. As you can see, all these long sentences in a row makes the paragraph difficult to read as well as boring. A sentence that goes on and on for a long time with no variety in length can be difficult for the reader to follow and understand. In almost all cases, a paragraph will be improved by alternating long sentences with shorter ones.**

This paragraph sounds much better when short sentences are inserted, as follows:

> **As you can see, this is an example of a paragraph that contains a variety of sentence lengths. Some sentences, such as the beginning sentence and this one, are quite long. Others are short. This provides a pleasant contrast for the reader. Both long and short sentences are used. This kind of paragraph is easy to read.**

B. Here is another paragraph that contains too many long, stretched-out sentences. Rewrite the paragraph on the lines below. Break up some of the long sentences into short ones to achieve variety.

> Some people in my family don't understand why I sometimes like to be alone. My three brothers and my parents are different from me and always like to be part of a group. I like to be with people, too, but I don't want to be with them all the time. Sometimes I need to be alone because that is when I can read or listen to music in privacy, which helps me get in touch with my inner self. I wish my family could realize that I can love them and still want private time.

_____

_____

_____

_____

_____

_____

*Answer on Activity Sheet 79B.

© 2000 by The Center for Applied Research in Education

Name _____ Date _____

DON'T STRETCH IT OUT
Paragraph—First Draft

A. ANSWER TO EXERCISE B ON ACTIVITY SHEET 79A:

There are several ways you can change this paragraph to create variety in sentence length. Here is one suggestion.

Some people in my family don't understand why I sometimes like to be alone. My three brothers and my parents are different from me. They always like to be part of a group. I like to be with people, too, but I don't want to be with them all the time. Sometimes I need to be alone. That is when I can read or listen to music in privacy. That helps me get in touch with my inner self. I wish my family could realize that I can love them and still want private time.

B. You are going to write a paragraph where you can practice using a variety of sentence lengths. First, choose one of these topic sentences.

❏ 1. Everyone is surprised when I say that winter is my favorite time of the year.

❏ 2. My parents sometimes plan family activities that are lots of fun.

❏ 3. Last season, there was one game that I will never forget.

❏ 4. There are three times during the school day that I like best.

Check the topic sentence you have chosen. Then, copy it below and complete a first draft of your paragraph. Follow these directions.

1. Your paragraph should contain four to six sentences.
2. Use long and short sentences.
3. This is just a first draft, so concentrate on getting your thoughts down on paper and don't be concerned about spelling or grammar.
4. Write your paragraph below.

_____

_____

_____

_____

_____

_____

© 2000 by The Center for Applied Research in Education

Name _____ Date _____

DON'T STRETCH IT OUT
Paragraph—Revising and Writing a Final Copy

A. Edit and revise the paragraph you wrote on activity 79B, using the following guidelines:

1. Does your paragraph have enough variety in sentence length?
2. Do you need to add more short sentences?
3. Do you need more long sentences?
4. Do you develop the topic stated in the first sentence?
5. Can you make the paragraph more interesting and fun to read?
6. Do all your subjects and verbs agree?
7. Do you indent at the beginning of the paragraph?
8. Check spelling with dictionary, if necessary.

B. Write the final copy of your paragraph below.

_____

_____

_____

_____

_____

_____

_____

_____

_____

_____

_____

_____

_____

_____

_____

© 2000 by The Center for Applied Research in Education

Name _____ Date _____

SIMPLE OR COMPLEX?
Explanation and Exercises

A. A paragraph can be improved by using a variety of sentence structures.

B. Sentences can be described by the number and type of clauses they contain, as follows:

→ 1. A *Simple Sentence* has one independent clause.

   Example: I went to the circus with my uncle.

→ 2. A *Compound Sentence* contains more than one independent clause.

   Example: There was a lot of traffic along the way, but we arrived in time to see the opening act.

→ 3. A *Complex Sentence* has one independent clause and at least one dependent clause.

   Example: Although our seats were far back, we were able to enjoy all the exciting performances.

   (**Note:** An *Independent Clause* can stand alone as a sentence, like both clauses in Example 2.

   A *Dependent Clause* cannot stand alone as a sentence, like "Although our seats were far back" in Example 3.)

C. The sentences used as examples in B can be put together to make a paragraph that contains all three types of sentences, as follows:

I went to the circus with my uncle. There was a lot of traffic along the way, but we arrived in time to see the opening act. Although our seats were far back, we were able to enjoy all the exciting performances.

D. Here are four sentences that can be combined into a paragraph. Under each sentence, tell whether it is a *simple, compound,* or *complex* sentence.

1. I think that Thomas Jefferson was the greatest American leader of all time.

   (Simple, Compound, or Complex?) _____

2. He was the third president of the United States, and he also founded the University of Virginia.

   (Simple, Compound, or Complex?) _____

3. Even if he had done nothing else, he will always be remembered for writing the Declaration of Independence.

   (Simple, Compound, or Complex?) _____

4. Our country is lucky to have had leaders like Thomas Jefferson.

   (Simple, Compound, or Complex?) _____

*ANSWERS ON ACTIVITY SHEET 80B.

© 2000 by The Center for Applied Research in Education

Name _____ Date _____

SIMPLE OR COMPLEX?
Paragraph—First Draft

> **A. ANSWERS TO EXERCISE D ON ACTIVITY 80A:**
> 1. Simple   3. Complex
> 2. Compound   4. Simple

B. Can you write a paragraph that contains all three types of sentences: simple, compound, and complex? Choose one of the following topic sentences:

- ❏ 1. My career choice would be to work with computers.
- ❏ 2. Our team won an important game last week.
- ❏ 3. I have a new best friend.
- ❏ 4. My mom has an interesting job.
- ❏ 5. I saw a good movie.
- ❏ 6. Halloween is my favorite holiday.

C. Write the topic sentence you have chosen on the lines below. Then, complete a first draft of the paragraph, as follows:

1. Your paragraph should have *at least four* sentences.

2. There should be *at least one* simple sentence, *one* compound sentence, and *one complex* sentence. Remember

   • a simple sentence has one independent clause.
   • a compound sentence has more than one independent clause.
   • a complex sentence has one independent clause and at least one dependent clause.

3. This is just a first draft, so concentrate on getting your thoughts down on paper. You can correct the grammar and spelling later.

_____

_____

_____

_____

_____

_____

_____

_____

© 2000 by The Center for Applied Research in Education

Name _____ Date _____

SIMPLE OR COMPLEX?
Paragraph—Revising and Writing a Final Copy

A. Edit and revise the paragraph you wrote in Activity 80B, using the following guidelines:

1. Do you begin the paragraph with the topic sentence?

2. Does the rest of the paragraph develop this topic?

3. Do you include at least one of each of these types of sentences: simple, compound, and complex?

4. Does your final sentence sum up the topic?

5. Can you add or change anything to make the paragraph more interesting and fun to read?

6. Do your subjects and verbs agree?

7. Do you indent at the beginning of the paragraph?

8. Check spelling with the dictionary, if necessary.

B. When your paragraph is as perfect as you can make it, write a final copy below.

© 2000 by The Center for Applied Research in Education

Name _____ Date _____

ASKING QUESTIONS
Explanation and Exercises

A. Make your paragraphs more interesting and fun to read with different types of sentences.

→ 1. Most sentences are *declarative* sentences. They make a statement, such as

   I am going to the zoo today.

→ 2. Some sentences ask *questions*. These can be especially useful at the beginning of a paragraph, as in

   Can you guess where I am going today?

→ 3. Some sentences are *exclamations* or *commands*. These can grab the reader's attention, as in

   Go to the zoo today!

B. Rewrite the following paragraph on the lines below. Make it more interesting by changing some of the declarative sentences to questions or commands.

> I think that every kid should be given an allowance. It is important that young people learn how to manage cash. How much they get depends on several things. Age is one consideration since older kids usually need more money. Family income is important, too. Obviously, rich parents can afford to give bigger allowances. Parents should also look at how responsible their kid is with money, but every kid deserves an allowance, no matter how small.

_____

_____

_____

_____

_____

_____

_____

_____

© 2000 by The Center for Applied Research in Education

Name _____ Date _____

ASKING QUESTIONS
Paragraph—First Draft

A. Here is an example of a paragraph that is made more interesting and readable by using questions and exclamations. Notice how effective a question is at the beginning of a paragraph.

> What's the best way to lose a friend? Sad to say, I learned the answer to that question when my best friend, Kim, dumped me. Do you know the worst part of the whole thing? It was my own fault! I took our friendship too much for granted. I criticized her clothes and even broke appointments with her when something better came up. Now, Kim is gone. So, learn from my mistake. Be good to your friends!

B. Choose one of the following topics to write a paragraph:

- ❏ 1. My Favorite Sport
- ❏ 2. A Walk in the Snow
- ❏ 3. My Favorite TV Show
- ❏ 4. A Place I'd Like to Visit
- ❏ 5. A Description of My Room

C. Check the topic you have chosen. Then write a first draft of a paragraph, using the following guidelines:

1. Your paragraph should have *at least five* sentences.

2. Include one sentence that asks a question and one exclamation.

3. Your topic sentence should indicate the subject (even if that sentence is in the form of a question).

4. This is a first draft, so concentrate on getting your thoughts down on paper. You can correct grammar and spelling later.

_____

_____

_____

_____

_____

_____

© 2000 by The Center for Applied Research in Education

Name _____ Date _____

ASKING QUESTIONS
Paragraph—Revising and Writing a Final Copy

A. Edit and revise the paragraph you wrote in activity 81B, using the following guidelines:

1. Do you begin the paragraph with a topic sentence?
2. Does the rest of the paragraph develop this topic?
3. Does your final sentence sum up the topic?
4. Do you include one sentence that asks a question?
5. Do you include one sentence that is a command or exclamation?
6. Can you add or change anything to make the paragraph clearer or more interesting?
7. Do your subjects and verbs agree?
8. Do you indent at the beginning of the paragraph?
9. Check spelling with a dictionary, if necessary.

B. When your paragraph is as perfect as you can make it, write a final copy below. (If you wish, you can write a title on the first line.)

_____

_____

_____

_____

_____

_____

_____

_____

_____

_____

© 2000 by The Center for Applied Research in Education

Name _____ Date _____

MAKING A CONNECTION
Explanation and Exercises

A. DEFINING TRANSITIONAL WORDS: A paragraph must flow smoothly. The message must be clear to the reader. If the paragraph jumps from one idea or thought to another without any sort of connection, the reader can get confused and be turned off. Here is what a paragraph can look like if the thoughts are not connected properly.

> I admire and respect my Uncle Dave. He is an important man with an important job. He always has time to play with the kids. He is patient and has taught me how to do lots of things well. He is not perfect and has some faults. He is often late and sometimes doesn't even show up. I like Uncle Dave better than anyone else in my family.

Now, see how this paragraph can be improved by using some transitional (connecting) words and phrases (These are *underlined.*)

> I admire and respect my Uncle Dave. <u>Although</u> he is an important man with an important job, he always has time to play with the kids. He is patient and has taught me how to do lots of things well. <u>Of course</u>, he is not perfect and has some faults. <u>For example</u>, he is often late and sometimes doesn't even show up. <u>Nevertheless,</u> I like Uncle Dave better than anyone else in my family.

B. Here are some common transitional words and phrases.

> also, besides, in addition, in the first place, moreover, still, too, in the same way, likewise, naturally, of course, certainly, in fact, although, at the same time, even so, however, in spite of, instead, nevertheless, on the other hand, otherwise, regardless, but, after all, for example, for instance, that is, all in all, finally, in other words, on the whole, that is, therefore, after a while, as long as, at last, at that time, eventually, meanwhile, next, now, since, soon

C. Practice using transitional words. Write five sentences below. Use a transitional word or phrase in each sentence.

1. _____

2. _____

3. _____

4. _____

5. _____

© 2000 by The Center for Applied Research in Education

Name _____   Date _____

MAKING A CONNECTION
Explanation and Exercises

A. The thoughts and ideas in a paragraph can be awkward and unclear if they are not connected smoothly. Here is a paragraph that suffers from unconnected ideas.

> I always wished I could have a dog. My mother never wanted one. She changed her mind. The whole family visited the animal shelter. They had all kinds of dogs. I saw a large shepherd I liked. Mom said that a small dog would be better. It took a long time for everyone to agree on a choice. We picked a cute terrier pup and named him Scotty. I had the dog I always wanted.

Rewrite this paragraph on the lines below, using transitional words and phrases where necessary to make it clearer and smoother. (Refer to the list of transitional words on Activity Sheet 82A.)

_____

_____

_____

_____

_____

_____

*ANSWER ON ACTIVITY SHEET 82C.

B. Here is another paragraph that needs some transitional words to make it more clear. Rewrite the paragraph on the lines below, adding transition words where necessary.

> Have you ever seen my brother's room? His clothes are all over the bed and floor. He has a hamper. He doesn't seem to use it. His books and papers are scattered around. I don't see how he can find anything. He says that he knows where everything is. I couldn't live that way. What a mess!

_____

_____

_____

_____

_____

*ANSWER ON ACTIVITY SHEET 82C.

© 2000 by The Center for Applied Research in Education

Name _____ Date _____

MAKING A CONNECTION
Additional Exercises

A. Answers to Exercises B and C on Activity Sheet 82B: Here are some suggestions for improving these paragraphs using transitional words. (Added transitional words are underlined.)

A. I always wished I could have a dog, <u>but</u> my mother never wanted one. <u>Suddenly,</u> she changed her mind. The whole family visited the animal shelter <u>where</u> they had all kinds of dogs. I saw a large shepherd I liked. <u>However,</u> Mom said that a small dog would be better. It took a long time for everyone to agree on a choice. <u>Finally,</u> we picked a cute terrier pup and named him Scotty. <u>At last</u> I had the dog I always wanted.

B. Have you ever seen my brother's room? His clothes are all over the bed and floor. <u>Even though</u> he has a hamper, he doesn't seem to use it. His books and papers are scattered around <u>also.</u> I don't see how he can find anything, <u>although</u> he says that he knows where everything is. <u>Certainly</u> I couldn't live that way. What a mess!

B. Fill in the blank spaces in the following paragraphs with transitional words or phrases.

1. There are some things I wish I could change about my appearance. _____, I don't like the color of my hair. _____, I think it is too frizzy. _____ there are my eyes. They are too close together. _____, there is nothing I can do about that. _____, I am going to begin wearing more stylish clothes. Maybe I'll be able to make myself over.

2. I did four stupid things yesterday. _____, I stopped to play with Mrs. Murphy's cat and was late to school. _____ I left my science homework home. _____, I was caught chewing gum during English class. _____, I spilled coke all over my new jeans during lunch. _____ it was a bad day.

*SEE ANSWERS BELOW.

Possible Answers: 1. In the first place, Besides, Then, However, Soon
2. First of all, Also, Then, Later, All in all,

© 2000 by The Center for Applied Research in Education

Name _____ Date _____

KEEP YOUR EYE ON THE BALL!
Explanation and Exercises

A. CHANGING THE SUBJECT: Your topic sentence states the subject. If you suddenly change the subject, the paragraph becomes disjointed and confusing, as in this example.

Have you ever been in a haunted house? I was, last Halloween, when my friend, Chuck, dared me to go into the old, empty mansion on the corner of our block. I pretended that I wasn't afraid, even though my knees felt wobbly. I went right up the steps and opened the door while Chuck watched from the street. Chuck is always daring me. I shouldn't pay any attention, but I always take him up on it. I've made up my mind that I'm not going to listen to Chuck anymore.

This paragraph is fine, up to the point where it says, "I went right up the steps and opened the door while Chuck watched from the street." After that, the paragraph wanders off into a different topic—how to deal with Chuck's dares, while the reader is waiting to hear more about the haunted house. The writer should have stuck to the subject, like this (the underlined portion is the part that has been changed):

Have you ever been in a haunted house? I was, last Halloween, when my friend, Chuck, dared me to go into the old, empty mansion on the corner of our block. I pretended that I wasn't afraid, even though my knees felt wobbly. I went right up the steps and opened the door while Chuck watched from the street. I even went inside, but just for a minute. As soon as I saw the dark room with huge cobwebs hanging all around like ghosts, I ran back outside. Thanks to Chuck's dare, however, I can now say that I have been inside a haunted house.

B. The following paragraph changes subject in the middle. Cross out the sentences that do not relate to the topic. Then rewrite the complete paragraph on the lines below, sticking to the topic all the way.

What would a perfect teacher be like? I think a teacher should really like kids. That's the most important thing. Then, he (or she) should be kind and patient like Mr. Harding, my art teacher. I like art because I am good at it. It is my best subject. Art is my last class, and I look forward to it all day.

_____
_____
_____
_____

*SEE ACTIVITY SHEET 83B FOR ANSWERS.

© 2000 by The Center for Applied Research in Education

Name _____ Date _____

KEEP YOUR EYE ON THE BALL!
Additional Exercise

A. ANSWER TO EXERCISE B ON ACTIVITY SHEET 83A:

This paragraph goes wrong after the words "Mr. Harding, my art teacher." Everything after that is about art class, when the topic is what makes a perfect teacher. A corrected paragraph, that *sticks to the point,* might read as follows:

What would a perfect teacher be like? I think a teacher should really like kids. That's the most important thing. Then, he (or she) should be kind and patient like Mr. Harding, my art teacher. Of course, teachers should know a great deal about the subject they teach and be able to explain it clearly. Anyone who has all these qualities could be a perfect teacher.

B. Here is another paragraph that is confusing because it doesn't stay on one subject. Cross out the sentences that don't belong. Then, rewrite the paragraph below, completing it correctly.

The Fourth of July is an important holiday. It celebrates the birth of the United States of America. On July 4, 1776, the Continental Congress issued the Declaration of Independence, which declared independence from England. Thomas Jefferson, who wrote the Declaration, was from Virginia. His home was called Monticello, and he became the third president of the United States. George Washington was the first president.

_____

_____

_____

_____

_____

_____

*See Answer Below.

© 2000 by The Center for Applied Research in Education

Answer: The subject changes suddenly after the words, "declared independence from England." Everything after that should be crossed out because the topic changes from the Fourth of July to Thomas Jefferson. The paragraph could be ended as follows: "This Declaration, written by Thomas Jefferson, is as true today as it was in 1776, and that is why we celebrate its anniversary with parades and fireworks."

Name _____ Date _____

WHO CARES?
Explanation and Exercises

A. IRRELEVANT DETAILS: In a paragraph, the topic sentence tells what the paragraph is about. All the sentences that follow should develop this topic. Sometimes, writers give too many unnecessary details that shift the focus away from the subject, as in this example:

> Last month, I got the biggest surprise of my life. I won first prize in a districtwide poetry contest. Not every school district has a poetry contest, but ours does. The title of my poem was "The Seagull." I was inspired to write it last summer when my family spent a week at the beach. We go away for a week every summer. Sometimes we go to the beach, and sometimes we go traveling. I liked watching the birds flying gracefully overhead or swooping into the water to catch fish. I tried to show that in my poem. I'm glad that the judges liked it.

This poem is about winning a poetry contest, but it contains a few sentences that are not truly relevant to the topic. These sentences are

Not every school district has a poetry contest, but ours does.
We go away for a week every summer.
Sometimes we go to the beach, and sometimes we go traveling.

See how much more effective the paragraph is without these irrelevancies.

> Last month, I got the biggest surprise of my life. I won first prize in a districtwide poetry contest. The title of my poem was "The Seagull." I was inspired to write it last summer when my family spent a week at the beach. I liked watching the birds flying gracefully overhead or swooping into the water to catch fish. I tried to show that in my poem. I'm glad that the judges liked it.

B. In the following paragraph, cross out any sentences that are not relevant.

> My career goal is to become a computer technician. Ever since I first had access to computers in first grade, I've enjoyed working with them. Some schools even have computers in kindergarten, but not ours. All my teachers say that I have a natural ability with computers. I usually know how to fix them when there are problems. We have Apple computers in our school, but we have an IBM at home, and I've used Compaq at my friends' houses. My Dad says that I think like a computer. I believe I could have a great career with computers.

SEE ANSWER BELOW.

Answer to Exercise B: You should have crossed out the following sentences, which are not relevant:
Some schools even have computers in kindergarten, but not ours.
We have Apple computers in our school, but we have an IBM at home, and I've used Compaq at my friends' houses.

© 2000 by The Center for Applied Research in Education

Name _____ Date _____

WHO CARES?
Explanation and Exercises

A. Don't crowd your paragraphs with details that are away from the topic, as in this example.

> I don't think that our school should have a dress code. Kids have the right to wear what they want. We shouldn't have to put on uniforms as if we were in the Army. My brother was in the Army, and he had to wear a uniform. Our clothes show that we are individuals. My friend, Marcie, and I buy all our clothes at the Gap. They have really neat styles there. I wouldn't be happy at a school where everyone dressed alike.

The following sentences don't belong because they take the reader's attention away from the main topic:

My brother was in the Army, and he had to wear a uniform.
My friend, Marcie, and I buy all our clothes at the Gap.
They have really neat styles there.

Now, see how much clearer the paragraph is when these irrelevancies are removed.

> I don't think that our school should have a dress code. Kids have the right to wear what they want. We shouldn't have to put on uniforms as if we were in the Army. Our clothes show that we are individuals. I wouldn't be happy at a school where everyone dressed alike.

B. Cross out the irrelevant sentences in the following paragraph. Then write the paragraph correctly on the lines below.

> No one gave our team a chance to win the game. The Pirates had already won five with zero losses. Our team, the Sharks, had not won a single game this season. We did pretty well last year, but some of the best players were no longer on the team. Mark moved to Idaho, and Armando didn't sign up again. Everyone was surprised when the game was tied at the end of the eighth inning. Imagine their astonishment when we scored a winning run in the ninth!

_____

_____

_____

_____

_____

*See Activity Sheet 84C for Answers.

© 2000 by The Center for Applied Research in Education

Name _____ Date _____

WHO CARES?
Paragraph—First Draft

A. ANSWER TO EXERCISE B ON ACTIVITY SHEET 84B:

You should have removed the following sentences:
We did pretty well last year, but some of the best players were no longer on the team. Mark moved to Idaho, and Armando didn't sign up again.

B. WRITING A PARAGRAPH—FIRST DRAFT

1. Choose one of the following topics for a paragraph, and check the one you have chosen.

   ❑ a.　　The Best Kind of Pet

   ❑ b.　　My Favorite TV show

   ❑ c.　　My Sports Idol

   ❑ d.　　Things I'd Like to Change about Myself

   ❑ e.　　Things I'd Like to Change about My Parents

On the lines below, write a paragraph about the topic you have chosen. This is a first draft, so just concentrate on getting your thoughts down on paper. You'll be able to fix up the grammar, spelling, etc., later.

Write the title on the first line. (Indent at the beginning of the paragraph.)

_____

_____

_____

_____

_____

_____

_____

_____

_____

_____

© 2000 by The Center for Applied Research in Education

Name _____ Date _____

WHO CARES?
Paragraph—Revising and Writing a Final Copy

A. Revise and edit the paragraph you wrote for activity sheet 84C, using the following guidelines:

> 1. Does your first sentence state the topic clearly?
> 2. Do the sentences that follow develop the topic?
> 3. Are there any irrelevant details that are not useful in developing this topic? Cross them out!
> 4. Do you stick to the subject throughout the paragraph? Cross out anything that changes the topic.
> 5. Does the last sentence conclude or sum up the topic?
> 6. Are your sentences complete? Do subjects and verbs agree?
> 7. Check spelling with a dictionary.

B. When your paragraph is as perfect as you can make it, write your final copy below. Write the title on the first line. (Indent at the beginning of the paragraph.)

_____

_____

_____

_____

_____

_____

_____

_____

_____

_____

_____

© 2000 by The Center for Applied Research in Education

Section Seven

ESSAY WRITING HELP

TEACHER'S GUIDE—
ALPHABETICAL LIST OF ESSAY WRITING PROBLEMS
AND ACTIVITY NUMBERS

Here is a list of the essay writing problems addressed in this section and the relevant activities.

Essay Writing	Activity Number
Concluding Paragraph	94A, B, C
Confusion: Getting Lost	95B
Confusion: Irrelevancies	95A
Developing the Topic	93A, B
Excessive Verbiage	96A, B
Introductory Paragraph	90A, B, C
Introductory Paragraph: Cautions	92
Introductory Paragraph: Topic Statement	91A, B
Organizing a Three-Paragraph Essay	85A, B, C, D
Prewriting Activities: Brainstorming	86A, B, C, D
Prewriting Activities: Clustering	87A, B, C, D
Prewriting Activities: Outlining	88A, B
Prewriting Activities: Writer's Block	89A, B

Name _____ Date _____

AS EASY AS 1, 2, 3
Explanation and Exercises

Do you know how to write a paragraph? If your answer is *yes*, then it will be easy for you to write an essay.

An essay is organized like a paragraph, with a beginning, middle, and conclusion. An essay is made up of paragraphs and is, therefore, longer. Anyone who can write a paragraph can put together a simple, three-paragraph essay.

It's as easy as 1, 2, 3.

→ 1. The beginning (introduction).

In a paragraph, this is the first sentence, such as

"My career goal is to be an archaeologist."

In an essay, this is expanded into a paragraph, as

People always ask me what I want to be when I grow up. I'm still only twelve, so I'm not sure. If I had to make up my mind right now, I'd choose archaeology.

Exercise 1: Write a beginning paragraph like the one above for an essay on your career goal.

_____

_____

_____

→ 2. The middle paragraph develops the subject that was introduced in the first paragraph with description, detail, or list of reasons, as

The thing I like best about archaeology is that I can spend a lot of time outdoors and not have to be cooped up at a desk all day. I also like the idea of traveling to far-off places. Wouldn't it be fun to dig up something important?

Exercise 2: Write a middle paragraph like the one above for an essay on your career goal.

_____

_____

_____

→ 3. The final paragraph concludes and sums up the topic, as

My ambitions may change, and I could eventually decide upon a different path. Right now, however, archaeology sounds fine to me as a career goal.

Exercise 3: Write a final paragraph like the one above to conclude and sum up your career goal.

_____

_____

_____

© 2000 by The Center for Applied Research in Education

Name _____ Date _____

AS EASY AS 1, 2, 3
Prewriting Exercises

It will be as easy as 1, 2, 3 to write a three-paragraph essay if you organize your ideas by following the steps on this brainstorming list.

BRAINSTORMING LIST

First decide upon a topic for your essay. Choose one of these topics. Put a check in the box next to the topic you have chosen.

- ❏ 1. The Best Day of My Life
- ❏ 2. The Worst Day of My Life
- ❏ 3. My Favorite Sport
- ❏ 4. Music I Like
- ❏ 5. My Favorite TV Show

→ 1. Write a beginning paragraph to introduce the topic. Try to make this introduction interesting and exciting to the reader. There should be two to four sentences in this paragraph.

_____

_____

_____

_____

→ 2. The middle paragraph will develop the topic. For "The Best Day of My Life," this could be a description of events. For "My Favorite Sport" it might be a list of reasons for your opinion. It is not necessary to write this paragraph now. Just make a list of the details you will use to develop the topic. Write your list on the lines below—include three or four details. You don't need complete sentences—just words or phrases.

_____

_____

_____

_____

→ 3. The final paragraph will conclude and sum up the topic in two or three sentences. Write a final paragraph below.

_____

_____

_____

© 2000 by The Center for Applied Research in Education

Name _____ Date _____

AS EASY AS 1, 2, 3
Paragraph—First Draft

Follow these easy steps and write a first draft of your essay.

---

1. *Reference:* Keep the brainstorming list you prepared in Activity 85B at hand.
2. *Title:* Copy the title on the title line below.
3. *Beginning:* Copy the beginning paragraph from your brainstorming list. Make changes wherever you think it can be improved.
4. *Middle:* Use the list you prepared to write and develop a middle paragraph.
5. *Conclusion:* Copy the final paragraph from your brainstorming list. Change it wherever you think it can be improved.

Note: This is just a first draft, so don't be too concerned about spelling or grammar. Just concentrate on getting your thoughts down on the paper. Be sure to indent at the beginning of each paragraph. Use the back of this paper if you need more room.

_____

_____

_____

_____

_____

_____

_____

_____

_____

_____

_____

_____

© 2000 by The Center for Applied Research in Education

Name _____ Date _____

AS EASY AS 1, 2, 3
Revising and Writing a Final Copy

A. Edit and revise your first draft, using the following guidelines:

> 1. Does your first paragraph introduce the subject? Can you make your introduction more interesting? Sometimes, beginning with a question or a surprising statement will catch the reader's attention.
> 2. Does the second paragraph develop the topic? Do you provide three or four detailed descriptions or statements to support the subject?
> 3. Does the final paragraph conclude and sum up the topic?
> 4. Are your sentences complete? Do subjects and verbs agree?
> 5. Check spelling with a dictionary.

B. When your essay is as good as you can make it, write the final copy below. Write the title on the first line. (Indent at the beginning of each paragraph. Use the back of this paper if you need more room.)

_____

_____

_____

_____

_____

_____

_____

_____

_____

_____

_____

_____

_____

© 2000 by The Center for Applied Research in Education

Name _____ Date _____

© 2000 by The Center for Applied Research in Education

FIRST, GET READY!
Research and Brainstorming Lists

A. RESEARCH—EXPLANATION: Do you know everything about every subject? Of course not! No one does. Sometimes you need to find out facts for an essay. This is called **research!**

B. EXAMPLE:

1. If you were writing an essay about the music of the 1940s, you would have to do research. Here are some places you could find the information you need.

   your school library   public library   Internet

2. Then you could write down all the information you find and organize it into a brainstorming list, as in this example.

BRAINSTORMING LIST FOR "MUSIC OF THE 40s"

*Types of Music—*swing, jazz, blues, ballads

*Some Popular Bands—*Glenn Miller, Tommy Dorsey, Jimmy Dorsey, Artie Shaw, Benny Goodman, Louis Armstrong, Louis Prima

*Some Popular Singers—*Frank Sinatra, Helen O'Connell, Tony Bennett, Vic Damone, Judy Garland, Nat "King" Cole, Dinah Shore, Bing Crosby

Some Hit Song—"I'll Be Seeing You," "White Christmas," "Serenade in Blue," "Chattanooga Choo Choo," "To Each His Own," "Nature Boy," "Little Brown Jug"

C. RESEARCH ACTIVITY

1. Choose one of the following essay topics and check the one you have chosen:

   ❑ a.   Popular Breeds of Dogs
   ❑ b.   Most Important Inventions of the 20th Century
   ❑ c.   The Boston Tea Party
   ❑ d.   Birds of the Seashore
   ❑ e.   Native American Tribes

2. Research your topic, using the library or the Internet.

3. Prepare a brainstorming list like the one above. Write it in the space below. (Use the back of this paper if you need more room.)

Name _____ Date _____

FIRST, GET READY!
Research and Brainstorming Lists

Use the brainstorming list you prepared in Activity 86A to write a three-paragraph essay, as follows:

→ 1. Your first paragraph should introduce the topic in an interesting way. Write your first paragraph (*two or three sentences*) below.

_____

_____

_____

_____

_____

→ 2. Your second paragraph should develop the topic with details from your brainstorming list. You don't have to include all the information you found in your research, just what you need to develop the topic fully. Write your second paragraph (*three to six sentences*) below.

_____

_____

_____

_____

_____

_____

_____

→ 3. Your final paragraph should restate and conclude the topic. Write your final paragraph (*two to four sentences*) below.

_____

_____

_____

_____

_____

© 2000 by The Center for Applied Research in Education

Name _____ Date _____

FIRST, GET READY!
Writing a Final Copy

A. Edit and revise the essay you wrote for Activity 86B, using the following questions as guidelines:

> 1. Does the first paragraph introduce the topic in an interesting way?
>
> 2. Does the second paragraph develop the topic? Do you include all the important information you discovered in your research?
>
> 3. Does the last paragraph restate and sum up the topic?
>
> 4. Are all your sentences complete? Do subjects and verbs agree?
>
> 5. Check spelling with a dictionary.

B. When your essay is as perfect as you can make it, write a final copy below. (Indent at the beginning of each paragraph.)

_____

_____

_____

_____

_____

_____

_____

_____

_____

_____

_____

_____

_____

_____

_____

© 2000 by The Center for Applied Research in Education

Name _____   Date _____

FIRST, GET READY!
Preparing Brainstorming Lists

A. It is *never* too hard to write an essay if you are prepared before you begin. Once you know what information to include and how to organize it, the actual writing is a *snap!* This activity will give you experience preparing brainstorming lists. Then, you will be well on the road to becoming an expert essay-writer.

B. Prepare a brainstorming list for an essay called "Choosing Your First Car," as follows:

1. Think of the essay as being divided into three parts.

2. *Part One* will discuss who buys a first car and why. In the box below, write words and phrases that describe people who are buying a first car.

| |
| |

3. *Part Two* will describe some of the cars that are available. In the first column below, list these cars. In the second column, next to each listing, write words and phrases describing this car.

| CAR | DESCRIPTION |
| | |

4. *Part Three* will recommend some good choices. In the first column list the cars you recommend. In the second column, next to each choice, write a phrase telling why it is recommended.

| RECOMMENDED CAR | REASONS |
| | |

5. With this brainstorming list, you would have no trouble writing the essay!

C. On a separate paper, prepare a brainstorming list for each of the following essays:

The People Who Live on My Street
The Best Shows on TV
A Day at the Mall

© 2000 by The Center for Applied Research in Education

Name _____ Date _____

PULLING OUT IDEAS
Explanation and Activities

A. WHAT IS CLUSTERING?

Clustering is one way to jot down and organize ideas. It is easy and fun to do.

B. DIRECTIONS AND EXAMPLE

1. Draw a large circle on a piece of paper. Using big lettering, write down the subject of the essay in the middle of the circle.

2. Using somewhat smaller print, write the main points about this subject that come into your mind. Write these near the subject in different parts of the circle.

3. Near each of these main points, write words and phrases that describe them. Use even smaller lettering for these.

4. Here is an example of clustering for an essay called "The People on My Block."

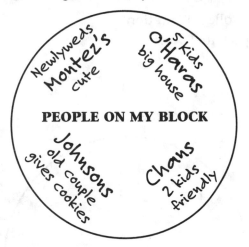

C. In the circle below, prepare a cluster for an essay called "My Social Studies Class." Use different-sized lettering for the subject, the main points, and descriptions, or you can use different colored pens for each.

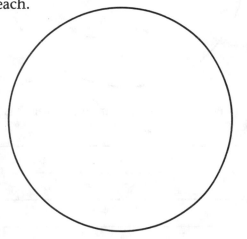

© 2000 by The Center for Applied Research in Education

Name _____ Date _____

PULLING OUT IDEAS
Clustering Activities

A. Setting down thoughts and arranging them in clusters makes essay-writing easy. Here are some useful hints for clustering.

→ 1. Don't be afraid to put down ideas as they occur to you. You don't have to use all the thoughts from your cluster in the essay. Just pick out the best ones. The bigger your cluster, the more you will have from which to choose.

→ 2. Remember to set the subject in the center of the circle. Write the main points around the subject as they come into your mind. Then, put down as many descriptive words as you can think of that relate to each main point.

→ 3. Use different-sized lettering (or different colored pens) for subject, main points, and descriptive words.

B. Choose one of the following essay topics, and check the one you have chosen:

❏ 1. The Importance of a College Education
❏ 2. The Most Exciting Spectator Sports
❏ 3. My Favorite Foods
❏ 4. Me, in the Year 2010

C. In the circle below, write a cluster for the topic you have chosen.

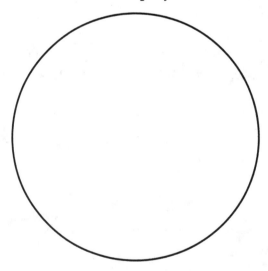

D. Using ideas from your cluster, write a topic paragraph for this essay.

_____

_____

_____

_____

© 2000 by The Center for Applied Research in Education

Name _____ Date _____

PULLING OUT IDEAS
Clustering—First Draft

A. Use the cluster you prepared in Activity 87B to write the first draft of an essay on the topic you have chosen.

---

1. Begin with the topic paragraph you wrote for Activity 87B

2. The body of the essay will contain two to four paragraphs. Write a paragraph for *each* main point in the cluster. You don't have to use all of them. Choose the ones that are most useful for your essay.

3. Include the details and descriptive words about each main point from your cluster.

4. Your final paragraph should state a conclusion to the essay.

B. Follow the directions above to write the first draft of a four- to six-paragraph essay on the topic you have chosen. This is just a first draft, so don't be concerned with spelling or grammar—just concentrate on getting your essay written. Indent at the beginning of each paragraph. (Use the back of this paper if you need more room.)

_____

_____

_____

_____

_____

_____

_____

_____

_____

_____

_____

_____

_____

_____

© 2000 by The Center for Applied Research in Education

Name _____ Date _____

PULLING OUT IDEAS
Clustering—Revising and Writing a Final Copy

A. Edit and revise the first draft of the essay you wrote for Activity 87C, using the following guidelines:

1. Does your first paragraph introduce the topic? Can you make this introduction more interesting so the reader will want to continue?

2. Does each paragraph in the body of the essay develop one of the main points? Are there unnecessary words that should be cut to make your thoughts clearer?

3. Does the final paragraph conclude the essay?

4. Are your sentences complete? Do subjects and verbs agree?

5. Check spelling with a dictionary.

B. Write the final copy of your essay below. Write the title on the first line. (Indent at the beginning of each paragraph. Use the back of this paper if you need more room.)

_____

_____

_____

_____

_____

_____

_____

_____

_____

_____

_____

_____

_____

_____

© 2000 by The Center for Applied Research in Education

Name _____ Date _____

MAKING A SKELETON
Writing an Outline—Explanation and Exercise

A. An *outline* is like a skeleton. It is the bare bones of an essay. After you make an outline, it is easy just to add the flesh that is needed for a complete essay.

Not everyone *needs* an outline in order to write an essay, but it can be a helpful step between brainstorming or clustering and the final product.

B. An outline can be long and detailed, or short and simple as is this example:

© 2000 by The Center for Applied Research in Education

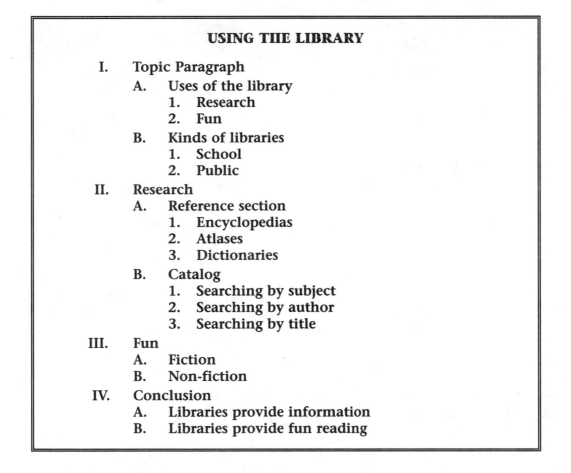

USING THE LIBRARY

I.   Topic Paragraph
   A.   Uses of the library
      1.   Research
      2.   Fun
   B.   Kinds of libraries
      1.   School
      2.   Public

II.   Research
   A.   Reference section
      1.   Encyclopedias
      2.   Atlases
      3.   Dictionaries
   B.   Catalog
      1.   Searching by subject
      2.   Searching by author
      3.   Searching by title

III.   Fun
   A.   Fiction
   B.   Non-fiction

IV.   Conclusion
   A.   Libraries provide information
   B.   Libraries provide fun reading

C. Follow the form above to write an outline for an essay on one of the following topics. Check the topic you have chosen.

❑ 1. Most Popular Pets

❑ 2. Cooking and Serving a Meal

❑ 3. The History of Baseball

❑ 4. Forms of Transportation

(Write your outline on the back of this activity sheet or on a separate paper.)

Name _____ Date _____

MAKING A SKELETON
Writing Outlines

Follow the guide on Activity 88A to write an outline for each of the following essays:

A. **"CAPITAL CITIES OF THE WORLD"**

B. **"AFTER-SCHOOL ACTIVITIES"**

C. **"COMPUTER PROGRAMS FOR KIDS"**

© 2000 by The Center for Applied Research in Education

Name _____ Date _____

BREAKING THE BLOCK
Freewriting—Explanation and Activities

A. EXPLANATION: Does your mind turn to mush when you are faced with a writing assignment? When you sit down to write an essay, does your brain feel like a big balloon filled with nothing but hot air?

This is called *writer's block.* It even happens to professional writers. Fortunately, there are ways to break that block! One of the most effective methods is called freewriting.

B. Freewriting is easy when you follow these five simple steps:

→ 1. Put aside the project on which you are working, and stop thinking about it!

→ 2. Find a writing position and tools that are most comfortable for you—sitting at the computer, curled up in a big chair with pen and notebook, even sprawled on the floor with colored pencils and scraps of paper.

→ 3. Begin to write anything that comes into your head—anything at all!—words, phrases, names. If you have trouble getting started, just write "I can't think of anything," then look around the room and write down whatever you see. Or describe the thoughts that come into your head, no matter how weird.

→ 4. Once you begin to write, keep on writing without stopping for *at least five minutes,* even if you have to write the same words over and over again.

→ 5. Now, that your pen (or computer) has been "warmed up," begin thinking about your writing project. Start by writing one word or phrase that has anything at all to do with the project. Then, keep writing for another *five* minutes. Don't stop even if the words and phrases you write don't seem to be connected to the topic.

C. Use the box below for your freewriting activity. Ask your teacher to time you or do it yourself. Then fill up the box with freewriting.

© 2000 by The Center for Applied Research in Education

Name _____   Date _____

BREAKING THE BLOCK
Explanation and Exercises

A. EXPLANATION: A writer's block can be as heavy and solid as a concrete block. It can hold you back from using the writing skill you already possess. Here are some exercises you can do to break that block!

B. Fill up the lines below with words that begin with the letter (or letters) at the beginning of the line.

r _____

e _____

th _____

st _____

b _____

gr _____

C. Fill up the lines below with words that end with the letter (or letters) at the beginning of the line.

n _____

r _____

er _____

ck _____

te _____

eat _____

D. Write as many words as you can think of to describe each of the following:

a car _____

a cat _____

a pizza _____

a tv show _____

a park _____

a circus _____

© 2000 by The Center for Applied Research in Education

Name _____ Date _____

HOOK THAT READER!
Explanation and Exercises

A. DEFINITION: The *introductory paragraph* of an essay is the first paragraph. It should do two things:

1. state the topic
2. get the reader's interest

Stating the topic is easy, but how can you do it in a way that will grab the reader's interest? Here are some suggestions.

→ 1. Begin with a question.

Example: Do you know what to do if there is an emergency in your home? Here are some steps you can take to handle this situation.

→ 2. Begin with a surprising or shocking statement.

Example: Yes, you can save a life! If there is an emergency in your home, here are the steps you should take to handle the situation.

→ 3. Begin with an anecdote (short story).

Example: My neighbor, Mrs. Ellison, almost died last week. Thanks to the quick-thinking of her eight-year-old son, however, Mrs. Ellison is alive and well today. You, too, could save a life if you follow these steps in a home emergency.

→ 4. Use the name of a famous person.

Example: Mara Greentree, the tv star, had an accident in her home recently. Fortunately, her brother was with her and knew exactly what to do. Here are the steps that everyone should know when there is a home emergency.

B. 1. On a separate paper, write an introductory paragraph for an essay called *"My Hero."* Get the reader's interest by beginning with a question. (Be sure to state the topic in this paragraph, too.)

2. Write another introductory paragraph for this essay. This time, begin with a surprising or shocking statement.

3. Write another introductory paragraph for this essay. Begin with an anecdote.

4. Write another introductory paragraph for this essay. Get the reader's interest by using the name of a famous person.

© 2000 by The Center for Applied Research in Education

Name _____ Date _____

HOOK THAT READER!
Explanation and Exercises

A. An introductory paragraph must grab the reader's interest as well as state the topic of the essay. Some ways of doing this are

→ 1. begin with a question
→ 2. begin with a surprising or shocking statement
→ 3. begin with an anecdote
→ 4. use the name of a famous person

B. Using each of these techniques, write four introductory paragraphs for an essay called, "A Typical Day at School."

1. (question) _____

_____

_____

_____

_____

2. (surprising statement) _____

_____

_____

_____

_____

3. (anecdote) _____

_____

_____

_____

_____

4. (famous person) _____

_____

_____

_____

_____

© 2000 by The Center for Applied Research in Education

Name _____   Date _____

HOOK THAT READER!
Explanation and Exercises

A. An introductory paragraph must grab the reader's interest as well as state the topic of the essay. Some ways of doing this are

→ 1. begin with a question
→ 2. begin with a surprising or shocking statement
→ 3. begin with an anecdote
→ 4. use the name of a famous person

B. Using each of these techniques, write four introductory paragraphs for an essay called, "A Day to Remember."

1. (question) _____

_____

_____

_____

_____

2. (surprising statement) _____

_____

_____

_____

_____

3. (anecdote) _____

_____

_____

_____

_____

4. (famous person) _____

_____

_____

_____

_____

© 2000 by The Center for Applied Research in Education

Name _____ Date _____

BE SPECIFIC!
Explanation and Exercises

> **A.** DEFINITION: A *topic statement* tells the reader what the essay is going to be about. It usually consists of one or two sentences in the introductory paragraph.

The topic statement is a guide for both the reader and the writer. It tells the reader what to expect. It gives the writer a framework for the essay—guiding the writer as to what to include and what to leave out.

B. EXAMPLES

1. A topic statement that says "Middle schools have been popular for a long time" indicates that the essay is about the history of middle schools. If, however, the topic statement is "The Northport Middle School offers many advantages for its student" the essay would be about the advantages of one particular middle school.

2. Here is another topic statement. *"The history of baseball proves it to be a truly American sport."* This essay is about the history of baseball. It might discuss when and how baseball began, how it developed, various teams and players, etc.

   A *different* topic statement on a similar subject might be *"There have been many great players in the history of baseball."* This introduces an essay that discusses baseball players only.

C. Write an introductory paragraph for an essay on each of the following topics. Introduce the topic in a way that will grab the reader's interest and also state clearly what the essay is about.

1. "My Favorite Authors"

   _____

   _____

   _____

   _____

2. "The Best Holidays of the Year"

   _____

   _____

   _____

   _____

© 2000 by The Center for Applied Research in Education

Name _____ Date _____

BE SPECIFIC!
Explanation and Exercises

A. The topic statement tells what the essay is about. It is like a frame. Anything that is not part of the picture must be left out. Be sure that the topic statement is true for *everything* you want to include in the essay.

B. Write an introductory paragraph for each of the following essays. Try to grab the reader's interest and include a topic statement that tells the specific subject of the essay.

1. "Modern Heroes, Real and Fictional"

_____

_____

_____

_____

_____

2. "Boys and Girls Are Equal in Every Way"

_____

_____

_____

_____

_____

3. "The Greatest U.S. Presidents"

_____

_____

_____

_____

_____

© 2000 by The Center for Applied Research in Education

Name _____ Date _____

HOW *NOT* TO INTRODUCE A TOPIC
Poor Introductions

Some techniques should *never* be used in introductory paragraphs.

→ **A. APOLOGIES OR PUTDOWNS:** Don't ever apologize or put yourself down, as in this example of a poor introductory paragraph.

> I'm not an expert on restaurants. My opinion may not mean much, but I like to eat in places where the service is fast and the food is tasty.

> *Two* phrases in the above paragraph are wrong: *I'm not an expert* and *My opinion may not mean much.* This announces to the reader that you don't know much about the subject, so why would they want to read this essay?

B. Write an introductory paragraph for an essay about restaurants. State the subject without apologizing or putting yourself down.

_____

_____

_____

_____

_____

→ **C. ANNOUNCEMENTS:** Never announce what you are going to do in the introductory paragraph. Here is an example of a poor introduction.

> In this essay, I am going to show that our school cafeteria needs improvement. We need more chairs, nicer people serving, and better food.

> The beginning of the first sentence, "*In this essay, I am going to show,* should be removed. You are supposed to write the essay, not talk about how you are going to do it.

D. Write an introductory paragraph for an essay about your school cafeteria. Do not put yourself down or announce what you are going to do.

_____

_____

_____

_____

_____

© 2000 by The Center for Applied Research in Education

Name _____ Date _____

PROVE YOUR POINT!
Explanation and Exercises

A. The body of the essay shows or proves what you have stated in the introductory paragraph. One way to do this is to give examples that prove your point. When writing the essay, you must make three decisions:

→ 1. *Number of examples to use*

Never use less than two examples.

→ 2. *Order in which examples appear in the essay*

Examples are usually given in order of importance, with the *most* important or strongest point first and the *least* important last. Sometimes, however, it can be effective to build up to your best shot, by saving the best example for last.

→ 3. *Number of paragraphs in the body of the essay: three-paragraph essay*

If you are writing a three-paragraph essay, the whole essay must be developed in the middle paragraph. All your examples will be included in this paragraph.

If you are writing a *five-paragraph essay,* you will have three paragraphs in which to develop the subject. You can have three examples—one for each paragraph of the body.

B. Write a paragraph for the body of a three-paragraph essay that begins as follows:

> Are you satisfied with the school cafeteria? Most students believe that the cafeteria could be improved. There are several steps that could be taken to make our lunch hour better.

(Write a paragraph below for the body of this essay. Give three examples to prove the point.)

_____

_____

_____

_____

_____

_____

_____

© 2000 by The Center for Applied Research in Education

Name _____ Date _____

PROVE YOUR POINT!
Explanation and Exercises

A. Sometimes, it can be effective to state the least important example in your essay first, and the most important last. That way, the *strongest* example will remain in the mind of the reader.

B. Here is the introductory paragraph of a five-paragraph essay. Decide on three examples for the body of the essay. Then, add three paragraphs, discuss one example in each paragraph. Save the most important example for the last paragraph. You could begin that paragraph with a transitional phrase that shows its importance, such as *"Most important of all."*

> Are you satisfied with the school cafeteria? Most students believe that the cafeteria could be improved. There are several steps that could be taken to make our lunch hour better.

Write three paragraphs for the body of this essay—one paragraph for each example. (Indent at the beginning of each paragraph.) Use the back of this paper if you need more room.

_____

_____

_____

_____

_____

_____

_____

_____

_____

_____

_____

_____

_____

© 2000 by The Center for Applied Research in Education

Name _____ Date _____

EFFECTIVE ENDINGS!
Explanation and Exercises

A. The concluding paragraph should

→ 1. Restate the topic in the introductory paragraph.
→ 2. Summarize the points in the body of the essay.
→ 3. Bring the essay to an end.

Example:

Our school has a good cafeteria, but it could be even better. Sturdier chairs, a friendlier serving staff, and food that is more appealing to kids would make a big difference. Every student in the school would be happy to see this happen.

B. Write a concluding paragraph for the following three-paragraph essay.

Do you feel proud when you see our country's flag? Francis Scott Key was so moved by the sight of Old Glory still flying after a terrible battle that he wrote "The Star Spangled Banner." The Stars and Stripes is important to me, too.

The flag is a symbol of our country. It expresses the hopes and ideals of the people who founded the United States of America in 1776. When we salute the flag, we are saluting our democracy and those who fought and even died to preserve it. It represents the liberty and freedom that we are guaranteed by the Constitution.

Write your concluding paragraph below.

_____

_____

_____

_____

_____

© 2000 by The Center for Applied Research in Education

Name _____ Date _____

EFFECTIVE ENDINGS!
Explanation and Exercises

A. The concluding paragraph of an essay should restate the topic, summarize the points in the body of the essay, and bring it to an end.

The concluding paragraph should *not*

1. include new information that has not been mentioned earlier.
2. mention something that has nothing to do with the topic.
3. leave the reader unsure whether or not the essay is concluded.

B. EXAMPLE: The following concluding paragraph would be incorrect for the essay about the flag that appears on Activity 94A;

> We can't all be composers and write national anthems. Other songs, such as "America the Beautiful," have also been written about the United States. Everyone knows the words to "America." Most of us take pride in the flag and in the ideals it represents, such as liberty, freedom, and our democratic Constitution. We also honor the Declaration of Independence.

Let us analyze this paragraph and see what is wrong with it.

1. The first sentence is fine, since the writing of the national anthem is mentioned in the introductory paragraph.

2. The next two sentences (*Other songs such as "America the Beautiful" have also been written about the United States* and *Everyone knows the words to "America"*) have nothing to do with the topic, which is the American flag, *not* patriotic songs. These sentences do not belong in this essay.

3. The Declaration of Independence is not mentioned anywhere in the essay. Therefore, it does not belong in the concluding paragraph.

4. There is nothing in this paragraph to indicate the essay has ended.

C. Rewrite this concluding paragraph correctly below.

_____

_____

_____

_____

_____

_____

© 2000 by The Center for Applied Research in Education

Name _____ Date _____

EFFECTIVE ENDINGS!
Explanation and Exercises

A. Writing a Concluding Paragraph for an Essay:

A concluding paragraph should

→ 1. Restate the topic in the introductory paragraph.
→ 2. Summarize the points in the body of the essay.
→ 3. Bring the essay to an end.

Be sure that you *do not:*

→ 1. Include information that has not been mentioned earlier.
→ 2. Mention anything that has nothing to do with the topic.
→ 3. Leave the reader unsure whether or not the essay is over.

B. Here is the introductory paragraph and the body of a three-paragraph essay about **sports**. Add a concluding paragraph on the lines at the bottom.

There is a sport for everyone! There are people who keep away from sports because they think they are not athletic. This is a big mistake because everyone benefits from participating in some sport.

The benefits are physical, mental, and social. Getting involved in sports activities will make your body stronger and healthier. The concentration that a sport requires helps sharpen the mind. Best of all, you will discover wonderful friends who share an interest in the same sport.

Write a concluding paragraph below.

_____

_____

_____

_____

_____

_____

_____

_____

© 2000 by The Center for Applied Research in Education

Name _____ Date _____

KEEP YOUR EYE ON THE BALL!
Explanation and Exercises

A. An *irrelevancy* is something that has nothing to do with the topic. When irrelevancies creep into an essay, the reader becomes distracted.

Can you spot the irrelevancies in this introductory paragraph?

> The difference between me and other pet owners is that I am devoted to my turtles. You would like them, too, if you knew their interesting personalities and habits. We had a cat once. Her name was Muffin and she had a disgusting habit of bringing dead mice into the house.

Did you find the irrelevancies here? Everything after the word "habits" is irrelevant. These sentences have nothing to do with the topic of the essay, which is "turtles."

B. The following introductory paragraph contains two irrelevant sentences. Rewrite the paragraph on the lines below without these irrelevancies.

> It is hard to imagine a time when there were no computers. Most kids now learn to use a computer at an early age. My parents did not have computers when they were growing up. The computer is useful in many different ways. My mom has an ancient typewriter that she still uses.

_____

_____

_____

_____

C. The following concluding paragraph contains two irrelevant sentences. Rewrite this paragraph correctly on the lines below.

> Computers are important in today's world. Years ago, people used to write everything by hand. School assignments, research, e-mail, and games are only some of the ways computers are used. Soon, it will be necessary for every home to have a computer. My friend, Jon, has two computers in his house. This is definitely the computer age.

_____

_____

_____

_____

*ANSWERS ON ACTIVITY SHEET 95B.

© 2000 by The Center for Applied Research in Education

Name _____ Date _____

KEEP YOUR EYE ON THE BALL!
Explanation and Exercises

A. ANSWERS TO EXERCISES ON ACTIVITY SHEET 95A:

EXERCISE B: The following irrelevant sentences should have been taken out: "My parents did not have computers when they were growing up." and "My mom has an ancient typewriter that she still uses."

EXERCISE C: The following irrelevant sentences should have been taken out: "Years ago, people used to write everything by hand." and "My friend, Jon, has two computers in his house."

B. GETTING LOST: Has your family ever gotten lost when traveling? That can be frustrating! It is just as frustrating for the reader when an essay goes off the main road (the topic) and begins to wander down side paths that cause confusion.

Here is part of an essay where the writer gets lost. Can you find the place where that happens?

> New Falls has an interesting history. Not many people know about it. Even lifelong residents are often not aware of the many historical sites around town.
>
> One such place is the old Thatcher house on Hickory Place. It was built in 1843 for the Thatcher family who owned the sawmill. The original house was small, with only two rooms. It was added on to through the years until 1904 when it became the size it is now. The Morrises who live there are direct descendants of the original Thatchers.
>
> Have you ever seen the water wheel on Third Street? That was built in 1876. Once I rode over there on my bike with my friend, Ray Santoro. We had a picnic on the grass near the water. Since then, we've gone there lots of times. I'll never forget the time my bike broke down and I had to carry it all the way home. Even after that, though, we kept going out there.

Did you find the place where the writer went off the topic and got lost? It occurs in the third paragraph, beginning with "Once I rode over there on my bike." The topic in the introductory paragraph is *historical places in New Falls*. The third paragraph, however, leads the reader onto a side road about bike trips the writer made with his friend and their various adventures.

C. On a separate sheet of paper, rewrite and complete the essay above.

1. The first two paragraphs can be the same.
2. Be sure to take out the side trip where the writer got lost.
3. Make up one or two additional historical sites for the town of New Falls and write a paragraph about each.
4. Be sure to write a concluding paragraph for this essay.

© 2000 by The Center for Applied Research in Education

Name _____ Date _____

CUT! CUT! AND CUT!
Explanation and Exercises

A. EXPLANATION: Have you ever seen a gardener pruning bushes? They cut branches and twigs to keep the bushes from becoming wild and overgrown. Writing needs to be pruned, too. Excess words can confuse the reader and make the meaning harder to grasp. Here are some suggestions for cutting. (This should be done when editing and revising an essay.)

1. *Unnecessary Detail.* Remove details that are not really needed. Don't bore the reader with unimportant details.

2. *Repetition.* Do not say the same thing more than once.

   Example: Repetitious—*"Last week, we went to the supermarket. When we went to the supermarket, we bought meat and fruit."*

   Better—*"Last week, we went to the supermarket. We bought meat and fruit."*

3. *Wordiness.* Do you say something in four or five words that could be told in one or two?

   Examples: *"In the event that this happens,"* would be better as, *"If this happens."*

   "On Tuesday, the date of which was November 25," would be better as *"On Tuesday, November 25,"*

4. *Unnecessary Words.* Here are some words that can usually be cut to make your writing sharper and clearer:

very	really	however	then
therefore	so	probably	also

   (Sometimes, of course, these words are necessary. More often, they are not needed and should be cut.)

B. Write a three-paragraph essay that you can use to practice cutting.

1. Choose a topic for your essay from the list below. Check the topic you have chosen.

   ❏ a.   What I Would Like to Change about Myself
   ❏ b.   What I Would Like to Change about My Parents
   ❏ c.   What I Would Like to Change about My School
   ❏ d.   What I Would Like to Change about My Neighborhood

2. Write a brainstorming list for this essay below. In each column write as many words and phrases as you can.

THINGS TO CHANGE	REASONS WHY CHANGE IS NEEDED

3. On a separate paper, write a first draft of your essay.
   Introduce the topic in the first paragraph.
   Develop the topic in the second paragraph.
   Restate and sum up the topic in the last paragraph.

© 2000 by The Center for Applied Research in Education

Name _____ Date _____

CUT! CUT! AND CUT!
Editing and Revising

A. Edit and revise the essay you wrote for Activity Sheet 96A, using the following as guide-lines:

1. Cut any unnecessary details that are not needed to make the point.
2. Cut any repetition. Do not say the same thing more than once.
3. Cut unnecessary words. (See list on Activity 96A).
4. Cut wordiness. Can you use fewer words to say the same thing?
5. Does your first paragraph introduce the topic? Can you grab the reader's interest by making this introduction more interesting?
6. Does your second paragraph develop the topic? Can you add anything to make your point more convincing?
7. Does the last paragraph restate and sum up the topic?
8. Are all sentences complete? Do subjects and verbs agree?
9. Check spelling with a dictionary.

B. Write the final copy of your essay below. (Indent at the beginning of each paragraph. Use the back of this paper if you need more room.)

_____

_____

_____

_____

_____

_____

_____

_____

_____

_____

_____

_____

_____

© 2000 by The Center for Applied Research in Education

Section Eight

LETTER WRITING HELP

TEACHER'S GUIDE—
ALPHABETICAL LIST OF LETTER WRITING
PROBLEMS AND ACTIVITY NUMBERS

The letter writing problems addressed in this section are:

LETTER WRITING PROBLEM	ACTIVITY NUMBER
Business Letter: Complete Form	100A, B
Business Letter Parts: Closing	99D
Business Letter Parts: Inside Address	99A, B
Business Letter Parts: Inside Address and Greeting	99C
Business Letter Parts: Return Address	98A, B
Job Application Letter	101A, B, C
Personal/Friendly Letter	97A, B, C

Name _____ Date _____

THANKS A LOT!
Example and Exercise

A. Nowadays, most people communicate by phone or e-mail, but sometimes the best way to send a message is by letter. Personal letters are used for thank-you notes, party invitations, and letters to friends.

Here is the correct form for a personal or friendly letter:

2504 Elm Street
Wexford, MA 56843
February 6, 2000

Dear Aunt Rachel,

You must be a mind reader! How did you know that a cd of "This Is It" by the group, Gang of Six, was what I wanted most for my birthday? I've already played it a hundred times.

Thank you for being the best aunt in the world.

Your loving niece,

Kim

Did you notice how this letter was set up?

→ 1. The return address is in the upper right. It has three lines:

　　　your street address
　　　your city, state, and zip
　　　the date *(The month is never abbreviated here.)*

→ 2. The greeting begins at the left margin. It is followed by a comma.

→ 3. The body of the letter is the message. Indent at the beginning of each paragraph.

→ 4. The closing is at the lower right (lined up with the return address.)

　　　Only the first word of the closing is capitalized.
　　　The closing is followed by a comma,

→ 5. Your name is signed under the closing.

B. On a separate piece of paper, write a "thank you" letter to someone who has done something nice for you or given you a gift. Follow the form above.

© 2000 by The Center for Applied Research in Education

Name _____ Date _____

THANKS A LOT!
Personal Letter—First Draft

A. You can buy invitations at a greeting card store, but wouldn't you like to receive a personal invitation to a party like the one below?

---

25 Blueberry Lane
Clapton, IL 34297
October 4, 2000

Dear Shandra,

    I am having a birthday party on Friday, October 17th, at the Ascot Bowling Lanes, 2 Ascot Road. We are going to have a great time bowling and eating lots of birthday cake and ice cream. It won't be fun without you, so please come!

        Your friend,

        Chris

B. Pretend you are going to have a party now or in the future (birthday, Valentine's Day, Halloween, or any other occasion). Write a first draft of a letter inviting one of your friends.

    This is just a first draft, so don't worry about spelling or grammar. Just concentrate on getting your thoughts down on paper.

    Follow the form for a personal letter above and write your first draft in the box below.

© 2000 by The Center for Applied Research in Education

Name _____ Date _____

THANKS A LOT!
Personal Letter—Revising and Writing a Final Copy

A. Edit and revise the first draft of your personal letter, using the following questions as guidelines:

→ 1. Did you write your return address in the upper right corner?

→ 2. Are there three lines in the return address?

       1st line—your street address
       2nd line—your city, state, and zip
       3rd line—today's date

→ 3. Did you write the greeting at the left margin? Did you put a comma at the end of the greeting?

→ 4. Did you indent at the beginning of each paragraph in the body of the letter (the message)?

→ 5. Did you write the closing at the lower right?

       Does the closing begin at the same point as the return address?
       Did you capitalize *only the first word* of the closing?
       Is there a comma after the closing?

→ 6. Did you sign your name under the closing?

B. Write the final copy of your personal letter in the box below.

© 2000 by The Center for Applied Research in Education

Name _____ Date _____

HERE'S WHERE I AM!
Explanation and Exercise

A. BUSINESS LETTERS FOR KIDS: Even kids write business letters at times. Here are some examples.

> applying for a job
> complaint about merchandise
> letter to the editor of a newspaper
> doing research for a school project

B. BUSINESS LETTER FORM—RETURN ADDRESS: There is a correct form for each part of a business letter. The first part of a business letter is called the return address.

→ 1. The return address is written in the upper right corner of the letter. It consists of three lines.

> The first line shows your street address.
> The second line shows your city, state, and zip. There is a comma between the city and state. Use the correct post office abbreviation for the state.
> The third line contains the date. The month should be spelled out in full.

→ 2. Here is an example of a return address.

> 245 South Street
> Albany, NY 10854
> March 4, 2000

C. Write *your* return address on the lines below.

_____

_____

_____

D. *Write a return address:* Antonio Rodriguez lives in San Diego, California. His house is at 25 Buena Vista Drive. His zip is 74356. Write a return address for Antonio on the lines below. Use today's date.

_____

_____

_____

*ANSWER ON ACTIVITY SHEET 98B.

© 2000 by The Center for Applied Research in Education

Name _____ Date _____

HERE'S WHERE I AM!
Explanation and Exercises

A. ANSWERS TO EXERCISE D ON ACTIVITY SHEET 98A:

25 Buena Vista Drive
San Diego, CA 74356
September 4, 2000

B. Return Address—Abbreviations

1. Do not abbreviate the name of the city.
2. Do not abbreviate the month.
3. Use the correct post office abbreviation for the state.
4. You may either spell out in full *or* abbreviate the type of street. (*Buena Vista Drive* could also be written *Buena Vista Dr.*)

Some common street abbreviations are

Avenue	Ave.	Drive	Dr.	Road	Rd.
Boulevard	Blvd.	Lane	Ln.	Square	Sq.
Circle	Cir.	Parkway	Pky.	Street	St.
Court	Ct.				

C. Write a return address for each of the following on the lines that follow. (Use today's date for each.)

1. Allison Banta lives in the city of New York. That is in the state of New York. Allison lives on 3550 Third Avenue. The zip is 20010.

   _____

   _____

   _____

2. Michael Ferris lives in Seattle, Washington. His street address is 250 Morris Parkway. The zip is 45934.

   _____

   _____

   _____

*SEE ANSWERS BELOW.

Answers to Exercise C: 1. 3550 Third Ave.
New York, NY 20010
May 4, 2000

2. 250 Morris Pky.
Seattle, WA 45934
May 4, 2000

© 2000 by The Center for Applied Research in Education

Name _____ Date _____

GOING WHERE?
Explanation and Exercises

A. BUSINESS LETTER FORM—THREE-LINE INSIDE ADDRESS: The inside address contains the name and address of the person to whom the letter is going.

> → The first line contains the person's (or company's) full name.
> → The second line contains the street address.
> → The third line contains the city, state, and zip.
>   *Never* abbreviate the name of the city. Use the correct post office abbreviation for the state.

B. EXAMPLES OF THREE-LINE INSIDE ADDRESS:

Campbell Model Toy Co. 23 Haverty St. Boise, ID 56483

Dr. Alan Farmer 465 Astor Ct. Crandale, NJ 07568

Here are some state abbreviations. (You can get the complete list at your post office.)

Alabama	AL	District of Columbia	DC	Maryland	MD
Alaska	AK	Florida	FL	Massachusetts	MA
Arizona	AZ	Georgia	GA	Michigan	MI
California	CA	Hawaii	HI	Missouri	MO
Colorado	CO	Idaho	ID	New Jersey	NJ
Connecticut	CT	Illinois	IL	New York	NY
Delaware	DE	Maine	ME		

C. Write the inside addresses for each of the following:

1. White and Grey Paper Co. Their street address is 468 Surrey Lane. The city is Denver. The state is Colorado, and the zip is 08431.

   _____

   _____

   _____

2. Dr. Zelda Black's office is in the town of Tamsbury in the state of Massachusetts. The street address is 14 Stateline Road, and the zip is 67834.

   _____

   _____

   _____

*ANSWERS ON ACTIVITY SHEET 99B.

© 2000 by The Center for Applied Research in Education

Name _____   Date _____

GOING WHERE?
Explanation and Exercises

A. ANSWER TO EXERCISE C ON ACTIVITY SHEET 99A:

1. White and Grey Paper Co.
    468 Surrey Ln.
    Denver, CO 08431

2. Dr. Zelda Black
    14 Stateline Rd.
    Tamsbury, MA 67834

B. FOUR-LINE INSIDE ADDRESS: When a letter is going to a person at a company, it usually requires four lines, as in this example.

> Mr. Alex Brophy
> Ambassador Publishing Co.
> 23 First St.
> Mobile, AL 08648

Sometimes you will use the person's title also. It goes on the first line, separated from the name by a comma, as

> Mr. Alex Brophy, Editorial Assistant
> Ambassador Publishing Co.
> 23 First St.
> Mobile, AL 08648

C. Here are additional rules for a business address.

→ 1. Always abbreviate Mr., Mrs., Ms., Dr. when used before a name.

→ 2. Do not abbreviate Miss.

→ 3. Capitalize each word of a person's title, such as: *Editor, President, Sales Manager, and Treasurer, Assistant Principal,* etc.

D. Write a four-line inside address for a letter to each of the following. (See Activities 98B and 99A for correct street and state abbreviations.)

1. Jack Hermana is the editor of the Elmwood News Dispatch. This newspaper is located at 25 Dispatch Square in Elmwood, Georgia. The zip is 97453.

2. Mrs. Anita Ostrow is the sales manager of the Cheap Jeans Co. Their address is 574 Washington Boulevard in the town of Ramsdale, which is in the state of Michigan. The zip is 97439.

a. _____   b. _____

   _____   _____

   _____   _____

   _____   _____

*Answers on Activity Sheet 99C.

© 2000 by The Center for Applied Research in Education

Name _____ Date _____

GOING WHERE?
Explanation and Activities

A. ANSWER TO EXERCISE D ON ACTIVITY SHEET 99B:

1. Mr. Jack Hermana, Editor   2. Mrs. Anita Ostrow, Sales Manager
   Elmwood News Dispatch   Cheap Jeans Co.
   25 Dispatch Sq.   574 Washington Blvd.
   Elmwood, GA 97453   Ramsdale, MI 97439

B. GREETING: The greeting appears below the inside address.

→ Begin the greeting at the left margin.

→ Use the last name only in the greeting preceded by Mr., Mrs., Ms., Miss, or Dr.

→ A common greeting in a business letter is Dear Sir: or Dear Sirs: or Gentlemen:
   (These are only for men.) The greeting in a business letter is followed by a colon (:).

C. EXAMPLES: The greetings that follow the inside addresses in *A* would be

> 1. **Dear Mr. Hermana:**
> 2. **Dear Mrs. Ostrow:**

D. Write an inside address and greeting for a letter to each of the following:

1. This is a letter to the Surplus Catalog Co. The person to whom you are writing is Ms. Toni Vamo. She is a marketing manager. Surplus Catalog Co. is located at 98 Main St. in Baltimore, Maryland. The zip is 46210.

   _____

   _____

   _____

   _____

   _____

2. Write the inside address and greeting of a letter to the research director at Flagler Institution. His name is Jonathan Wexler. The Flagler Institution is in Gainesville, Florida. It is at 89 College Boulevard. The zip is 06423.

   _____

   _____

   _____

   _____

   _____

*ANSWERS ON ACTIVITY SHEET 99D.

© 2000 by The Center for Applied Research in Education

Name _____ Date _____

GOING WHERE?
Explanation and Exercises

A. ANSWERS TO EXERCISE D ON ACTIVITY SHEET 99C:

1. Ms. Toni Vamo, Marketing Manager
   Surplus Catalog Co.
   98 Main St.
   Baltimore, MD 46210
   Dear Ms. Vamo:

2. Mr. Jonathan Wexler, Research Director
   Flagler Institution
   89 College Blvd.
   Gainesville, FL 06423
   Dear Mr. Wexler:

B. The closing in a business letter is written after the message.

1. The closing begins in the middle of the line at the same point as the return address.
2. The closing is always followed by a comma (,).
3. The first word of the closing begins with a capital.
4. All other words in the closing are written lower case.

C. Some common closings for business letters are

> Yours truly,
> Sincerely,
> Yours very truly,
> Sincerely yours,
> Very truly yours,

D. Each of the following closings is incorrect. Write it correctly on the line.

1. Yours Truly, _____
2. sincerely _____
3. Sincercly yours _____
4. Yours very Truly, _____
5. Very Truly Yours _____

SEE ANSWERS BELOW.

Answers to Exercise D: 1. Yours truly, **2.** Sincerely, **3.** Sincerely yours, **4.** Yours very truly, **5.** Very truly yours,

© 2000 by The Center for Applied Research in Education

Name _____ Date _____

SET IT UP!
Example, Prewriting, and First Draft

A. HERE IS THE CORRECT FORM FOR A BUSINESS LETTER:

(Writer's street address)
(City, state, and zip)
(Current date)

(Name of person or company to whom you are writing)
(Their street address)
(City, state, and zip)

Dear Sir (or name of person):

Your message will appear here. This is called the body of the letter. State your message clearly.

Yours truly,

(Sign your name here)

Enc. (This indicates that you are enclosing something.)

B. PREWRITING: You are going to write a letter to the Smithsonian Institution. The address is 10th St. & Constitution Ave. NW in Washington, D.C. The zip is 20560. You need information for a report on Native American tribes of the Southwestern United States (You are not really going to write a report, just the letter!) Make your prewriting notes for this letter as follows:

1. Write your return address here. _____

    _____

    _____

2. Write the inside address here. _____

    _____

    _____

3. Write a greeting here. _____:

4. Write the first sentence of your letter on the line below.

    _____

C. On a separate paper, write a first draft of your letter. Follow the business letter form in A above. This is just a first draft, so don't be concerned about spelling or grammar. Concentrate on getting down your thoughts and using correct business letter form.

© 2000 by The Center for Applied Research in Education

Name _____ Date _____

SET IT UP!
Revising and Writing a Final Copy

A. Edit and revise the letter you wrote for activity 100A, using the following guidelines:

1. Is the return address in the upper right?

   Did you write your street address on the first line?
   Did you write your city, state, and zip on the second line?
   Did you write today's date on the third line?

2. Does each line of the inside address begin at the left margin? Does it look like this?

   Smithsonian Institution
   10th St. & Constitution Ave. NW
   Washington, DC 20560

3. Since you are not writing to a person, your greeting should be Dear Sirs: or Gentlemen:

4. Does the message tell what information you want and why you need it?

5. Does the closing begin in the middle of the line under the return address? Is there a comma after the closing?

6. Did you sign your name under the closing?

B. Write the final copy of your letter in the box below.

© 2000 by The Center for Applied Research in Education

Name _____ Date _____

I CAN DO IT!
Explanation and Prewriting Activities

A. JOB APPLICATION LETTER: A letter is important when applying for a job. In it, you must

→ 1. state the job for which you are applying.
→ 2. describe your qualifications for the job.
→ 3. offer references, if possible.
→ 4. persuade the reader that you are the best person for the job.
→ 5. produce a letter that is correctly written and set up.

B. Here are three ads from a local newspaper, *The Sharpville Herald,* in Sharpville, AL 35207.

❏ Counselors-in-training needed for community day camp, ages 12+. Must be excellent swimmers and good with young children. Box #89

❏ Newspaper delivery routes available. Must be reliable and able to make early morning deliveries. Box #56

❏ Mother's helper to assist with two boys ages 4 and 2. Four days weekly after school, hours to be arranged. Write, giving age and experience. Box #93.

C. Check one of these ads; then complete this brainstorming list.

BRAINSTORMING LIST

1. In the box below, list any experience you have had doing this kind of work. (You don't need sentences—just words and phrases.)

```


```

2. In the box below, list any skills and knowledge you have that will be useful in this job. (Just words and phrases)

```


```

3. In the box below, state your reasons for wanting this job.

```


```

4. In the box below, name any who could give you a reference.

```


```

5. Write an opening sentence for your letter on the line below.

_____

© 2000 by The Center for Applied Research in Education

Name _____ Date _____

I CAN DO IT!
Writing a First Draft

A. Write the first draft of a letter applying for one of the jobs listed in Activity 101A.

1. Use the box number in the ad as the first line of the inside address.
2. Since this is a box number, use Dear Sir: as your greeting.
3. Begin your message with the opening sentence you wrote in your brainstorming list.
4. In the next paragraph, state your skills, knowledge, experience, and references, if any.
5. In the third paragraph, state your reasons for wanting this job and why you think you should get it.
6. Follow the guide below for correct business letter form.

Write your first draft below.

© 2000 by The Center for Applied Research in Education

_____
(Write your street address above)

_____
(Write your city, state, and zip here)

_____
(Write today's date here)

_____
(Write the Box # above)

_____
(Write the name of the newspaper here)

_____
(Write the city, state, and zip here)

_____
(Write the greeting here)

_____
(Begin the message here)

_____

_____

_____

_____

_____

_____
(Write the closing here)

_____
(Sign your name here)

Name _____ Date _____

I CAN DO IT!
Revising and Writing a Final Copy

A. Edit and revise the first draft of your letter of application for a job, using the following questions as guidelines:

→ 1. Does the first paragraph tell why you are writing?
→ 2. Does the second paragraph state your skills and experience?
→ 3. Does the third paragraph state clearly why you should get the job?
→ 4. Does the inside address and the greeting begin at the left margin?
→ 5. Did you indent at the beginning of each paragraph?
→ 6. Are the parts of the letter correct?
   a. Do you use the correct abbreviation for the state in the return address and the inside address?
   b. Is there a comma between the city and state?
   c. Did you spell out the month in the date?
   d. Is there a colon after the greeting?
   e. Does the first word of the closing begin with a capital letter?
   f. Did you put a comma after the closing?

Write the final copy of your letter below.

© 2000 by The Center for Applied Research in Education